Alternative Voices in Contemporary Economics

Series Editor:

Professor Steven Pressman, Monmouth University, USA

The Alternative Voices in Contemporary Economics series provides an important platform for new and innovative approaches to economic analysis within the following traditions: Post-Keynesian, Feminist, Institutional, Marxian, Sraffian, Radical, Austrian, and Behavioural. This series offers researchers working in these heterodox traditions the opportunity to address methodological, theoretical or empirical issues. The series editor works closely with authors and editors to ensure the quality of all published works.

Britain, the Euro and Beyond

MARK BAIMBRIDGE
University of Bradford, UK

and

PHILIP B. WHYMAN
University of Central Lancashire, UK

ASHGATE

Published by
Ashgate Publishing Limited
Gower House
Croft Road
Aldershot
Hampshire GU11 3HR
England

Ashgate Publishing Company
Suite 420
101 Cherry Street
Burlington, VT 05401–4405
USA

Ashgate website: http://www.ashgate.com

British Library Cataloguing in Publication Data
Baimbridge, Mark
  Britain, the Euro and Beyond. - (Alternative voices in
  contemporary economics)
  1. Economic and Monetary Union 2. Euro area 3. Monetary
  policy - Great Britain
  I. Title II. Whyman, Philip
  322.4'94

Library of Congress Cataloging-in-Publication Data
Baimbridge, Mark.
 Britain, the Euro and beyond / by Mark Baimbridge and Philip B. Whyman.
   p. cm.
 Includes bibliographical references and index.
 1. European Union--Great Britain. 2. Great Britain--Foreign economic relations--European Union countries. 3. European Union countries--Foreign economic relations--Great Britain. I. Whyman, Philip. II. Title.

HC240.25.G7B35 2008
337.1'420941--dc22

2007030954

ISBN 978-0-7546-4414-9

Printed and bound in Great Britain by TJ International Ltd, Padstow, Cornwall.

Contents

List of Figures

List of Tables

Preface

There are many people to thank for their input into making of this book possible. Most obviously, we must thank our Commissioning Editor at Ashgate, Brendan George, for his immediate support for this project. Secondly, the *Alternative Voices in Contemporary Economics* series editor, Professor Steven Pressman for his judicious comments which have served to improve the text. Thirdly, we would like to thank our colleagues at the universities of Bradford and Central Lancashire for their comradeship and general support for our research on European economic integration. Finally, we owe a deep sense of gratitude to our families and partners for their forbearance during the preparation of this book. It is to them that this book is dedicated: MB: Mary, Ken, Beibei and Douglas; PW: Barbara, Boyd and Claire.

Any remaining errors and omissions we gladly attribute to each other.

Haworth and Heaton Norris
June 2007

European Integration Timeline

From its beginnings, half a century ago, in the immediate aftermath of the Second World War, through the expansion of the seventies and eighties and the great debate surrounding the Maastricht Treaty, here we highlight some of the key events which have shaped the development of the EU towards closer integration.

1948	The Organisation for **European Economic Cooperation (OEEC)** is set up in Paris in April 1948, co-ordinating the distribution of the Marshall Plan financial aid which will amount to $12.5 billion from 1948 to 1951. The OEEC consists of one representative from each of the 17 Western European countries which join the organisation. In May 1948 in The Hague, the Congress of Europe (a meeting of delegates from 16 European countries) agree to form the **Council of Europe** with the aim of establishing closer economic and social ties.
1951	The **European Coal and Steel Community (ECSC)** is established by the signing of the Treaty of Paris in April 1951. Along with France and West Germany, Italy, Belgium, Luxembourg and The Netherlands have also chosen to join the organisation. Members of the ECSC pledge to remove all import duties and quota restrictions on the trade of coal, iron ore, and steel between the member states.
1952	The **European Defence Community (EDC)** Treaty is signed by France, West Germany, Italy, Belgium, Holland and Luxembourg in May 1952. It includes the provision for the formation of a parallel **European Political Community (EPC)**. However both initiatives are destined to founder since the French National Assembly never ratifies the EDC Treaty, finally rejecting it in August 1954.
1955	The process of further European integration is given fresh impetus by a conference of ECSC foreign ministers at Messina, Italy, in June 1955. The meeting agrees to develop the community by encouraging free trade between member states through the removal of tariffs and quotas. Agreement is also reached to form an Atomic Energy Community to encourage co-operation in the nuclear energy industry.

1958	The two Treaties of Rome are signed, establishing the **European Economic Community (EEC)** and the **European Atomic Energy Community (Euratom)**. As well as stipulating the eventual removal of customs duties on trade between member countries (over a period of 12 years) the EEC Treaty sets out allow the free movement of workers, capital and services across borders and to harmonise policies on agriculture and transport.
1960	At the Stockholm Convention in January 1960 Austria, Britain, Denmark, Norway, Portugal, Sweden and Switzerland form the **European Free Trade Association (EFTA)**. The objective of EFTA is to promote free trade but without the formal structures of the EEC.
1961	UK applies to join the EEC.
1963	British application for EEC membership fails.
1967	UK submits second application to join EEC.
1968	Customs union completed and Common Agricultural Policy enacted.
1972	In October, following the recommendations of the Werner Report, the EEC launches its first attempt at harmonising exchange rates. The mechanism adopted is the so called 'snake in the tunnel' whereby participating governments are required to confine the fluctuations of their currencies within a range of +/- 1 per cent against each other. The value of the group of currencies (the snake) is also to be maintained within a range of +/- 2.25 per cent against the US Dollar (the tunnel). Countries requiring assistance to keep their currencies within the required band may receive help only in the form of loans.
1973	Denmark, Ireland and the UK join the EEC.
1975	UK referendum supports staying in EEC.
1978	At a summit in Bremen in July, the French and West German governments announce their intention to create the **European Monetary System (EMS)**. At the centre of the EMS is the **European Currency Unit (ECU)**. The value of the ECU is to be derived from a weighted basket of all participating currencies with the greatest weighting against the West German mark.
1981	Greece joins the EC.
1986	Portugal and Spain join the EC.

1986	In October, following the recommendations of the Werner Report, the EEC launches its first attempt at harmonising exchange rates. The mechanism adopted is the so called 'snake in the tunnel' whereby participating governments are required to confine the fluctuations of their currencies within a range of +/- 1 per cent against each other. The value of the group of currencies (the snake) is also to be maintained within a range of +/- 2.25 per cent against the US Dollar (the tunnel). Countries requiring assistance to keep their currencies within the required band may receive help only in the form of loans.
1990	UK joins EMS.
1992	At a summit of the European Council in Maastricht, Holland, the **Treaty on European Union (TEU)**, also known as the Maastricht Treaty, is signed. Originally intended to include a declaration of an intention to move towards federal union, at Britain's insistence this aspect is played down. Subsequent to the signing of the Maastricht Treaty, the European Community is referred to as the European Union (EU). UK leaves EMS.
1993	The Single European Market takes effect. Trade tariffs are scrapped, but Duty Free shopping remains until 1999.
1994	Stage 2 of EMU is initiated on January 1st with the establishment of the **European Monetary Institute (EMI)** to oversee the co-ordination of the monetary policies of the individual national central banks. The EMI will also work towards the introduction of stage 3 by organising the creation of the European Central Bank.
1995	Austria, Finland and Sweden join the EU, bringing membership to 15. The Schengen agreement comes into force and scraps border controls. UK and Ireland stay out of the agreement.
1997	Heads of Government draft a new agreement in Amsterdam which updates the Maastricht Treaty and prepares the EU for its eastward expansion. Qualified majority voting is introduced into new areas, reducing individual countries' powers to veto new measures.
1998	At the beginning of May, at a summit of EU officials and heads of state in Brussels, the announcement is made as to which countries will participate in the launch of the euro the following January. In June the **European Central Bank (ECB)** is established in Frankfurt, Germany. The ECB together with the national central banks of the 15 EU member states form the **European System of Central Banks (ESCB)** which will be responsible for setting monetary policy for the euro countries and managing those countries' foreign reserves. The EU opens accession negotiations with Hungary, Poland, Estonia, the Czech Republic, Slovenia and Cyprus.

1999	Romania, Slovakia, Latvia, Lithuania, Bulgaria and Malta are invited to begin accession negotiations. Eleven countries adopt the euro as their official currency (although national currency notes and coins remain in circulation), but Sweden, Denmark and the UK stay out.
2000	The Nice summit agrees to limit the size of the Commission and increase the President's powers. Qualified majority voting is introduced in new areas, but members keep their vetoes on social security and tax. A timetable for taking forward accession negotiations is endorsed.
2001	The Laeken European Council establishes the Convention on the Future of Europe.
2002	Euro notes and coins are introduced in twelve EU countries. The European Commission announces that ten countries are on course to meet the criteria for accession to the EU in 2004.
2003	The UK has been a member of the EU for 30 years.
2004	EU enlargement to 25 member states with addition of Slovakia, Latvia, Lithuania, Malta, Hungary, Poland, Estonia, the Czech Republic, Slovenia and Cyprus.
2005	EU Constitution ratification ended by referendum defeats in France and the Netherlands. The UK holds EU Presidency, but fails to make progress on new 2007–13 budget. Accession negotiations are opened with Turkey and Croatia.
2006	Slovenia's entry into the euro on 1 January 2007 is confirmed. Accession negotiations with Turkey are suspended.
2007	EU enlargement to 27 member states with addition of Bulgaria and Romania. The Treaty of Lisbon, replacing the Treaty on establishing a Constitution for Europe, is signed.

Glossary of Terms

Asymmetric and symmetric external shocks   External shocks refer to the impact upon the domestic economy generated by activities beyond the control of UK authorities, for example a sudden rise in oil prices or change in global demand for raw materials. If an external shock has a similar effect amongst upon a given group of countries, it is said to be a symmetric shock since the policy response will be largely the same for all countries. Asymmetric shocks, alternatively, refer to those changes in the external environment which have significantly different effects upon different countries, requiring very different policy responses by each country in order to respond effectively.

Bundesbank   German central bank – equivalent to the Bank of England, although operating with greater independence from government.

Common Agricultural Policy (CAP)   EU agricultural support scheme which accounts for majority of EU budget until 1997. The protection of EU food producers has led to food prices rising significantly higher than world prices.

Commonwealth   The Commonwealth of Nations, usually known as The Commonwealth, is an association of independent sovereign states, almost all of which are former territories of the British Empire. The Commonwealth is primarily an organisation in which countries with diverse economic backgrounds have an opportunity for close and equal interaction. The primary activities of the Commonwealth are designed to create an atmosphere of economic cooperation between member nations, as well as the promotion of democracy, human rights, and good governance in them. The Commonwealth is not a political union of any sort, and does not allow the UK to exercise any power over the affairs of the organisation's other members. The Commonwealth encompasses a population of approximately 1.8 billion people, making up about 30 per cent of the world's total, whilst its land area of the Commonwealth nations equals about a 25 per cent of the world's land area.

Cyclical and structural convergence   Economic convergence refers to potential EMU participants becoming economically similar prior to membership. Cyclical convergence occurs when the business cycles of boom and recession become increasingly similar amongst participating economies, so that a recession in the UK would occur approximately at the same time as a comparable slow-down in Germany, rather than one or two years in advance as at present. Similarly, structural convergence refers to changes in industrial and financial structure of the participating economies which have the effect of ensuring similar reactions to external forces over the long term.

Deflation/Reflation   Deflation may be defined as a reduction in economic activity in the economy which is associated with a sustained reduction in inflation, output and employment. Reflation refers to an increase in economic activity which stimulates output, employment and inflation in varying degrees.

Devaluation/revaluation/over-valuation   Devaluation refers to a reduction in the value of a given exchange rate relative to other rates, whilst revaluation concerns the increase in the exchange rate. For example, if the exchange rate on a given day was £1 equals $1.67, if the value of sterling increased so that £1 could now buy $2 worth of goods, the value of the pound would be said to have appreciated, whereas if the value fell to perhaps $1.5, sterling would be said to have fallen in value or devalued. Over-valuation refers to the circumstance where the value of sterling is so high that British exporters find it difficult to compete and possibly lead to a trade deficit were more is imported than exported. Too high an over-valuation could lead to economic recession as export companies reduce output and lay off workers. This then may spread to the remainder of the economy.

Economic and Monetary Union (EMU)   As a matter of definition, monetary union occurs when exchange rates are permanently and irrevocably fixed and may therefore precede the introduction of a single currency. However, the two terms are generally used interchangeably. Economic union involves a further transfer of macroeconomic policy to the federal level – particularly monetary policy but typically also 'co-ordination' of fiscal policy within prescribed limits.

European Central Bank (ECB)   This supersedes national central banks in those EU nations participating in EMU. Based in Frankfurt, the ECB will be in sole charge of exchange rate and monetary policy for all EMU countries, setting one common interest rate which will apply irrespective of the particular needs of individual countries at any period of time. Its sole policy goal is to achieve price stability without a similar responsibility to assist employment creation or economic growth. Policy conflict between ECB and the wider economic responsibilities of individual governments is difficult to resolve since the ECB is beyond the control of both member states and the EU Commission.

European Company Statute (ECS)   Still under discussion, this would enable companies to register at EU, rather than national, level.

European Economic Area (EEA)   The European Economic Area (EEA) came into being on 1 January 1994 following an agreement between the European Free Trade Association (EFTA) and the EU. It was designed to allow EFTA countries to participate in the European SIM without having to join the EU. In an obligatory referendum, Switzerland's citizens chose not to participate in the EEA. Instead, the Swiss are linked to the EU by bilateral agreements, with a different content than that of the EEA agreement. Thus, the current members, contracting parties, are three of the four EFTA states (Iceland, Liechtenstein and Norway) and the EU25. The EEA is based on 4 'freedoms': the free movement of goods, persons, services and capital between the EEA countries. The non EU members of the EEA have agreed to enact legislation similar to that passed in the EU in the areas of Social Policy, Consumer Protection, Environment, Company Law and Statistics.

European Free Trade Association (EFTA)   The European Free Trade Association (EFTA) was established on 3 May 1960 as an alternative for European states that were not allowed or did not wish to join the EU. The treaty was signed on January 4, 1960 in Stockholm by seven states (United Kingdom, Denmark, Norway, Sweden, Austria, Switzerland and Portugal). Finland became an associate member in 1961 (later becoming a full member in 1986), whilst Iceland joined in 1970. The United Kingdom, Denmark and Ireland joined the EU in 1973, and hence ceased to be EFTA members, whilst Portugal left EFTA for the EU in 1986. Liechtenstein joined in 1991 (previously its interests in EFTA had been represented by Switzerland). Finally, Austria, Sweden and Finland joined the EU in 1995 and hence ceased to be EFTA members. Currently, only Iceland, Norway, Switzerland and Liechtenstein remain members of EFTA. The EFTA States have jointly concluded free trade agreements with a number of countries worldwide. EFTA has the following institutions: the Secretariat, the EFTA Council, the EFTA Surveillance Authority, and the EFTA Court.

European Monetary Institute (EMI)   The forerunner of the European Central Bank (ECB).

European System of Central Banks (ESCB)   The central banks of all member states participating in EMU, which will act as subsidiaries of the ECB, implementing its policies.

European Union (EU)   Formally the European Community (EC) and Common Market, the change of name occurred after ratification of the Maastricht Treaty, signifying a changed relationship between the twelve (now twenty-five) participating nation states (called 'member states' in EU terminology), from a loose trading community towards a federal state encompassing one currency, central bank and discussion of parallel moves towards political union.

European Works Councils (EWCs)   Originating from EU Directive, EWCs are to be established in large multinational European companies, based in one or more member states, in order to encourage consultation with and between workers from all productive units.

Euro-X Committee   A committee of those member states participating in EMU where discussions may include market-sensitive preferences for interest and exchange rates.

Excessive Deficit Procedure (EDP)   The EDP is a feature of the Maastricht Treaty, where a budget deficit is deemed excessive if it exceeds 3 per cent of GDP, and if government debt exceeded 60 per cent of GDP.

Fiscal federalism   Fiscal federalism involves a redistribution of resources from more successful to weaker regions of a federal state or, in the case of the single currency, between regions or member states participating in EMU. In practice, fiscal federalism acts in a similar manner to regional transfers in a nation state, whereby it seeks to stabilise the entire EMU by reducing inflationary pressure in booming areas and kick-starting recoveries in depressed areas through a transfer of tax revenue from the former into public expenditure (or a tax cut) in the latter. Fiscal federalism may, therefore, assist macroeconomic management, particularly due to the existence of regional-spillovers or externalities thereby preventing individual regions from 'going it alone'. It may also aid social cohesion by acting as an inter-regional public insurance scheme, preventing 'unlucky' areas bearing a disproportionate financial burden.

Fiscal policy   Fiscal policy refers to the interaction between government expenditure and taxation. Under EMU, fiscal policy will remain under the control of national economic authorities, although constrained by the MCC and Stability and Growth Pact rules.

G7/G8   An informal grouping of seven of the largest industrialised economies (USA, Canada, Germany, France, UK, Australia and Japan). On occasions Russia has been invited to participate in recent summits, giving rise to the G8.

Gold Standard   A currency arrangement whereby the central bank is obliged to give a fixed amount of gold in exchange for its currency. If a number of countries all fix their currencies relative to gold, they must, by definition, fix their exchange rates amongst themselves. The Gold Standard that existed between the majority of the industrialised economies during the thirty years-or-so before the First World War, imposed certain rules upon participating economies, the most important of these was a distaste of 'debasing the currency' by devaluing. Moreover, a participating nation experiencing a balance of payments deficit, would have to take corrective deflationary action, thus preferring external over internal balance. The increased international volatility caused by war conditions terminated the system and its replication in 1925 was disastrous for the UK as it occurred upon pre-WWI parities which no longer represented the true economic balance between nations.

Gross Domestic Product (GDP)/Gross National Product (GNP)   These are two methods of measuring the value of the total flow of goods and services produced by an economy over a specified period of time – usually a year. The difference between the two is that GNP equals GDP plus net income earned by domestic residents from overseas investments.

International Monetary Fund (IMF) Established in 1944, by 2004 it possessed 184 members. It is intended to encourage international co-operation in monetary matters and the removal of foreign exchange restrictions. Members are required to contribute a quota calculated upon the basis of GDP, and its fund can then be utilised to help members over temporary balance of payments difficulties, although usually in parallel with adopting corrective economic policies, such as domestic deflation and devaluation, intended to stimulate exports and reduce imports.

Maastricht Convergence Criteria Established by the Maastricht Treaty to ensure economic convergence amongst potential participants prior to their entry to EMU, there are five criteria which each country must achieve before they are permitted to participate in the single currency. They are: (i) each country's rate of inflation must be no more than 1.5 per cent above the average of the lowest three inflation rates in the EMS; (ii) its long-term interest rates must be within 2 per cent of the same three countries chosen for the previous condition; (iii) it must have been a member of the narrow band of fluctuation of the ERM for at least two years without a realignment; (iv) its budget deficit must not be regarded as 'excessive' by the European Council, with 'excessive' defined to be where deficits are greater than 3 per cent of GDP for reasons other than those of a 'temporary' or 'exceptional' nature; (v) its national debt must not be 'excessive', defined as where it is above 60 per cent of GDP and is not declining at a 'satisfactory' pace.

Monetary policy Monetary policy is typically concerned with the level of interest rates, the availability of credit, banking regulations and the control of the money supply by the central bank. Under EMU, monetary policy will be transferred from national authorities to the ECB.

Nominal and real wage rigidity Nominal wages refer to money wages, whereas real wages refer to the purchasing power of those wages. Thus, a 3 per cent rise in nominal wages during a period of 2 per cent inflation produces a 1 per cent rise in real wages. Wage rigidity refers to a situation when wages are observed not to be perfectly flexible in response to a change in economic circumstances, for example, if wages should fail to fall sufficiently to price people back into work during a recession.

Non-accelerating inflation rate of unemployment (NAIRU) NAIRU is the rate of unemployment, whether it be 1 per cent or 8 per cent, where inflation remains stable. The importance of this measure is that, if unemployment falls below its NAIRU rate, inflation will accelerate whilst if above the NAIRU, inflation will fall.

North American Free Trade Agreement (NAFTA) The North American Free Trade Agreement (NAFTA) came into effect on 1 January 1994 and links Canada, the United States, and Mexico in a free trade sphere. NAFTA called for immediately eliminating duties on half of all US goods shipped to Mexico and gradually phasing out other tariffs over a period of about 14 years. Restrictions were to be removed from many categories, including motor vehicles and automotive parts, computers, textiles, and agriculture. The treaty also protected intellectual property rights (patents, copyrights, and trademarks) and outlined the removal of restrictions on investment among the three countries. Provisions regarding worker and environmental protection were added later as an expansion of the earlier Canada-US Free Trade Agreement of 1989. Unlike the EU, it does not create a set of supranational governmental bodies, nor does it create a body of law which is superior to national law. NAFTA, as an international agreement, is very similar to a treaty. The agreement was initially pursued by free-trade governments in the US and Canada. Some opposition persists to the present day, although labour unions in Canada have recently removed objections to the agreement from their platforms.

Optimum currency area (OCA) theory   This theory is utilised by economists to identify those factors which indicate the optimum size of a currency arrangement. Consequently, the theory proposes that objective tests can be employed to decide whether it is in the common interests of, for example, Ireland and Italy, or France and Germany, whether they should join together in EMU, or whether it is in their mutual advantage to retain separate currencies and monetary systems. Similarly, the theory could be used to identify whether regions, rather than countries, should form a currency union. Thus, the South-East of England may have more in common with certain wealthy regions of Germany and France than either Wales or Northern Ireland, and in theory it may make economic sense to form a currency arrangement accordingly. In practice, however, whilst nation states remain the principal form of government for the majority of the world's population, OCA theory will be concerned in deciding where monetary integration should and should not be formed between groups of countries.

Organisation of Economic Co-operation and Development (OECD)   The 'rich nations' club, based in Paris, famous for economic research and forecasting.

Single European Act (SEA)   The 1986 Single European Act introduced the single internal market, but also extended qualified majority voting within the Council of Ministers and further committed the EU to 'the objective of the progressive realisation of European and Monetary Union'.

Single European Market (SEM)/Single Internal Market (SIM)   Resulting from the 1986 Single European Act, the single market refers to the removal of trade, capital and physical barriers across Europe, supposedly achieved by 1 January 1993, which allows the free competition across the entire EU market.

Stability and Growth Pact (SGP)   Proposed by Germany to avoid excessive fiscal profligacy by individual member states within EMU, it limits budget deficits to 3 per cent of GDP (as per MCC prior to membership). If this limit is ignored, and the country is not in recession (defined as GDP falling by 0.75 per cent), fines of between 0.2 and 0.5 per cent of GDP will be levied by the EU financial authorities. The Stability and Growth Pact additionally suggests that budget deficits be limited to 1 per cent of GDP in the long-term, thus increasing fiscal tightening.

Chapter 1

Introduction

The relationship between Britain and the European Union (EU) has been a difficult one over many decades, beginning with disinterest upon its formation, increasing desperation to gain membership when this appeared to guarantee superior economic performance, and latterly disquiet about the net drain that membership has upon the vitality of the national economy. There is no doubt that an organisation that has recently expanded to twenty-seven (and counting) member states is a significant player in the world economy. It has a larger population size and gross purchasing power than the USA. The introduction of Economic and Monetary Union (EMU) between twelve member states, in its initial phase, is without precedent in world economic history, since it has occurred without first attaining political integration intended to govern the single economy so created. Therefore, the EU is certainly a powerful economic and trade bloc, and all medium sized nations should desire to form some type of relationship with this organisation in their own interests. Nevertheless, this does not necessitate membership or the signing of formal treaty arrangements, but may involve a relatively informal statement of co-operation on a range of topics for mutual benefit.

One factor underlying the difficulty of the relationship between Britain and the EU arises from the fact that the former has tended to regard European integration as primarily (or entirely) an economic process, whilst leading federalists have taken a more holistic viewpoint, balancing more towards economic integration with aspects of political union. Thus, British membership of the then 'Common Market' has been transformed as the organisation has taken on more powers and trappings of a super-national state, most powerfully reflected in the introduction of EMU amongst the majority of pre-2004/2007 accession existing member states, but also reflected in moves towards the establishment of a federal system including a constitution and unified foreign policy stance. These initiatives have move ahead of the majority of British citizens, who express surprise (and more than a little hostility) towards this policy drift. This divergence between those seeking a narrow or broad direction for the EU has therefore dogged its development, with moves to pursue a federalist agenda, rejected by a majority of British voters due to a failure to first debate the future of Europe and thereby gain consent (or otherwise) for the preferences of the political elite.

The importance of the EU for British economic development has, additionally, been called into account due to the increasing impact of globalisation. The dramatic reduction in world tariffs on manufactured goods and many types of services, together with international deregulation of controls on currency movements and national financial sectors, have facilitated the expansion of international trade, greater financial market integration, and the development of the trans-national organisation of production facilities. The process has enabled the rapid economic development of Asian economies, including Taiwan, Singapore, South Korea, Hong Kong, China and India. In such circumstances, the question has been raised over the relative importance that Britain, or any other medium-sized economy, should give towards *regional* economic integration, as opposed to pursuing a policy of *global* trade and other economic links. Indeed, it is certainly true that, in more recent years, the former economic dynamism associated with the EU appears to have declined, and the burdens of economic failure (i.e. long-term, large-scale unemployment) have been keenly experienced in many continental European nations.

The question of Britain's relationship with the EU is further complicated since it cuts across traditional political divisions, so that advocates and opponents of deeper political and/or economic integration can be found on both sides of the party political divide. Neo-liberal conservatives may support the creation of a large free trade area, free from all political interference with the agenda of big business, but may oppose most forms of regulation (particularly social policy) and discussion of political integration that originate in Brussels. Similarly, a left-of-centre supporter of European integration is likely to hold their views because of the importance of establishing regional regulation of capital, and promotion of a social dimension to an otherwise narrowly economic perception of European integration, whilst they may be less enamoured by the power that the 'project' gives to trans-national corporations and the resultant weakness of trade unions and national governments. Consequently, the greater the emphasis all parties place upon the negative features, the more likely they are to be described as 'Eurosceptics', and the net advocates of the process 'Europhiles'. Yet, the important point to note is that honest commentators within each grouping accept that the debate over the future relationship between Britain and the EU is not wholly one-sided and that their conclusions are reached due to their analysis of the problem and preferred solutions.

This book seeks to provide an analysis of the economic relationship between Britain and the EU and thereby facilitate discussion of the future direction in which this relationship might develop. In the process, it will examine historic and contemporary costs and benefits in seeking to arrive at an estimation of whether, to date, EU membership has been a burden or an assist for the British economy. Additionally, it assesses current trends and developments, most notably in the area of EMU participation and the consequences that this, reinforced by the impact of its institutional framework, would have upon the British economy. Questions of fiscal federalism, the development of a minimum level of social policy for Europe, together with the likely impact upon business and trade unions, are additionally considered. The book finally turns to consider alternatives to the current arrangements between Britain and the EU, whether involving a degree of re-negotiation of rights and responsibilities, or adopting some other means of relaxing the uniformity necessitated by current membership rules, so that, either Britain alone, or indeed the entire EU organisation, can enjoy enhanced flexibility and autonomy within a loose membership arrangement. In the terminology, this would create a united conglomeration of individual, sovereign states, and not a 'United States of Europe'. Additionally, the final section of the book examines the consequences that might arise if Britain withdrew from the EU, either to be free of the costs and restraints imposed by membership, or through desiring to create different forms of trade and/ or macroeconomic strategy aimed at more optimally promoting national economic development than under the current EU model. Hence, conclusions are reached relating to a range of alternative economic policies that could be adopted, both within and without formal EU membership, which might improve the economic development of the British economy.

PART I
Britain as an Awkward Partner

Chapter 2

Britain and the EU:
A Difficult Relationship

Introduction

This chapter provides an overview of the historical relationship between the UK and the EU. Firstly, it summarises why the EU is a distinctive entity compared to the other international organisations to which Britain is aligned (e.g. NATO, UN, IMF etc). It is from this perspective of the unique interrelationship between Britain and the EU that many, if not all, of the tensions emanate from. Secondly, we briefly review the turbulent 'on-off' relationship that characterised the post Second World War period. We follow the assessment of Harrison (1996) that the relationship has processed through several distinct phases. Significant for this book overall, the most recent of these can be traced back to the 1988 Bruges speech of Mrs Thatcher and formalised under the leadership William Hague in 1997. The victory of the Eurosceptic wing of the Conservative Party over the Europhile camp, represented by Kenneth Clarke in the 1997 leadership election, has developed to the point where UK membership is being openly questioned. Thirdly, we examine the potential causes for the often-fractious relationship between Britain and its Continental neighbours. Possible reasons for this include the UK's unbroken history, the legacy of empire and war, the presence of a distinctive legal system, unique capitalist structure and an individualistic culture. It is argued that these play an important role in contributing to the frequently conflicting aspirations of both people and politicians on each side of the English Channel.

A Short History of European Integration

The EU is a unique institution, which is continually evolving in bursts of activity interspersed with relative passivity. The intention to peacefully integrate European economies has precedents as long ago as the fourteenth century, although the particular form taken by the EU is largely determined by its emergence out of the period of political and economic reconstruction following World War II. Its aim, as specified in the founding 1957 Treaty of Rome, has been to 'lay the foundations of an ever closer union among the peoples of Europe and by pooling resources is to preserve and strengthen peace and liberty'. Thus, the EU was established as a political organisation to enhance security through mutual reconstruction, whilst avoiding excessive nationalism so recently exhibited by European nation states.

From the beginning, the EU has evolved principally through the promotion of economic co-operation and integration preceding ever-closer political ties. Thus, it was foundered through a merger of the European Coal and Steel Community, the European Atomic Energy Community and the European Economic Community. Subsequently, it created a customs union before further integration established a single internal market. Indeed, the creation of EMU between twelve EU member states should be perceived as another step on this road of further integration. However, the principal reason why the architects of this 'new' Europe have preferred economic integration to precede political union is the result of a political conflict between competing visions of the mechanism(s) of achieving closer ties between nations.

Throughout the development of the EU there have been disagreements and fluctuating alliances between federalists, advocating the replacement of individual nation states by a larger democratic structure, internationalists, preferring a global not regional focus, and nationalists, who prefer a community of nation states engaged in free trade. As a result, it has typically been easier to reform trading relations between member states than generate unanimity on more politically sensitive issues such as tax harmonisation, border controls, together with the establishment of a unified army, foreign policy and police force.

The organisational model adopted by the EU reflects its creation as a 'cold war' entity, dominated by Europe's political and business elite. It is the EU Commission, civil servants who *initiate* topics for discussion and provide subsequent drafts of propose legislation, who are thereby able to influence the future agenda. The Council of Ministers comprises representatives of national governments, whose agreement is required for proposals to become legally binding Directives. Thus, the future framework of the EU is determined between two self-selected groups, which are substantially more open to lobbying by business interests than by civic groups (Balanyá *et al.*, 2000). The third EU institution, the European Parliament is comprised of directly elected representatives in approximate proportion to a nation's relative population size. However, parliament is a relatively new phenomenon, grafted onto the existing elite model to enhance popular support of the EU institutions whilst simultaneously countering claims of a democratic deficit at the heart of the organisation. Although able to review proposals, the parliament can only affect most issues through the power of its persuasion, with the twin exceptions being the power to reject the annual budget and the ability to sack the entire Commission. Thus, the EU organisational model still suffers from a democratic deficit in terms of direct influence afforded to European citizens over the decision-making process of the principle institutions.

Thus, the main impetus for the formation of a co-operative movement amongst countries in Western Europe was the experience of the Second World War. Indeed, the need to avert further conflicts and consolidate peace is a goal that the process of European integration has certainly helped to achieve alongside the role of NATO, which should not be underestimated. The first initiative, drawn up by Jean Monnet, the head of the French Commission for Economic Planning, was to ensure that reconstruction in the heavy industries of West Germany should not endanger peace. The result was the European Coal and Steel Treaty (ECST) in 1951, which had three key objectives. Firstly, to ensure integration through the removal of customs duties and quotas over a five year transition period, modernisation and expansion of these industries through investment, the restriction of protectionist state aids and the provision of a common external commercial policy. Secondly, such detailed agreements were subservient to the political goal of achieving stability between France and Germany. Finally, the Treaty was instrumental in setting up supra-national institutions (e.g. the Council of Ministers, European Court of Justice), which would begin the process of closer co-operation between European partners. For her part, Germany was more than happy to accept the possibility of regaining control over its key industries as well as the prospect of rehabilitation, whilst the French, who largely engineered this initiative, along with Belgium, Italy, Luxembourg and the Netherlands also warmly received the proposals. More importantly, this agreement would also come to represent the first tentative steps toward European integration (Baimbridge *et al.*, 2004).

Six years later the European Economic Community (EEC) Treaty was ratified, which laid the foundations for a Common Market for the free movement in services and factors of production and the nurturing of free competition. In 1968, the six original members made further advances by the blanket removal of intra-community trade tariffs, the formation of a common external tariff (CET) on trade with third countries and the adoption of a common commercial policy. The EEC Treaty continued to follow the supra-nationalist model employed in the ECST by creating a framework within which these institutions could more effectively enact EEC legislation and law pertaining to the principles of the single market. However, almost twenty years passed until further steps in European integration materialised in the form of the Single European Act (1986). This legislature would contribute significantly to the integration process through the introduction of qualified majority voting (QMV).[1]

In the 1990s, the objectives of European integration broadened from that of a European Community to a European Union (EU). In the Treaty on European Union (TEU) (commonly known as the Maastricht Treaty) in 1992, three pillars of European decision-making were formalised. The first pillar was essentially the European Community involving the adoption, modification and implementation of a legislative framework for the operation of the single market. The ethos behind the second and third pillars was to encourage intergovernmental co-operation in the areas of Foreign and Security Policy, and Justice and Home Affairs respectively.[2] In this context, the role of the Commission and the European Parliament is limited, where decision-making is made on the basis of Member State representatives in the forum of the Council of Ministers. The EU was, however, still faced with the cumbersome procedure of having to ratify important international agreements with third countries both in the capacity of a single body and as a collection of member states (Baimbridge *et al.*, 2004).

---

1   Except, *inter alia*, in the area of tax harmonisation that still relies on unanimity.

2   Despite the formulation of a common foreign and security policy, the experience has, at best, been mixed with failure to forge a coherent policy towards the Balkans, whilst there were well publicised splits over Iraq.

Accordingly, a key feature of the Treaty of Amsterdam in 1997 was to ordain the Council with powers to represent the EU thus providing a more focused point of reference on the world stage. This Treaty also shifted matters pertaining to external border controls, immigration and asylum from the third to the first pillar in an attempt to solidify the concept that full implementation of a single market required a working space that protected the rights and provided security for both EU and non-EU citizens alike. The other major achievement in the 1990s (within the TEU) was the formalisation of guiding principles and mechanisms for Economic and Monetary Union (EMU), which would eventually lead to the adoption of a single currency (Baimbridge *et al.*, 2004).

The other notable development over this fifty year time frame has been the growth in EU stature on the world stage as membership in the original club of six has expanded, beginning with Denmark, Ireland and the United Kingdom joining in 1973. Enlargement to the 'South' previously had been deemed inconceivable due to the political affiliations of the ruling parties. Indeed, up until the early to mid-1970s, Greece, Portugal and Spain were governed by a non-elected body, which was considered as an unofficial (until TEU formalised this requirement) obstacle to entry. However, with the return of democracy, each sought and gained membership throughout the 1980s, starting with Greece (1981) followed by Portugal and Spain (1986). Finally, in 1996, the EU enlarged again with the accessions of Austria, Finland and Sweden. In 2004, the Union embraced another ten members: Cyprus, The Czech Republic, Estonia, Hungary, Latvia, Lithuania, Malta, Poland, Slovakia, Slovenia; with Bulgaria and Romania following in 2007. Further enlargements are to be expected, as Croatia has already applied for Candidate status whilst a number of Western Balkan states (Albania, Bosnia-Herzegovina, Macedonia, Serbia, Montenegro) are each aspiring for membership over the coming years, not forgetting the long-standing position of Turkey as an aspirant member.

Why the EU is Distinctive

Prior to examining in detail the historical relationship between Britain and the EU, the unique aspect of the features of the EU that make it a distinctive entity need to be reviewed. Firstly, the scale of the EU's activities and its impact on British life is illustrated by its geographical reach, population and trading capacity of the EU. However, it can also be seen from the extent of EU policy competences from an organisation originally designed to promote competition and trade, it has developed a wide range of policy responsibilities, whilst EMU and the attempt to introduce a Constitution has moved the EU closer to actual statehood. Even the policy areas where national governments have guarded their sovereignty (e.g. foreign policy and justice issues) have become the subject of increasing supranational collaboration. Secondly, the EU comprises a complex set of institutional structures and policy arrangements. Thirdly, it is unlike most supranational organizations (where relationships are mediated through national governments) in the extent to which the EU seeks a progressively more direct relationship with the civil societies and citizens of its member states. For example, the Treaty of Amsterdam of 1997 made the citizens of member states citizens of the EU, thereby establishing the dual loyalty and identity found in federal systems. Indeed, the EU Constitution represented a further extension in this direction until is derailing by the electorate of France and the Netherlands in 2005. Thus on some measures, the structures of the European Union are already well advanced towards the federal model and display greater integration than those of well-established federations such as the United States (McKay, 1999, 2001).

The EU is also distinctive among international organisations in being able to act autonomously of its national members whereby much EU legislation has direct and immediate effect. Subsidiarity (the principle that decisions should be taken at the lowest possible level) often appears more honoured in the breach than in the observance, and a more powerful dynamic within the EU seems to be one pushing policy towards the European level of decision-making. Most important of all, perhaps, in giving the EU a distinctive and controversial character is that there is no consensus between its member states regarding its final goal; whether its aim is confederation, federation or simply a closer union of independent nation states (Peele, 2004).

The Formal Political Relationship

The most important source of external influence on British politics since 1973 was not a single country but what is now the EU. On the European issue the Liberals (latterly Liberal Democrats) are alone among the parties to show consistency, nourished by their distance from power after 1945. In contrast, Labour and Conservative have pursued electoral advantage through syncopations of policy over seven broad phases between 1945 and the present (Table 2.1). Harrison (1996) labels the initial six phases as: Conservative Europeanism (1945–51), British isolationism (1951–61), revived Conservative Europeanism (1961–7), all-party Europeanism (1967–70), revived Conservative Europeanism (1970–5), and revived all-party Europeanism (1975–1997), which continues for the Labour Party. However, a seventh phase can be identified, namely that of Conservative euroscepticism (1997–).

Table 2.1   Summary of UK-EU relationship

Phases of UK-EU relationship	Comment
Conservative Europeanism (1945–1951)	Winston Churchill demonstrated more sympathy than Labour with Europe's aspirations to unity, but this did not entail any choice between Europe and the 'open seas'.
British Isolationism (1951–1961)	On taking office Churchill disappointed some Conservative 'Europeans' by opting clearly for the open seas, thereby launching the second (isolationist) phase.
Revived Conservative Europeanism (1961–1967)	The first application for entry in 1961 launched the third phase. Although Britain had at last reached the situation where the government was in favour of membership and Macmillan's bid failed with de Gaulle partly because of the conflict between the low-key domestic campaign conducted and the need to convince the French that Britain was psychologically 'ready' for the change. Moreover, de Gaulle realised that Macmillan had not abandoned pursuit of the 'special relationship' on defence and other matters with the United Sties. In Heath, however, the Conservatives found a leader who was 'not inclined to postpone choices, whose instincts on foreign policy were far more radical, and who was ready to use his influence within his Party energetic to push Euro-sceptics into a minority' (Harrison, 1996).
All-Party Europeanism (1967–1970)	Wilson's application for entry launched the fourth phase, during which for the first time Europeanism encompassed both government and opposition, indeed the Conservatives took the unusual step of imposing a three-line whip in favour of Wilson's decision to apply. However, whilst the leaders in both parties now favoured membership, their rank and file contained dissidents. In particular, Labour dissidents were determined to exploit the European issue as a way of repudiating the Wilson government that had disappointed them on other issues.
Revived Conservative Europeanism (1970–1975)	Hence, in the fifth phase, Europeanism reverted to being a single-party alignment. Once in power in 1974 Labour set about restoring all-party agreement on EEC membership, negotiating amended terms of accession, subject to the referendum that emerged as a device for holding its pro- and anti-EEC wings together. The two-to-one referendum victory placed Labour's Euro-sceptic left on the defensive such that Party activists, who prided themselves on being more closely in touch with opinion than the leaders they criticized, received a severe shock.

Revived All-Party Europeanism (1975–1997)	Although both Labour and Conservative governments saw themselves as European throughout this phase, both parties were divided. Labour at first remained sufficiently Eurosceptic for defence of Britain's continued EEC membership to fuel the SDP's secession. By summer 1980 Labour's Europeans were on the defensive, and three members of the future 'gang of four' (Williams, Owen, and Rodgers) issued a statement deploring the revived threat to leave the EEC. However, the subsequent Party conference ignored David Owen's plea and voted to take Britain out of the EEC without a referendum.

On the Conservative side of the political divide as long as the EEC saw itself as a community of nation states that provided an enlarged free market for British goods, Thatcher had no difficulty with membership. She was able to silence the developing divide in her Party after 1979 by her desire to improve the financial basis of Britain's membership in relation to the Community budget. However, two developments in the 1980s made this position difficult to sustain. Firstly, the contrast between a free-market Britain and an interventionist EEC progressively widened under the Thatcher revolution and secondly, while the EEC moved from being a free-trade area to economic and then political union. Indeed, by the mid-1980s Labour was becoming more sympathetic to the EEC given that socialism was now on the defensive at home, the EEC began to seem for Labour a last redoubt for these values. Simultaneously, Thatcher was losing a sequence of important ministers (Heseltine, Lawson, and Howe) who disliked the anti-European direction she now seemed to be taking.

Conservative Euroscepticism (1997–)	Hence, commencing under the Premiership of Thatcher and her 1988 Bruges speech, there has been a discernable drift away from the Heath inspired Europeanisation of the Conservative Party. This was further highlighted by the Treaty on European Union ratification process between December 1991 and July 1993 and elsewhere in the government of John Major (1992–97). However, it was with the leadership of William Hague (1997–2001) that the final rupture in the post-1975 all-party Europeanisation consensus could be most clearly pinpointed. Thus we identify a seventh phase of Conservative Euroscepticism in which the seeds had been sown almost a decade prior, but which came to fruitition under the leadership of William Hague in 1997. Hague sought to make the EU, and in particular the adoption of the euro, a key issue of difference ('clear blue water' being the catchphrase of the time) between New Labour and the Conservatives. Whilst this caused tensions in his party, it also led to it doubling its seats (to 36) in the 1999 European Parliamentary elections suggesting it to be a popular stance. However, it proved less effective in the 2001 General Election when the issue of Europe registered lower than the traditional concerns of the economy, health and education etc. However, two leaders latter and this distinctive Eurosceptical focus remains at the forefront of Conservative policy. Indeed, they fought the 2005 General Election with the most Eurosceptic manifesto of the three main national parties.

Source: Adapted from Harrison (1996).

The question therefore becomes: what does this seven-fold sequence reveal about the two main political parties? Firstly, because they compete for electoral advantage through seeking new sources of support, full ventilation for Eurosceptic and Europhile opinion has been assured, even at the expense of party consistency on policy. Secondly, Britain's EU story reveals the importance of divisions within, as well as between, parties in the process of seeking opinion likely to be electorally helpful. Thirdly, although the EU is difficult to fit into the traditions of both Conservative and Labour parties, it did not in itself prompt the emergence of a centre party (although it has arguably led to the rise of the UK Independence Party, ironically aided through the instigation of proportional representation for European Parliament elections) still less an electoral system favouring centrist government. Indeed, the two-party system has been tenacious enough to survive continuous comparison with the proportional representation and centre-government coalition systems in the EU. Fourthly, there is the two-party system's capacity to present an image of indecision, inconsistency, and even bad faith. This has done nothing to boost Britain's reputation within the EU, though such wavering and hesitation probably accurately reflects the state of British opinion on the issue since the 1950s.

This raises the rather different question of how public opinion on the European issue has impinged on the political system since 1945. Harrison (1996) argues that pressure groups directly concerned with the matter have been relatively unimportant. Interest and cause groups concerned with specific areas of policy, gravitating as they instinctively do to the centres of power, have of course been active at the European level. Yet Britain's three applications to join the (then) EEC did not result from pressure-group activity. Thus, if pressure groups were relatively unimportant, why did public opinion not only accept that Britain should not only enter the (then) EEC, but also the steady extension of its aspirations? The answer is that general public have seldom been overtly enlisted in the process. There has been only one referendum, and General Elections have never centred upon the European issue, bar perhaps the one-sided attempt by Hague in 2001. Although the 1975 referendum did at least involve the public in reaching a decision, many commentators argue that Wilson's handling of the entire issue since 1970 had loaded the decision in favour of entry and continued membership (Butler and Kitzinger, 1996). However, as previously described, there has been a perceptible rise in Euroscepticism both within the major parties and through the emergence of smaller parties such as the UK Independence Party and the Green Party of England and Wales. Hence, public disenchantment with the EU has begun to find specific outlets (voice) within the political arena. Thus, at the time of writing both the scheduled EU-related referendums regarding the EU constitution and UK membership of EMU are appearing that (if held at all) they will reverse the continuous process of EU integration on the part of Britain.

Reasons for British Difficulties with the EU

There is both a scholarly and a political debate about why Britain has so often appeared to be at odds with its European neighbours (George, 1992, 1998). These can be summarised as the frequently expressed questions of: Why does Britain not appear to share the vision of the other member states? Why does the UK so often resists common policies? Why is it that it always seems to be Britain that wants special treatment? Why in spite of its size and international influence is the British government perceived as trying to block or dilute the impact of initiatives from Brussels? Here we seek to summarise the many and complex reasons for Britain's lack of enthusiasm towards the European project when the rest of Europe seems keen on economic and political integration.

The first theme revolves around the notion of an unbroken history. In particular, this relates to the lack of invasion, absence of revolution and being an 'old' state in a 'new' world. Firstly, given a lack of invasion, it is impossible to understand Britain's place in Europe without appreciating the importance of the institutional continuity of British political structures. Most of continental Europe has been swept by invading armies several times in the last couple of hundred years, but England has not been invaded since 1066. Secondly, there has been an absence of revolution, whereby Britain has not undergone a dramatic revolutionary upheaval, such as that which transformed France (1789) or Russia (1917). The closest was the Civil War (1642–1648) and the Glorious Revolution (1689) that established the principle of parliamentary sovereignty and a constitutional monarchy, but crucially it reformed the institutions of governance rather than replacing them with new ones.

As an old state in a new world, when we look at the rest of Europe, most states are either relatively new, or have gone through upheavals in the fairly recent past as a result of wars or revolutions. For example, Germany was only unified as a single state in 1870, but it was then divided again in 1945, and was finally reunified as recently as 1990. Whilst Spain, Portugal and Greece were under military dictatorships as late as the 1970s, so their contemporary political institutions and structures are relatively new. Italy was only unified in the nineteenth century, while Yugoslavia came into being after the First World War and has since disintegrated into its constituent parts. Moreover, some of the countries who have recently joined the EU (Hungary, Poland, and the Czech Republic), have recently been reconstituted following the end of the Russian occupation, and other areas, like the three Baltic states (Latvia, Lithuania and Estonia) have only established their independence since the implosion of the Soviet Union at the start of the 1990s.

A second aspect unique to Britain relates to the twin concepts of empire and war. Here both the legacy of empire and the pretence of global influence are regarded as explanatory causes of Britain's non-alignment with the rest of Europe. Although its empire disappeared in a very short time after the Second World War, what the empire left behind, however, was a pattern of international trade and cooperation that looked away from Europe and towards the Commonwealth. One of the major considerations when Britain joined the EEC in 1973 was the abandonment of its Commonwealth partners, who now found their goods and services outside the CET particularly in agricultural products (Burkitt and Baimbridge, 1990).

Whilst Britain can no longer realistically pose as a top power, however, in international diplomacy it still tends to 'punch above its weight', through holding onto its permanent seat on the United Nations Security Council, and maintaining a level of military spending that allows it to join the USA as a junior partner. Hence, Britain's reflex reaction is still to look to its 'special relationship' with the USA, rather than to deeper cooperation in Europe. Moreover, when American and European positions collide Britain is still usually to be found, isolated among its European partners, siding with the Americans. However, economically and politically, Britain cannot pretend to be the major player even in Western Europe given that eight of the other EU member states are wealthier than Britain, the EU itself is dominated by a strong Franco-German axis, and Britain is left trying to come to terms with a future as an island at the extreme north-western edge of an emerging federal European superstate.

The third element is the development of a distinctive legal system, whereby Britain operates a very different legal system from that found on the continent, where the Napoleonic Code forms the basis of law. Consequently, Britain has to make major adjustments that the other EU nations do not have to make. Indeed, if in future the development of a single European state required close harmonization of national legal systems, then it would be Britain that would have to make the shift.

In particular, the British system of law differs in many important respects from that in most of Continental Europe. For example, the jury system is not generally found in Europe, where magistrates and judges tend to bring in a verdict as well as conducting a trial. Furthermore, the adversarial system of justice is also alien to the European inquisitorial tradition, where an examining magistrate questions witnesses on all sides in an attempt to uncover the truth of a particular case. Finally, Continental law also makes much more use of general enabling legislation, that which hands over to the European Commission the right to issue related directives which have the status of new laws and which do not require parliamentary approval. Instead, the British system relies on common law, leaving it to judges to interpret how statutes should apply in particular cases, and binding them to a tradition set by the precedent of earlier rulings.

A further aspect to the contrasting legal systems concerns the different rights of citizenship. Such that perhaps the most important difference between the British and continental traditions concerns the different conceptions of citizenship based in the two different legal systems. There is a presumption in continental European law that citizens' rights are granted and safeguarded by the state because it is enshrined in a constitutional document. Legal rights in this tradition are therefore prescriptive. In Britain, by contrast, it has been assumed that individuals have the right to do whatever they choose provided law does not explicitly prohibit it. Legal rights in this tradition are only hampered by proscriptive legislation. This explains why the UK has no equivalent to a Bill of Rights, for in principle we are born with our freedoms and do not look to the state to grant them to us.

A fourth identified difference is that Britain possesses a distinctive type of capitalism typified by the City of London, liberalised markets and its welfare state regime. Hence, whilst the primary emphasis in the move to closer European integration was economic, such that all the EU nations pursue the capitalist market system, British-style capitalism is distinctive compared with that in continental Europe. Hence, with the requirement that twenty-five European economies should converge, it is the British economy that once again appears most out of step.

Through the City of London, the size and significance of its financial services market is a unique feature of the British economy. Not only does London host hundreds of banks, insurance companies and other financial institutions, but its stock exchange and its futures and bonds markets are also the major trading markets in Europe for shares and securities.

The City of London is an indicator of a much more profound underlying difference between the British and continental capitalist systems, the degree of liberalised markets. For example, Albert (1993) contrasts many of the features found in 'Rhine' model countries with those characteristic of the more liberal systems (neo-American model) of capitalism and identifies three key differences in these alternative capitalism systems. Firstly, share capital plays a much more significant role in funding private investment and thereby promoting a short-term perspective in contrast to relying on bank loans to fund new investment. Secondly, the development of a credit culture where the 1980s regulation of financial services facilitated an increase of credit far greater than anything witnessed in other EU countries. This also contrasts with more of a 'savings culture' in Rhine model countries (excluding private pension funds). Finally, the emergence of a competitive ethos compared to an emphasis on cooperation based on corporatist structures between government, capital and organised labour.

Such differences form the background to Britain's emphasis to greater supply-side reforms in the European economies through removing subsidies to industry, ending support to agriculture, opening up competition and reducing labour market controls and regulation. However, such reforms are alien on the Continent with the Social Chapter, for example, illustrating how Britain is expected to fall into line with the rest of Europe.

Additionally, welfare state regimes further illustrate the divide between the British and continental European capitalist systems. A key study by Esping-Andersen (1990) has identified three distinctive 'welfare regimes' in Europe. Firstly, liberal regimes (e.g. Britain) where there is an emphasis on social security as a 'safety net' rather than universal provision. Here the key concern is that welfare provision should not undermine labour market flexibility through an over-generous provision of benefits. Secondly, corporatist welfare regimes (e.g. Germany) where the emphasis is on socially inclusive forms of insurance, but in accordance to people's position in the labour market. Finally, social-democratic welfare regimes (e.g. Scandinavia) where the emphasis is on equality resulting in benefits being both high and universal.

A final general difference between Britain and other EU countries is its distinctively individualistic culture, both traditional and contemporary. Anglo-Saxon individualism has been identified in the pioneering studies of Hofstede (1980) relating to how different countries ranked on an individualism/collectivism scale. Within the Western group of countries the most individualistic countries were the USA, Australia, Britain and Canada. In contrast, most EU countries came considerably further down the scale. Such individualism found in contemporary English-speaking cultures, it is argued, can be traced back to the end of feudalism with its restrictions on the sale and purchase of land, which remained in force in parts of continental Europe up to and beyond the time of the French Revolution. Hence, people were used to selling their labour for a wage, and to exchanging goods and services in return for money, such that market-based individualism seems to have predated Protestantism and the Reformation by several centuries. It is interesting to note in this regard that it was British thinkers (e.g. John Locke, David Hume, Adam Smith, David Ricardo and John Stuart Mill) who first developed the ideas and principles of liberalism in relation to individual liberty, the free market and the minimal state.

Contemporary individualism can be seen as the pervasive culture that underpins many aspects of British economic and social life in contrast to European norms. Again, privatised provision signals a more individualistic culture illustrated in Britain by a much higher proportion of its population in private or occupational pension schemes, a higher rate of private home ownership and a stronger system of private education. As a corollary, public provision is generally weaker in Britain than elsewhere in Western Europe.

Effects of Membership on British Politics

This final section reviews the aspects in which the EU has fundamentally influenced the British political system. These are briefly discussed in relation to its constitution, parliament and elections.

In terms of Britain developing a written constitution by signing the Treaty of Accession in 1972 and subsequent treaties (Maastricht, Amsterdam and Nice etc) Britain incorporated a lengthy written element in her constitution that take precedence over 'ordinary' statute law. Consequently, the supremacy of European law is a major limitation on Parliament's sovereignty although Parliament may at any time repudiate EU membership and the obligations consequent on that membership and leave the EU. Furthermore, EU membership also entailed a significant change to the conduct of elections in Britain. Firstly, a nationwide referendum was held for the first time in 1975 on Britain's continued membership of the EEC one unanswered question was what would have happened if Parliament had voted one way and the electorate another.

Secondly, since 1979 there are five-yearly elections to the European Parliament where the most significant feature of the elections is the derisory turnouts leading to questions of a 'democratic deficit'. This raises problems for the legitimacy of the European project, implying that the enterprise found largely among political elites rather than the broader public. Indeed, identification with and awareness of representative institutions remains much higher at national than European level.

Table 2.2 illustrates the mean turnout statistics over the 1979–2004 period for the EU(15) and the EU as a whole both pre- and post-2004.[3] The consequence of continuous compulsory voting is clearly evident, together with its legacy post–1993 in Italy. There follows a cluster of 5 member states averaging between 50–60 per cent turnout, whilst the remaining 6 are resolutely below the significant 50 per cent barrier, including Britain.

---

3   For the calculation of EP election turnout the initial 'out of sequence' EP elections of accession countries (Spain, Portugal, Sweden, Austria and Finland) are counted as per the immediate prior EP election, otherwise these results would be omitted from the quinquennial calculations. Moreover, the unweighted member state turnout is used in all tables and calculations.

Table 2.2   Summary of EP election turnout (1979–2004)

	Number of elections	Average turnout (per cent)
Belgium*	6	91.13
Luxembourg*	6	88.48
Italy	6	78.08
Greece*	6	73.28
Spain	5	58.30
European Union (1979–2004)	89	56.66
Ireland	6	55.57
Germany	6	55.50
Austria	3	52.97
France	6	51.45
Denmark	6	49.62
Portugal	5	47.56
Finland	3	44.27
Netherlands	6	43.38
Sweden	3	39.20
UK	6	33.38

*Compulsory voting.
Source: Baimbridge (2005).

Thirdly, both Houses of Parliament have created committees to consider the increasing body of draft European legislation. As more decisions are made in the Council of Ministers by majority voting, so British ministers become less responsible to Parliament for Council decisions that they are not able to veto. In terms of administration, Whitehall is becoming more European-minded with civil servants liaising with Brussels to take account of the European dimension of policies, and an increasing number are being seconded to the EU. Ministers are also spending more time negotiating with their ministerial counterparts in the other member states and the views of departments are coordinated through the European Secretariat in the Cabinet Office (Bulmer and Burch, 1998).

For Britain's judiciary they are required under the treaties to give precedence to European law. Not only do British statutes have to be amended to remove any conflict, but also plaintiffs are also able to claim damages against national governments that do not give effect to European laws.

Evidently, a consequence of EU membership has been that the state has lost a significant degree of autonomy in a whole range of policy areas. Thus, despite the argument that parliamentary sovereignty is retained because the UK has the right to leave the EU if it so chooses, the reality is that the role of Parliament is often to ratify decisions made in the EU. Consequently, the EU appears to undermine the territorial integrity of its member states; decisions made outside the nation-state at the European level are being implemented within Britain. These factors seem to suggest that the autonomy of the British state is greatly restricted by EU membership, and that policy-making has increasingly become a partnership between the British government, other member states, and the institutions of the EU. The scope and depth of policy-making at the EU-level have dramatically increased. The EU has almost completed the internal market and has absorbed the institutional reforms of the Single European Act (1986), which established qualified majority voting in the Council of Ministers and increased the power of the European Parliament. The TEU further expanded EU competencies and the scope of qualified majority voting in the Council, and provided the European Parliament with a veto on certain types of legislation. The way the EU is designed, the difficulty of controlling the Commission, the problems with agreeing to restrain the process of integration, the unique informational base of the Commission, the regulatory powers of the Commission and the European Court of Justice, and the unintended consequences of institutional change all make it difficult for national governments to control the EU.

Table 2.3   Summary of policy competences

Policy competence predominantly located in the EU	Policy competence, a combination of EU and national governments	Policy competence predominantly located in national governments or through intergovernmental agreement
Agriculture	Environmental	Foreign affairs
Trade	Transport	Macro-economic policy
Fishing	Social policy	Health
Competition	Regional policy	Education
Consumer protection	Research and technology	Defence
Monetary policy (EMU)		Drugs
		Welfare benefits
		Law and order

Source: Richards and Smith (2002).

Table 2.3 illustrates how most policy areas now possess an EU element and, in particular, a significant number are either wholly or partially devolved from national governments.

Euroscepticism

One feature both of contemporary British politics and of Britain's attitude towards European integration is Euroscepticism, which has deeply divided the Conservative and Labour parties since the first moves towards integration in the early post-war years (Geddes, 2004).[4] In relation to the EU as a whole, it is generally stronger in Northern European countries, both member states such as Denmark, Sweden and the UK (Spiering, 2004; Sunnus, 2004), non-members (Iceland and Norway), together with Switzerland (Church, 2004). However, there is also a vocal sceptical opposition in founding member states such as France (Hainsworth *et al.*, 2004; Milner, 2004), Germany (Busch and Knelangen, 2004) and the Netherlands (Harmsen, 2004). Additionally, the phenomenon is also visible amongst the 2004 accession member states from Central and Eastern Europe is that the EU's bureaucracy and perceived socialist tendencies may be sustainable for mature Western European economies, but could weaken their fragile post-communist economies (Kopecky, 2004; Szczerbiak, 2004).

However, the notion of 'Euroscepticism' is fraught with difficulties in relation to its analytical purchase and as a descriptive tool, being rarely defined by the academia. Forster (2002: 2) seeks to breakaway from the narrow definitions through suggesting that it needs to be understood 'as a particular manifestation of a school of sceptical thought about the value of Britain's involvement with moves towards supranational European integration' which over time has remained constant in its fundamental concerns of sovereignty, national identity and economic and political independence. Thus, whilst Euroscepticism might initially be regarded as emerging from the late 1980s / early 1990s, is possesses a substantial historical context in which current EU developments are merely the latest in a long line of issues.

One of the initial difficulties of discussing Euroscepticism is the range of standpoints that it encompasses. Figure 2.1 illustrates the thought-action spectrum from weak versions of seeking to prevent deepening, if not widening, of European integration to outright disengagement and withdrawal if a member state or refusal to join if not (e.g. Norway, Iceland and Switzerland). However, matters are rarely this simple. Firstly, it would be misleading to equate Euroscepticism with anti-Europeanism, since it feasible to feel European in a geographical and cultural sense, but to oppose the EU as an entity. Secondly, for most it is not a bipolar choice between support and opposition of European integration, but scepticism regarding the direction in which it is developing (Behnisch, 2002). Thirdly, it is, of course, perfectly feasible for an individual or even a political party to find themselves moving along this spectrum given changing circumstances (Forster, 2002).

---

4   For a detailed analysis of this phenomenon within British politics, see Forster (2002).

Weak---Hard				
EU integration should extend no further	Roll back EU influence to position prior to TEU	Questioning benefits of EU membership	Argue for opt-outs and partial exemptions from areas of EU competence	Rejection of EU membership and advocate withdrawal from the EU

Source: Adapted from Forster (2002) and Flood (2002).

Figure 2.1   Spectrum of Euroscepticism

A further complicating factor when discussion Euroscepticism is that it frequently leads to paradoxical political unions across party and ideological divisions. However, subtle differences emerge in the detailed criticisms levied by commentators on each side of the divide. On the left, the traditional opposition of socialist and communists has more recently been supplemented by Green critiques. These are combined to attack the EU in terms of its economic commitment to neo-liberal capitalism (deregulation, free trade, globalisation etc), which is regarded as inimical to the well being of disadvantaged sections of both EU societies and those across the world. In political terms the key issues are seen as the EU's excessive subservience towards NATO and US military hegemony. For the right and extreme right, political objections focus upon the maintenance of national sovereignty, whilst economic issues centre on insufficient liberalism highlighted by excessive regulation and invention, together with budgetary burden for redistributive programmes (structural funds, the Cohesion Fund and the CAP). A further concern is the loss of control over national borders to regulate migration given its implications for labour markets, the welfare state and national identity (Flood, 2002).

The academic debate surrounding the concept of Euroscepticism has frequently been secondary to the more general debate regarding Britain as the perennial 'awkward partner' in terms of EU integration (George, 1992, 1998). Forster (2002: 3) argues that this is largely due to 'the predominance of pro-integrationists in the academic community, especially in the field of European integration, which for a variety of reasons has treated Euroscepticism in an asymmetrical way to pro-integration groups … The academic community has therefore routinely overlooked Eurosceptics and Euroscepticism and by design or default has often failed to treat it as a serious phenomenon or object of study'. Empirical studies utilising the Eurobarometer surveys indicate that lower levels of support for the EU are found amongst the retired, the unemployed and manual workers as opposed to white-collar workers, the self-employed and managers. Indicating a degree of association between socioeconomic and education levels and support for the EU (Flood, 2002).

Finally, in addition to the common difficulties of inconsistency and incoherence a significant deficiency identified by commentators regarding Euroscepticism has been the inability to 'articulate a clear alternative to the EU and Britain's membership of it' (Forster, 2002: 137). However, the evidence presented in this book argues that EU membership and the momentum towards deeper political and economic integration, has consistently undermined UK national interests. The EU was designed by the founding members to accommodate their perceived shared objectives, which are quite different from those of the UK, *inter alia*, the dominance of CAP expenditure, the UK's inequitably large net budget contributions, the persistent sizeable trade deficit with the EU and the creation of an immigration policy based on land-locked continental countries rather than an island nation. Further measures of integration, including the abolition of exchange controls, the design of the single market, and giving away economic sovereignty through entering the ERM and EMU, may be rational consequences for those EU nations which possess strong interdependency through trade and a shared culture, but are irrational for the UK.

Conclusion

Although European leaders have always made clear their view that the European project recognizes and even celebrates cultural diversity, however, the European project is building on a continental cultural heritage which is contrary to Britain's historical links to North America and its former empire reinforced by a common language, its individualistic culture and its system of law. However, of particular importance for this book is the fundamental difference in economic structures. Britain's economy depends to a much greater extent on its financial sector; it has a much smaller and more capital-intensive agricultural sector; it still trades significantly non-EU countries; and its liberal competitive instincts align it much more closely with the United States than with the corporatist traditions of Western Europe.

In summary, as the EU moves closer to complete political and monetary union, it is Britain that continues to make the most adjustments. In particular, British law is out of step with the emerging system of European law and the British economy is out of step with European regulated labour markets and corporatist management structures. Given this record of difficult adjustment to European integration and it is understandable if there is an increasing desire for Britain to slow down, pause, or even rethink the whole EU project.

Chapter 3

Historical Cost-Benefit Analysis of EU Membership

Introduction

The UK's relationship with the EU has been controversial ever since the Treaty of Rome established the latter. Indeed, public opinion polls since 1992 demonstrate a majority opinion amongst the UK electorate that remains critical of the EU, with a not insignificant number desiring withdrawal. In the face of such apparent hostility towards further economic and political integration, the British establishment has remained remarkably united in not only in supporting continued membership of the EU, but in fostering wider and deeper economic integration. Successive governments claimed that the benefits of EU membership are 'self-evident' (e.g. Lord Hanley, 3 July 1995, House of Lords), so that the UK must remain at the heart of Europe; otherwise it would lose crucial political influence and millions of jobs. Moreover, the UK government is committed to holding two Euro-referendums, relating to the newly negotiated European constitution and potential membership of EMU, and yet has thus far avoided undertaking the kind of information distribution and political campaign that is required if informed decisions are to be taken by British citizens. Furthermore, the claim is repeatedly made that even a slight weakening in the trend towards greater unification would cost the UK jobs and influence, never mind what would occur if the UK voted to withdraw from EU membership. Yet, governments of all colours have been remarkably reticent to undertake an independent cost-benefit analysis of UK membership.

The reason for this apparent conundrum is that at least in purely economic terms, it is doubtful that the UK has received a net benefit from EU membership. Indeed, even when taking political considerations into account, former Chancellor of the Exchequer, Norman Lamont who argued that

> The advantages of the European Union are remarkably elusive... I cannot pinpoint a single concrete economic advantage that unambiguously comes to this country because of our membership.

The following two chapters therefore seek to test Lamont's claim by compensating for the absence of an official cost-benefit analysis and reviewing the evidence relating to the historical advantages and disadvantages arising from EU membership for the British economy. This chapter concentrates upon trade-related matters, whereas Chapter 4 focuses upon the impact of EU institutional arrangements.

The Balance of Trade

After the UK's accession, tariffs on trade in manufactures between Britain and EU member countries were eliminated in five equal steps of 20 per cent implemented on 1 April 1973, 1 January 1974, 1 January 1975, 1 January 1976 and 1 July 1977. UK quantitative restrictions on EU trade were abolished on 1 January 1973, except for a few based on non-economic grounds, such as public morality and security. The UK was compelled to apply the Common External Tariff (CET) to imports from all countries not belonging to, or enjoying special arrangements with, the EU. The CET was applied in four stages of 40 per cent on 1 January 1974, 20 per cent on 1 January 1975, 20 per cent on 1 January 1976 and 20 per cent on 1 July 1977.

When Britain joined the EU, it was accepted that entry would impose a balance of payments cost in the form of contributions to the EU budget and higher prices for imported food. These effects indeed occurred, but were intensified by a sharp deterioration in the UK balance of trade with the EU. It fell from a surplus of £385 million in 1970 (effectively the last pre-entry year) to a deficit of £12.6 billion by 1988. According to the governments' own figures, published in the annual Balance of Payments Accounts (*The Pink Book*), the UK suffered a total accumulated trading deficit of £90.6 billion with the EU during the 27 years to 2000. Over the same period, the UK enjoyed a trading surplus of £70.9 billion with the rest of the world. In fact, the deficit is larger than official statistics suggest. First, they are a summation of historical statistics, not adjusted for inflation. Second they take no account of the Antwerp-Rotterdam effect, which incorrectly allocates approximately 10 per cent of British exports to the EU rather than to the rest of the world, because they go initially to the Continent for containerisation before being dispatched internationally.

Such a substantial volume of resources, drained from the British economy, has led to deflationary budgetary and monetary policies to restore balance of trade equilibrium by lowering relative production costs. However, output and employment simultaneously fall, which in turn generates less favourable investment prospects. The resulting loss of efficiency further worsens the balance of trade, which necessitates more deflationary policies, causing lower growth. It is difficult for this spiral of relative decline to be reversed whilst the UK remains subject to a very large trade deficit with other EU member states. Orthodox policies to reduce trade deficits involve the deflation of the economy, thereby relying upon rising unemployment to choke off demand for imported goods. Unfortunately, this will leave the UK economy growing more slowly, and carrying higher rates of unemployment, than would otherwise have occurred, thus contradicting the economic advantages that were advocated in the 1970s relating to the trade benefits of EU membership.

A second argument used to justify UK membership of the EU claims that this is the source of a majority of UK trade and therefore withdrawal from the EU trade bloc, or even refusal to participate in the Euro-zone, would have disastrous consequences for UK exports and hence employment prospects. Unfortunately, this claim is based upon a misleading premise, because Table 3.1 indicates that it is only true if statistics are used selectively – i.e. if trade is restricted to goods and services, and the remainder of the current account (i.e. investment income and transfers) is discounted. However, a detailed analysis reveals that only 48 per cent of the UK's current account relates to the EU, and 43 per cent occurs with Euro participants. Indeed, just as much trade takes place with the USA as France and Germany combined. Thus, although the UK is deeply involved in trading to EU member states, it remains a minority of total trade. Moreover, the EU trade remains in significant deficit, whereas non-EU trade generates a surplus, signifying that a reallocation of trade-creating resources to non-EU areas may contribute towards reducing the UK's overall trade deficit.

Table 3.1 **UK current account exports by region, 1992–1999 (per cent of total category credits)**

	(1)	(2)	(3)	(4)	(5)	(6)
	Total	Goods	Services	Goods and services	Investment income	Transfers
Eurozone	43.1	54.1	31.7	48.4	35.8	19.4
Total EU	48.1	57.9	35.4	52.2	38.6	54.8
Total Europe	56.5	64.4	44.3	59.3	50.2	59.8
USA	17.1	12.6	23.3	15.3	20.2	19.9
Rest of the Americas	5.2	3.5	5.3	4.0	7.5	5.4
Asia	16.2	14.8	19.7	16.1	17.3	10.2
Australasia and Oceania	2.4	1.7	3.2	2.0	2.9	3.2
Africa	2.7	3.0	4.1	3.3	1.6	2.0
International Organisations	0.1	0.0	0.2	0.1	0.2	0.0
1999 £bn	357.0	165.7	64.0	229.6	109.1	18.3

Source: UK Balance of Payments Accounts (2000).

The significance of the US dollar is an additional factor impacting upon the importance of the EU for UK trade. Many commodities (including oil, gas, information technology, pharmaceuticals and high-technology electronic equipment) are priced and exchanged in dollars. Recently released currency invoicing statistics from HM Customs and Excise demonstrate that only 19 per cent of British goods' exports are invoiced in euros or other EMU 'legacy currencies', compared to 27 per cent in dollars and 53 per cent in sterling. Table 3.2 provides the evidence. Even within the Euro-zone, as much UK trade (around 25 per cent) occurs in dollars as in the Euro-zone currencies. Furthermore, these statistics relate to goods only, so that they inevitably overstate the role of the euro. Given the greater importance of the dollar than the euro to UK trade, and noting that over the last decade the pound-dollar relationship has proved to be the most stable currency exchange rate in the world, it is clear that joining the euro will increase volatility in the UK's trade and investment.

Table 3.2   The currency of invoicing UK goods exports, 1999 (per cent)

Currency	%
Sterling	53
US Dollar	27
EMU Currencies	19
Other Currencies	1

Source: HM Customs and Excise (2000).

In the long term, the share of British trade with the current members of the Euro-zone is likely to decline. The population of the Euro-zone is projected by the US Census Bureau to fall by over 7 per cent to 2050, whilst the population of most of the rest of the world is still rising. In some parts of Asia and the Middle East annual population expansion is predicted to be as high as 3 per cent. Assuming that per capita growth rates are the same across EU and non-EU countries, the EU's share of the British current account will fall to less than 40 per cent by 2050. If the non-EU nations enjoy higher per capita growth, which is probable on recent trends, then the EU's share will decline below 30 per cent. Although the Euro-zone will remain a significant trading bloc, future world changes in population and income levels will erode its importance. It is ironic that, as the UK ponders abandoning the pound for the euro, the importance of the Euro-zone is declining.

The Common Agricultural Policy

Since the abolition of the Corn Laws in 1846, Britain's policy was to allow free entry to the lowest cost foodstuffs, which benefited industry because workers obtained their food at prices competitive with our rivals in manufacturing. Additionally the British public possessed more income to spend on other goods, whilst the countries from which the UK imported food spent on commodities produced in Britain. This beneficial cumulative process was destroyed by the UK's accession to the EU.

The desire of France and Germany to protect farmers from external competition, coupled with the French intention to secure outlets for the products of their former colonies, initially held the EU together. The French in particular were determined that the UK should never be allowed to join unless it abandoned its cheap food programme. A Common Agricultural Policy (CAP) was incorporated within the EU integration strategy to maintain the balance of interests between its original six members. They initiated a CAP operated by EU officials, who fix a common minimum price for given foods whatever the world level of prices for agricultural commodities, by manipulating the quantity to which consumers enjoy access.

The constraints imposed by the CAP raised the British cost of living, whilst encouraging an inefficient transfer of resources into agricultural output away from more productive manufacturing and services. Moreover, because the UK has traditionally been a net importer of foodstuffs, higher food prices represented a deterioration in the UK's terms of trade, whilst the inflationary impact upon UK exports damaged the balance of payments. Throughout the 1980s EU food prices were on average 7 per cent greater than those prevailing on the world market (Burkitt *et al.*, 1992). According to a National Consumer Council estimate, in September 2000 the CAP cost an average UK family of 2 adults and 2 children £22.50 in a larger weekly food bill than if food was bought in world markets. Total CAP agricultural support, including the taxpayers' contribution to farming via the EU budget and the expense of destroying surplus produce, cost the average British family £36 per week. Combining the effect of the higher prices caused by the CAP with the impost upon the taxpayer of maintaining the system, the average burden upon British employees is one quarter the size of their income tax and national insurance contributions (Burkitt *et al.*, 1996).

The CAP is an expensive, inefficient method of supporting agriculture; for every £100 that farmers gain from it, consumers and taxpayers' pay £160. A return to the deficiency payments system that operated in Britain from 1947 to 1973 is the most efficient alternative. The saving upon food expenditure and taxation, combined with the availability of cheaper food, would be counter-inflationary, as it lowers the retail price index and increases demand, thus reducing unit costs. Moreover, lower food prices lead to smaller pay increases, so cutting labour costs throughout the economy, whilst the transfer of income from the poor to the rich, through higher food prices, would end. One solution to the recent crisis in British agriculture is to embrace organic, environmentally sustainable land management and farming techniques. It is a solution that the CAP precludes.

The Common Fisheries Policy

The Common Fisheries Policy (CFP) constitutes an example of how the UK gave away control of its resources due to EU accession. Immediately prior to Britain's entry, the six original members, without sanction from the Treaty of Rome, devised the CFP as a way of gaining access to the 60 to 80 per cent of fish in EU waters, which lay within the British Territorial Limit. In his eagerness to join the EU, Edward Heath agreed to this self-interested manoeuvre, accepting fish to be 'a common European resource' which any member could catch anywhere in the Community. Through such acceptance, he gave away part of UK citizens' birthright and sowed the seeds for the decline of the UK fishing industry.

Whilst the number of fish consumed in 1988 was approximately equal to the 1997 level, the proportion provided by UK vessels fell from over 85 per cent to only 61 per cent, with imports rising threefold. When transitory agreements expired, the UK had to negotiate hard to prevent more than 40 Spanish boats from fishing in the 100,000 mile 'Irish Box' at any one time. Spain possesses the world's largest fishing fleet, with a tonnage of 587,173 in 1997, but enjoys relatively few domestic waters, so that it sought to take advantage of the CFP to fish intensively in British waters.

Over-fishing is the consequence of limited stocks supporting an influx of new fleets, embodying improved technology, which enables larger catches. In 1972 some 300,000 tonnes of cod were taken from the North Sea, but in 1999 fisherman only managed to catch 60 per cent of the total EU quota of 81,000 tonnes. The EU response to this plundering of a scarce natural resource was not to re-establish national fishing rights, but to impose a system of quotas, or 'total allowable catches', to restrict the number of fish landed in a year. As each fishing vessel receives its share of the quota, the right for non-UK vessels to fish in UK territorial waters is enshrined. However, quotas only relate to the landing of certain categories of fish. The EU has made no cut in industrial quotas, so allowing the Danish fleet to continue removing vast quantities of the small fish on which larger species, such as cod and haddock, depend for food.

Unless drastic action is taken to stop over-fishing there will be no more cod, haddock, or monkfish left anywhere from the North Sea to the Irish Box. The EU administered its quotas with such corruption, cynicism and incompetence that barely an edible fish remains within its jurisdiction. By contrast, Iceland, having won the Cod War in the 1970s, took its scientists' predictions seriously and introduced measures that ensure it still enjoys a sustainable supply of fish. The EU could, if it wanted, close down fisheries temporarily and compensate (or retrain) fishermen until stocks recover. Apart from a token reduction in fish quotas (which are bound to be broken because they are never enforced), the EU has decided that the short-term need of vested interests are more important than the long-term survival of an industry and a whole eco-system.

The Save Britain's Fish Campaign argues that the quota failure should be replaced by a conservation strategy, based upon the utilisation of new technology which can control the size and species of fish caught in trawler nets. This technology is deployed by the Canadian and Norwegian governments, but is rejected by the EU. In view of the CFP's failings, the reluctance of the EU to reform and the urgency of minimising further losses of fish stocks, it appears inevitable that the UK should withdraw from the CFP if it is to protect its few remaining fisheries effectively.

The Royal Society of Edinburgh (2004) forwarded three major recommendations regarding the impact of the CFP. Firstly, that the existing 12 mile limits be made permanent instead of being subject to renewal every ten years. Secondly, it recommended that arrangements for use of EU Structural Funds in order to make maximum use of the Financial Instruments for Fisheries Guidance and other Funds for the economic diversification of fisheries dependent areas are reviewed. Thirdly, the position of the EU's exclusive competence for conservation of marine biological resources should be reconsidered, with a view to having this deleted from the proposed EU Constitution so that the principle of subsidiarity applies to fisheries, as it does to other matters.

The CFP has been an unmitigated disaster for UK fishermen, and UK consumers who faced price rises due to restricted supply and lower utilisation of vessel capacity. In 1973 between 60 per cent and 80 per cent of fish within EU waters lay within the British Territorial Limit, yet by 1996 the UK's share of catches within the EU was only 12.7 per cent. A year later, the UK's share of catches within the EU's fishing tonnage was a mere 12.3 per cent (Eurostat Yearbook, 1998–1999). These statistics provide a crippling indictment of the CFP's impact upon the UK fishing industry. The conclusion is inescapable; Britain's fishermen are being betrayed in the pursuit of EU integration by those elected to defend them.

Single Internal Market

The Single European Act (SEA), which was adopted by the UK parliament in 1986 and became European Law in 1987, was intended to create a single, unified internal market covering all member states by 31 December 1992. By this date, all formal trade barriers had to be removed, including border controls, whilst ensuring the free movement of capital, people, goods and services between members.

The economic rationale was presented in a report prepared for the EU Commission (Cecchini, 1988), which claimed that consumers would be able to buy cheaper goods after the removal of non-tariff barriers due to increased competition between firms and greater exploitation of economies of scale made possible by a larger market place. The report suggested these benefits would increase EU GDP by 7 per cent and create 5 million new jobs across the Union. This prediction, however, assumes that the potential for greater economies of scale actually exists, and that a single market will not lead to increased monopolisation and consequent retention of monopoly profits. Since non-tariff barriers did not present large obstacles to trade amongst the EU nations before the single internal market (SIM), it was unlikely that their removal would lead to significant economies of scale being achieved, which had not already been attained.

In addition, a substantial part of Cecchini's estimated benefits were supposed to come from supply-side effects that reduced inflation and balance of payments constraints. Thus greater economic activity would provide increased resources for reflationary government expenditure. To the extent that the loosening of restraints on growth depend upon increasing competition and utilising economies of scale, if these advantages fail to materialise, eventual supply-side benefits will be lower than predicted. Furthermore, Cecchini's assumption of concerted reflation amongst EU nations was always implausible and has been superseded by deflationary imperatives demanded by ERM membership and the Maastricht Treaty's fiscal convergence criteria that all members are committed to achieving. Without co-ordinated reflation, a considerable proportion of Cecchini's predicted benefits flowing from the SEA would not materialise (Burkitt and Baimbridge, 1990, 1991).

The SIM is the prime economic reason for the UK's participation in the EU. For Britain's political and business establishment, the belief that it generates enormous benefits has become an unqualified article of faith. However, how accurate is this assessment?

In the relatively protectionist world of the 1960s and 1970s, significant potential benefits accrued from EU membership, due to the absence of previously high tariffs *within* the single market. Whilst the successive rounds of GATT reduced average tariffs on manufactured goods from their immediate post- 1945 levels of over 40 per cent, they remained above 20 per cent. The attraction of free trade within the EU, whose member economies grew above the industrial average before 1973 (but failed to do so subsequently), appeared considerable despite the economic and political burdens imposed by accession. However, successive waves of trade liberalisation suggest that the UK would not join the EU for trade reasons today. The Uruguay Round of world trade negotiations from 1986 to 1994 reduced the average tariff on trade manufactures between developed countries to a mere 3.8 per cent, scarcely a barrier for any exporters enjoying sizeable profit margins. In the twenty-first century, the developed world is closer to free trade than it has ever been.

For the UK, serious questions arise from the operation of the SIM. Why have British exports to the EU been growing more slowly than to the rest of the world? Why did the UK incur a cumulative current account deficit of £64 billion with the EU between 1992 (the inception of the SIM) and 1997, whilst achieving an aggregate surplus of £48 billion with the rest of the world over the same period? Such trends imply that any benefits from the SIM in the post-Uruguay world would hardly compensate for the costs of EU membership.

To demonstrate the point, a crucial question must be answered; have UK exports to the other fourteen EU members grown more rapidly as a result of the SIM? The weight of evidence indicates a negative answer (Stewart-Brown, 1999a and b). The 'ideal' test would be to compare the growth of UK exports to the EU since the inauguration of the SIM with what would have occurred had Britain remained outside. Obviously such a test is impossible, so that the most accurate available substitute is to compare the rate of growth of UK exports to the EU with that of non-member countries. Table 3.3, illustrates that of the thirteen countries whose merchandise exports to the EU exceeded ten billion dollars in 1997, nine enjoyed substantially faster export growth rates to the EU (without any help from the SIM) than did the UK. Only Japan and Switzerland possesses significantly lower ones. Therefore being outside the SIM does not constitute a barrier on the available evidence.

A pertinent comparison is with the USA, the only other country whose merchandise exports to the EU exceed 100 billion dollars. Table 3.4 provides a comprehensive analysis of UK and USA merchandise export growth both to the EU and to the rest of the world. Four points merit attention:

1. The US export growth to the EU, without 'access' to the SIM (4.2 per cent), was barely less than the UK's (4.4 per cent);
2. The UK and the US both experienced substantially lower export expansion to the EU than to the rest of the world;
3. The share of total exports going to the EU declined less for the USA than for the UK;
4. After completion of the SIM, the direction of British merchandise exports underwent a major shift away from the EU towards the rest of the world.

Thus experience to date provides no support for the establishment belief that the SIM provides significant benefits for the UK. With the significant exception of Japanese car producers (who account for only 1.5 per cent of foreign direct investment into Britain), manufacturers enjoy access to the SIM, wherever they are located, as Tables 3.3 and 3.4 demonstrate. The weight of evidence is clear; the assumption of the British governing class, articulated by Charles Kennedy in *The Times* on September 26th 1999 that 'Britain gains so much from membership of the European Union, it is hard to believe that anyone can still question that it is in our national interest', lacks any empirical basis in the contemporary, low tariff world.

Table 3.3 Leading exporters to the EU(14): merchandise exports (FOB)

Exporter	1992 (US $ billion)	1997 (US $ billion)	Annual growth rate (per cent)
UK	113.7	141.4	4.4
US	84.9	104.4	4.2
Japan	54.8	52.0	-1.0
Switzerland	38.1	40.8	1.4
Norway	19.4	26.9	6.8
Russia	17.9	25.2	7.1
China P.R., Hong Kong	16.1	21.2	5.7
China P.R., Mainland	7.1	20.0	23.0
Czech and Slovak Republics	6.9	16.9	19.6
Poland	7.7	15.6	15.2
Singapore	8.2	13.3	10.2
Hungary	6.4	13.0	15.2
South Korea	8.0	11.2	7.0

Source: Directory of Trade Statistics Yearbook 1998, International Monetary Fund.

Table 3.4 UK and US world merchandise exports (FOB)

	1992 (US $ billion)	1997 (US $ billion)	Annual growth rate (per cent)
UK exports:			
To EU (14)	113.7 (59.8 %)	141.1 (50.6 %)	4.4
To Rest of the World	76.3 (40.2 %)	137.7 (49.4 %)	12.5
US exports:			
To EU (14)	84.9 (19.0 %)	104.4 (15.2 %)	4.2
To Rest of the World	362.5 (81.0 %)	583.2 (84.8 %)	10.0

Source: Directory of Trade Statistics Yearbook 1998, International Monetary Fund.

Cambridge Econometrics (1990) presented an alternative prediction for the effects of the SIM which was based upon more realistic assumptions than those used by Cecchini and which produced more pessimistic conclusions concerning its impact upon the UK economy. The Cambridge scenario expected the SIM to generate rationalisation of European industry through mergers and concentration of production. These were predicted to result in the loss of 300,000 manufacturing jobs in the UK, possibly offset by a gain of about the same number of service jobs, although the assumed expansion in financial sector employment appears optimistic amidst general job cutting after over-expansion during the 1980s liberalisation. Growth of service employment to compensate for the loss of well paid, skilled manufacturing jobs producing tradable goods may either not appear or be concentrated in low paid, part time sectors.

In addition, the Cambridge Econometrics model assumed that the SIM will exacerbate existing regional differences throughout the EU as a whole and within the UK economy. Thus the greater part of any expansion in growth and employment opportunities resulting from the effects of the single market will disproportionally favour the South East region of the UK, whilst the loss of manufacturing jobs will affect already disadvantaged northern regions. Moreover, since the South Eastern region tends to possess relatively tight labour and housing markets, the possible additional demand generated by the SEA might simply lead to inflationary wage and house price pressures rather than generate significant gains in terms of economic growth and employment opportunities.

Table 3.5   Medium-term macroeconomic consequences of the SIM

Model and data	CPB	CPB + EU data	EU
Volume of private consumption	2.6	3.2	3.1
Volume of private investments in fixed assets:			
Housing	3.1	4.3	4.7
Other	2.0	2.6	7.0
Volume of goods and services exports	7.6	16.1	10.5
Volume of goods and services imports	7.1	14.7	7.2
Volume of GDP	2.3	3.4	4.5
Labour productivity	2.4	2.3	3.0
Employment	-0.1	0.9	1.5
Rate of capacity utilisation	0.7	1.2	2.5
Financial surplus of government	0.0	1.2	2.2
Balance of payments current account	0.1	0.6	1.0

Source: Bakhoven (1989).

A study undertaken by Bakhoven (1989), using a world econometric model, predicts significantly more negative results than the Cecchini Report (see Table 3.5). This model predicts that employment across the EU will *fall* by some 0.1 per cent over the first six years of SIM operation, meaning approximately 400,000 people will lose their jobs as a direct result of the SIM. Moreover, Cecchini's prediction that the SEA would lead to budget surpluses of some 2.2 per cent of GNP, which could be used to finance a co-ordinated reflationary strategy, is also disputed by the Dutch results, which anticipate no such budget surplus and therefore no additional resources available to finance an employment-generating programme.

Because the single market only fully began operations on 1 January 1993, it is too soon to draw firm conclusions concerning the actual effect it has had on the UK, and to test whether the predictions made by the Cecchini Report models were correct. However, early indications suggest that the SIM is likely to widen, not diminish, the UK's trade deficit with other EU nations. Employment will be lost in manufacturing. In the absence of the reflationary policies assumed by Cecchini, which are essentially Keynesian measures which could be implemented without the SEA, the final effect on UK growth and employment rates is at best marginal, and at worst will further damage the UK economy at a time when the dynamics of EU membership are increasingly adverse.

Regulation

One area where the EU is often criticised is in its supposed over-regulation of the SIM, together with associated areas of health and safety protection and social policy. The rationale for EU-level regulation is that this harmonises measures across the single market, thereby promoting price transparency and hence competition, and in the process reduce any implicit protectionism realised through differential rules or regulations. However, regulations impose costs for firms in that, by its nature, it is intended to restrict the autonomy of investors, producers and employers, thereby increasing costs, causing inflationary pressure and restraining potential economic growth rates. Thus, many commentators argue that the sum total of EU regulation constitutes an unnecessary burden upon European economies.

Deva (2002) calculated that until May 1997 approximately 40 per cent of the legislation that affects Britain was initiated and authored in Brussels or Strasbourg, yet since New Labour came to power this ratio has risen to some 55 per cent. Should Britain join the euro, the proportion is projected to increase to 70 per cent. In relation to these developments, Lord Weatherill, a former Speaker of the House of Commons, recently said,

> I am increasingly alarmed by the way in which our constitution is today overridden with a flood of EU directives and regulations, which are seldom, if ever, debated in Parliament and yet are binding on us.

The argument made by neo-liberal economists is that over-regulation is associated with the concept of 'Eurosclerosis', which describes the perception of many continental European economies as suffering high unemployment and low rates of economic growth in recent years because they have damaged the dynamism of their economies through over-regulation, too much public spending (with its associated taxation) and the dempening of incentives to invest and work due to an over-expansion of welfare states.

Not surprisingly, this picture is challenged by other economists, largely adopting a Keynesian point of view, who argue that the entire idea of 'Eurosclerosis' is without proper empirical foundation. Rather, public expenditure can stimulate aggregate demand when the private sector is reluctant to spend or invest due to difficult economic circumstances, and indeed much of the problems faced by many of the leading EU member states during the past two decades have arisen primarily because of toow restrictive macroeconomic policies, deflationary exchange rate regimes and a resultant loss of productive capacity.

Irrespective of the 'Eurosclerosis' argument, EU regulation has been further criticised because it is designed and applied at super-national level. This implies that it has not been democratically determined, at least not directly, due to the democratic deficit at the heart of the European project. Moreover, it may be that such regulation would be better left to individual nation states – the subsidiary principle – so that it may better reflect the preferences of individual nation states. Thus, the Germans could persist with their beer purity rules without these being watered-down by weaker EU regulation, whilst other nations could impose stronger animal rights or environmental protection legislation than possible to persuade all EU member states to enact.

The EU Budget

The pattern of EU expenditure and the sources of its revenue are structured so that the UK consistently contributes a greater proportion of EU finances than it receives in return or than is warranted by its national income relative to that of other member states. This phenomenon did not arise by accident, but from the inherent structure of the EU budget. Therefore it will persist in the future.

The EU budget is financed through four mechanisms: agricultural levies, customs duties, a proportion of VAT receipts based on a nationally harmonised basket of goods and services, and a calculation based upon the size of each nations' GDP. These means of raising tax revenues are defined as the EU's 'own resources', accounting for 2.2 per cent, 22.6 per cent, 15.1 per cent and 60.1 per cent respectively towards the EU budget in 1999. As recently as 1990, VAT receipts made the largest contribution. However, they were biased against members like the UK, whose historically higher-than-average consumption rates caused overpayment to the EU in comparison to the GDP per capita calculation. Furthermore the EU ignores VAT exemptions that require member states to transfer the same amount of revenue to the EU budget whether or not the commodities paid full rates of VAT. This method of funding was neither fair nor transparent, so that the EU eventually restructured its revenue collection by ensuring that the fourth resource is the principal contributor to financing the budget.

The figures for national contributions to the EU are available for 1999, when Britain remained the second net largest contributor to the EU. The statistics are those of the EU's Court of Auditors; HM Treasury calculations would raise the UK's gross contribution to £11 billion rather than £7.3 billion shown in Table 3.6. Although £17.7 billion pounds is taken from member states, only £9.7 billion is received by the contributing nations. The remainder (£7.9 billion) is absorbed by the EU bureaucracy.

The Fontainebleau reduction in UK budget contributions was secured in 1984 by Mrs Thatcher, as partial compensation for the net payments Britain was making to the EU budget. The original agreement was to run until 1999, but is still in operation. The EU Commission and other member countries periodically threaten its continued existence.

Table 3.6   National contributions to the EU budget in 1999 (£ millions)

Country	Receipts	Payments	Net Gain or Loss
Germany	6,392	13,869	-7,477
UK	3,814	7,296	-3,482
Netherlands	1,141	3,351	-2,210
Italy	5,933	7,086	-1,153
Belgium	1,264	2,104	-840
Sweden	739	1,546	-808
France	8,445	9,212	-767
Austria	802	1,352	-550
Finland	593	797	-204
Denmark	995	1,090	-95
Luxembourg	53	128	-75
Spain	8,483	4,102	+4,381
Greece	3,286	889	+2,397
Portugal	2,571	808	+1,762
Ireland	1,897	698	+1,200

Source: EU Court of Auditors (1999).

The UK's contribution is not a constant amount of a static total, because the EU budget grew over the period of UK membership. EU expenditure rose by an average of 9 per cent per annum between 1979 and 1998, when annual inflation across the EU was just 5.7 per cent. This represents a substantial real increase in EU resources at a time when national governments were restraining their budgets; from 1995 to 1998 the EU budget increased by 13.7 per cent, far above the 5.4 per cent average EU inflation rate. Over the 27 years to 2000 the UK's net contribution (i.e., total payments minus total receipts) came to £47.8 billion (not allowing for inflation), of which £4.7 billion was paid in 2000 alone. The magnitude of these sums is highlighted by the average cost of building an NHS hospital at £180 million.

The accession of Austria, Finland and Sweden partially facilitated the expansion of revenues, because all three countries were richer than the EU average. However, this has been superseded by the recent Eastern enlargement of the EU, admitting member states whose GDP per capita is typically less than half the EU average. Moreover, the expanding EU budget caused a number of existing members, including Belgium, Denmark and Luxembourg, to become net contributors after earlier enjoying net benefits. Previous net contributors have been forced to increase payments to the EU budget, with the UK's net contribution more than doubling (by 133 per cent) between 1993 and 1998. Britain's payment to the EU budget amounted to 96 ECU per person in 1999 compared to 46 ECU, in 1993.

The distribution of EU funding changed over the years, with agricultural support declining from over two-thirds to just half of EU expenditure, whilst various redistributive transfer schemes (such as the regional, cohesion and social funds) increased in value. The UK receives relatively little from agricultural support, due to its greater concentration on non-agricultural sectors. Moreover, areas of expanded spending, namely transfers to the poorest member states, by definition exclude the UK. Reform of the EU budget is long overdue, for it still requires the UK to pay for the storage of unsold, overpriced agricultural products, which East European outlets could supply at a lower cost simultaneously contributing towards these countries' economic regeneration.

Table 3.7 demonstrates the large and growing burden placed upon Britain by EU membership, evidenced by a rise of 84.2 per cent in its net contribution to the EU budget between 1990 and 1998. Other reasons for such an increase include a fall in the Fontainebleau abatement of 18.8 per cent, whilst European Regional Development Fund Payments declined by 19 per cent.

Table 3.7   UK official transactions with EU institutions (£ millions)

	1990	1994	1998	Change 1990–1998
Total UK Receipts of which:	4,084	5,258	5,705	39.7%
European Social Fund	225	320	783	248.0
Fontainebleau abatement	1,697	1,726	1,377	-18.8
European Regional Development Fund	441	608	357	-19.0
Total UK Payments of which:	6,559	8,431	10,265	56.5
Import Duties	1,710	1,981	1,823	6.6
VAT Contribution	4,148	4,189	4,189	-9.4
UK Net Contributions to EU Budget	2,475	2,173	4,560	84.2

Source: UK National Accounts (1999), *Blue Book, ONS* (Yearbook Editions).

British taxpayers, individual and corporate, through the mechanism of contributions to the EU budget, paid an effective disguised tariff on UK exports to the EU of 6.8 per cent (gross) or 3.4 per cent (net) in 1998. Table 3.8 indicates that this tariff has risen by 2.0 per cent (gross) and 1.5 per cent (net) since 1996, thus undermining claims for the establishment of a single internal market within the EU. If Britain's net payments to the EU ceased immediately, the Chancellor could cut 2 pence off the standard rate of income tax without increasing the public sector borrowing requirement.

Low-growth EU

One of the initial attractions of EU membership was the fact that the original six EU states had achieved higher economic growth than the OECD average. For example, between 1958 and 1973, the original six members enjoyed a combined average growth rate of 5.1 per cent per annum (Nevin, 1990). However, by the time the UK joined, the underlying conditions creating this preferable development had become exhausted, and the EU's restrictive policies produced lower growth and higher unemployment. Thus, the EU became a low-growth area and the UK, despite the benefits of North Sea Oil, has been a low-growth economy within the EU. As a consequence of two decades of relatively low growth, the EU suffers from very high levels of unemployment.

Table 3.8   **The tariff on UK exports to EU '14' due to UK contributions to EU budget**

		£ billion
1996	A- Gross UK Contribution to EU Budget	7.39
	B- Net UK Contribution to EU Budget	2.83
	C- Total UK Exports + to EU. '14'	151.68
Effective	Tariff on UK Exports:	
	A÷C	4.8%
	B÷C	1.9%
1998	A- Gross UK Contribution to EU Budget	11.00
	B- Net UK Contribution to EU Budget	5.51
	C- Total UK Exports + to EU. '14'	161.96
Effective	Tariff on UK Exports:	
	A÷C	6.8%
	B÷C	3.4%
	+ = Visibles plus invisibles excluding	
	receipts from EU institutions.	

Source: Milne, I. (1998 and 1999), *UK Trade in 1996 and UK Trade in 1998 and Growth 1992–1998*, The June Press.

Table 3.9   **Growth and unemployment in EU and non-EU industrialised economies (1994–1998)**

	GDP growth (%)	Unemployment (% of total labour force)			
	(1994–1998)	1995	1996	1997	1998
OECD	2.1	7.7	7.7	7.4	7.1
USA	3.0	5.6	5.4	4.9	4.5
UK	2.2	8.7	8.2	7.0	6.3
France	1.6	11.7	12.4	12.3	11.7
Germany	1.2	8.2	8.9	9.9	9.4
Italy	1.3	11.9	12.0	12.1	11.8
EU15	1.9	10.7	10.8	10.6	9.9
EMU11	1.9	11.4	11.5	11.5	10.9

Source: NIESR (2000), European Commission (2000).

Table 3.9 illustrates the rates of relatively slow growth and high unemployment characterising the EU, and particularly affecting the larger continental member states. UK and USA performance was clearly superior during this period. Furthermore, the entirety of Western Europe only represents 31 per cent of total world GDP, implying that three-quarters of world demand occurs outside of the EU.

Table 3.10   Distribution of world GDP income (1997–2005)

	World GDP			
	Share distribution (%)			**Contribution to economic growth (%)**
	1997	**1999**	**2005**	**1997–2005**
North America	28.5	29.8	28.3	27.3
Western Europe	30.2	32.7	31.4	35.7
Asia:	10.9	9.5	11.6	14.4
China	3.1	3.6	4.7	11.1
India	1.4	1.4	1.7	3.1
Indonesia	0.7	0.5	0.6	0.3
Latin America	6.9	7.6	8.4	14.4
Australia/New Zealand	1.6	1.5	1.5	1.1
Africa and Middle East	3.9	3.7	3.7	3.0
Eastern Europe	3.6	3.8	4.3	7.0
Japan	14.3	11.4	10.8	-3.0

Source: Problémes Economiques (1999).

Table 3.11 indicates that, during this period, the US economy remained (in both GDP and per head GDP) the major world contributor of economic growth relative to EMU, whilst the UK additionally demonstrated superior economic growth performance during this period of analysis. Moreover, Table 3.12 predicts that Europe will suffer a decline in world demand and purchases of imported goods from Britain and other nations, whereas USA, China, India and Latin America are likely to offer much better prospects for UK exports. Hence, established UK trading relations with the USA will continue to generate greater benefit than trade concentrated on EU countries, as the USA continues to expand faster than most of the latter. However, the world's most rapidly growing areas are found amongst the developing countries. Indeed, during the last decade, the EU's share of world trade has *fallen* by one quarter; the high value-added technology sector is over one-third larger in the USA and Japan than in Europe. Indeed, EMU countries seem to have a comparative disadvantage relating to High-Tech exports, as these comprised only 15 per cent of total manufacturing exports, whereas comparable shares in Britain, USA and East Asia/Pacific represent 28 per cent, 33 per cent and 28 per cent of total manufacturing, respectively (Table 3.12).

Table 3.11   Summary of economic and development indicators by selected area (1990–1998)

Country	GDP (1998, $ millions)	GDP per capita 1998 ($)	GDP, annual average, % (1990–98)*	High-tech exports (% of manufactured exports, 1998)	Internet hosts per 10,000 people, 1999
UK	1,357,197	23,003	3.7	28	270.60
USA	8,230,397	30,483	4.5	33	1,508.77
EMU	6,457,663	22,191	1.8	15**	157.53
East Asia and Pacific	1,693,340	932	6.9	28	2.39
South Asia	565,131	433	3.2	4**	0.17
World	28,736,978	4,873	3.3	22	94.47

*Own calculations based on data in World Bank (2000).
**1997 figure.
Source: World Bank (2000).

Table 3.12   Imports and demand as proportion of world imports and demand (1995–2005)

	Demand for consumer goods				Demand for equipment goods				Demand for intermediaries goods			
	Imports		Demand		Imports		Demand		Imports		Demand	
	1995	2005	1995	2005	1995	2005	1995	2005	1995	2005	1995	2005
North America	19.7	23.9	27.0	29.9	23.9	27.3	28.7	29.1	15.7	16.8	22.9	22.4
Western Europe	51.6	44.2	27.8	24.3	39.9	34.1	24.3	18.1	50.2	40.3	28.3	24.9
Asia	11.2	13.5	15.3	19.8	21.3	19.7	16.0	26.8	18.6	24.2	19.1	26.0
China	2.5	5.8	5.2	10.2	3.1	6.0	6.0	11.9	3.0	7.3	7.7	15.5
India	0.6	1.2	2.6	3.7	0.7	1.0	1.4	1.9	1.2	1.9	2.1	2.7
Indonesia	0.5	0.6	1.4	1.2	1.0	0.8	0.6	0.6	1.2	1.1	1.5	0.9
Latin America	3.4	5.7	6.5	9.1	4.8	7.5	3.9	7.0	4.8	8.0	6.6	9.1
Australia and New Zealand	2.1	1.9	1.4	1.3	2.5	3.8	1.4	2.1	2.0	2.2	1.4	1.6
Africa and Middle East	1.6	1.5	1.3	1.2	1.3	0.9	0.9	0.7	1.4	1.2	1.5	1.5
Eastern Europe	2.6	3.2	2.3	2.7	1.8	2.9	1.4	2.4	2.0	3.3	2.2	3.4
Japan	7.8	6.1	18.4	11.7	4.4	3.8	23.5	14.8	5.3	4.0	18.0	11.1

Source: Problémes Economiques (1999).

Furthermore, the significance of Higher-Tech industry for Britain is highlighted in Table 3.13. Of the first fifteen EU employers in Higher-Tech manufacturing and services industries, UK regions are represented 8 times and vary from Bedfordshire, Oxfordshire to Strathclyde, Isle of Wight.

The European economy is therefore pursuing integration as a defensive not offensive measure; it is seeking to offset its economic weakness through greater economies of scale. The economic framework adopted as part of EMU, however, is likely to perpetuate a decade of mass unemployment, deflation and slow economic growth. Thus, if the UK decided to lock itself within a trading bloc, it could choose one more successful than the EU.

Table 3.13   Top 15 regions, per cent of total employment in all higher-tech manufacturing and services (1997)

Regions	% of total employment
Stockholm (S)	9.4
Berkshire, Buckinghamshire and Oxfordshire (UK)	8.8
Bedfordshire and Hertfordshire (UK)	8.1
Ile de France (F)	6.9
Hampshire and Isle of Wight (UK)	6.6
Uusimaa (FIN)	6.6
Ostra Mellansverige (S)	6.5
Pohjois-Suomi (FIN)	6.4
Avon, Gloucestershire and Wiltshire (UK)	6.4
Vlaams Brabant (B)	6.3
Surrey and East-West Sussex (UK)	6.3
Dumfries and Galloway, Strathclyde (UK)	5.9
Borders, Central, Fife, Lothian and Tayside (UK)	5.8
Greater London (UK)	5.7
Oberbayern (D)	5.6

Source: Eurostat (2000).

The Cost of ERM Membership

The European Monetary System (EMS) was created after the break-up of the Bretton Woods fixed exchange rate system. The Exchange Rate Mechanism (ERM) was established in 1979 within the EMS; it involved participating countries fixing their currencies against each other, and thus against the European Currency Unit (ECU), which was a composite of member currencies. Bilateral rates for each currency were circulated against all others and consequently against the central ECU rate. On 1 December 1999, the ECU was replaced by the single currency, the euro. Therefore, non-members of Economic and Monetary Union (EMU) can, should they so desire, fix their currencies to the euro through the ERM.

Within a fixed exchange rate mechanism, when a currency falls to its permitted minimum, the government is forced to change economic policy to avoid breaking the imposed band. Such a strategy can take the form of using official reserves to purchase one's own currency (if too low in value) or purchase other currencies (if too high). The ERM was designed to provide exchange rate stability through mutual cooperation between participating countries' central banks to safeguard their currencies against short-term speculation, whilst removing uncertainty from trade. Exchange rate movements within the permitted band ensured that a currency did not become fundamentally misaligned, with devastating consequences for employment and output.

However, in the run-up to establishing the single currency, the ERM underwent a significant evolution. Individual currencies were no longer protected by exchange controls, but realignments were all but forbidden on the ground that a nation should demonstrate the stability of its currency with other participants prior to EMU entry. At this point the UK decided to become a member of the ERM in October 1990, at a fixed central parity of 2.95 deutschmarks to the pound, a rate intended to put pressure upon the UK economy to reduce inflation rather than setting a competitive exchange rate. Unsurprisingly, this chosen rate, and ERM membership itself, proved to be a mistake.

The period of ERM membership, from October 1990 top September 1992, was a disaster for the British economy. From expanding at a rate of 2 per cent per annum prior to entry, the restraints imposed upon productive activity due to an over-valued currency were so severe that the economy headed into recession. During the two years of membership, GDP shrunk by 3.8 per cent, being associated with six out of eight quarters of negative growth. Under these circumstances, unemployment rose by 1.2 million to a total of 2.85 million on official government figures.

Whilst it would be exaggerated to claim that this period of economic decline was caused solely by ERM membership, it is worth noting that the economy expanded by an average of 2 per cent per annum immediately prior to membership and also in its aftermath. Moreover, the unemployment rate was 5.5 per cent before sterling joined the ERM, rose sharply afterwards, but started to fall again once the UK departed. Of course, other factors influenced these developments (e.g. German reunification), but it was the restrictions imposed upon macroeconomic policy by the ERM, which prevented the UK from responding to deflationary pressures by expansionary fiscal and monetary policy to limit the damage inflicted upon jobs and output.

Measuring the extent to which ERM membership damaged the UK economy, the first calculation focuses upon rising unemployment. The UK Treasury believes that the average unemployed person costs the state £9,000 a year in terms of benefits paid and taxes foregone. Combining that figure with the 1.2 million increase in unemployment during the UK's two year membership of the ERM the cost to the Treasury can be estimated at £10.8 billion, equivalent to 1.8 per cent of the then UK GDP!

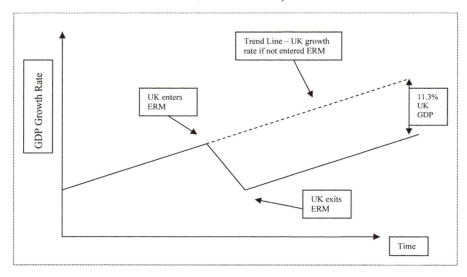

Figure 3.1   Illustration of UK's lost GDP resulting from ERM membership

A second element refers to the potential increase in output and living standards that were foregone during these two years. It includes not only the 3.9 per cent absolute decline in GDP during ERM membership, which amounts to £23.1 billion at 1992 prices, but additionally incorporates an estimate of the growth that the economy would achieve in a normal year. The long-term trend of the UK economy is estimated to be approximately 2.5 per cent per annum, so that any deviation from this trend must be taken into account. Without ERM membership, UK GDP would have been expected to be around 5.0 per cent higher (i.e. two years' expansion at 2.5 per cent a year), whilst during those two years it fell by 3.9 per cent. When these two statistics are added together, the cost of lost output lies in the region of £53.4 billion in 1992 prices (9 per cent of national income).

Third, to the unemployment and output costs must be added the price of defending sterling within its ERM parity. Although ultimately unsuccessful, the UK government spent an estimated £15 million of its foreign reserves, trying to resist the speculative attack that ended the UK's ERM membership. After Britain left the ERM and sterling devalued by 20 per cent, the Bank of England sought to rebuild its foreign exchange holdings, but discovered that each pound now bought 20 per cent less than previously. Therefore, the £15 billion reserves were devaluated by a fifth, costing Britain an additional £3 billion.

In summary, adding the costs borne by the UK Treasury (£10.8 billion), lost output (£53.4 billion) and the fall in value of the UK's official reserves (£3 billion), the ERM experiment cost £67.2 billion or 11.3 per cent of 1992 UK GDP. Such sums illustrate the price exacted by fixed exchange rate mechanisms, an ominous indication of the burden imposed on those countries operating the single currency.

In an ever-changing economic environment, the optimal value of the exchange rate, which facilitates full employment of domestic resources and an external trade balance simultaneously, will vary. Therefore, it is crucial for each country to retain control over all national policy instruments. Speculative fluctuations must be smoothed and the exchange rate managed by a democratically accountable central bank to prevent disruption of international trade. However, such a strategy does not require fixed, unchangeable exchange rates as under ERM or EMU. The optimum strategy is for international (as opposed to merely European) central bank cooperation on exchange rate levels to achieve a combination of maximum short-term stability with maximum long-term flexibility.

The Loss of Democratic Economic Self-Government

The Maastricht Treaty committed the EU to evolve towards eventual political, economic and monetary union, which would convert the Parliament at Westminster into a regional assembly of a larger, super-national political authority, tasked to refine and implement EU legislation and negotiate on matters of national interest with a remote bureaucracy in order to secure concessions rather than dictate policy as an autonomous, sovereign nation state. However, even before the Treaty was enacted, EU membership decisively limited the scope for self-government previously enjoyed by the UK. Whilst ever Section 2(2) of the 1972 European Communities Act remains on the statute books, all UK governments will be compelled by British courts to reverse policies which conflict with EU law. Such a loss of accountable self-government to unelected EU institutions is not a one-step process, but is subject to an accelerating 'ratchet effect'. This arises from applying the EU doctrine of *acquis cummunautaire*, whereby the powers that the EU has arrogated to itself over the years have to be accepted in total by all new aspirant member states and cannot be repatriated to its member states. From summit to summit and treaty to treaty, it strengthens itself at the expense of democratically elected governments, whilst the Commission and the European Court of Justice (ECJ) are constantly striving to extend their jurisdiction.

These trends demonstrate the momentum behind the Treaty of Rome's commitment to 'ever closer union'. The Treaty of Nice, negotiated in December 2000, accelerated these trends, stating that on 39 new treaty items, some minor but others not, qualified majority voting rather than unanimity resting on the veto will now prevail (see Table 3.14). The British government agreed to such changes, whilst also relinquishing its emergency brake controlling 'enhanced cooperation' between some but not all member states. Enhanced cooperation is the rebranded name for a two-speed EU In an association of 15 countries, let alone an enlarged institution of 25, flexibility is vital, but it is unwise to assume that, without safeguards, integrationists will respect Britain's viewpoint. Failure at Nice to veto the new Charter of Fundamental Rights, viewed by all other member states as a prototype for the EU constitution, and likely to be interpreted as such by the ECJ before its ratification, demonstrates the British establishment's acceptance of the principle of 'pooled sovereignty'.

The fact that the Treaty of Nice represents a further move towards closer political and economic integration, of economies, politics and institutional frameworks, reflects the broad consensus amongst EU political leaders in this area. However, on a range of issues, British interests and concerns diverge from those of the EU. For example, UK trading relations, energy resources, military capacity, agriculture and investment patterns, together with a distinctive history, law and language, all provide a generally contrasting perspective from that of the UK's continental neighbours.

Table 3.14   Additional areas where Britain can no longer veto EU legislation

(i)	the appointment of the EU 'foreign policy supremo'
(ii)	agreements on foreign, justice and home affairs
(iii)	anti-discrimination measures
(iv)	measures enabling freer movement within EU
(v)	procedures for checks of external borders
(vi)	travel conditions for non-EU residents
(vii)	implementing common rules on asylum (basic rules remain unanimous)
(viii)	implementing rules on standards for protecting refugees (basic rules stay unanimous)
(ix)	implementing rules between EU countries receiving refugees (basic rules continue to be decided unanimously)
(x)	illegal immigration measures
(xi)	simplifying systems for cross-border exchange of documents
(xii)	measures promoting compatibility of conflicting member states' legislation
(xiii)	eliminating obstacles to efficient functioning of civil proceedings
(xiv)	measures to allow member states to cooperate on justice and home affairs issues
(xv)	emergency aid to member states
(xvi)	emergency financial assistance to member states
(xvii)	epresenting the Commission at world level in areas affected by monetary union
(xviii)	rules governing the Council of the European Central Bank
(xix)	international agreements on services and intellectual property
(xx)	industrial policy
(xxi)	actions of social and economic cohesion outside structural funds
(xxii)	structural funds rules
(xxiii)	cohesion funds
(xxiv)	some environmental measures (e.g. water resource management), except for taxation
(xxv)	economic and technical cooperation with third countries
(xxvi)	MEP's statue (unanimity clause for taxation)
(xxvii)	regulations for European political parties
(xxviii)	secretary-general of the Council
(xxix)	deputy secretary-general of the Council
(xxx)	rules of procedure of the Court of Justice
(xxxi)	rules of procedure of the Court of First Instance
(xxxii)	members of the Court of Auditors
(xxxiii)	rules of the Court of Auditors
(xxxiv)	members of the Social and Economic Committee
(xxxv)	members of the Committee of Regions
(xxxvi)	financial regulations of the EU budget
(xxxvii)	rules governing Financial Controllers
(xxxviii)	appointment of the Commission President

The British Government possessed no distinctive, popular mandate for agreeing to the terms of the Nice Treaty. Indeed, recent opinion polls reveal a consistent pattern; at least one-third of the electorate would vote for withdrawing from the EU if given the opportunity, whilst around two-thirds oppose joining the euro, the main integrationist initiative currently in train. This is not because the British people are un-typically insular or xenophobic. Most enjoy travelling to the continent (France and Spain accounted for over 40 per cent of UK citizens' voyages abroad in 2001), where many possess jobs or friends. Moreover, the vast majority want to enjoy close relations with other European countries, respect the cultural diversity across the continent and support the maintenance of European peace. However, they do *not* desire to relinquish self-governing democracy, nor their ability to manage their economy and neither their traditions. Moreover, UK public opinion appears to favour a looser, decentralised EU organisation, with more emphasis upon trade and jobs than micro-managing additional areas of life, perhaps better left to the auspices of national governments.

The standard justification for the substantial extension of QMV at Nice is that the veto would 'imperil the single market' after enlargement. However, the Commission has come to define the 'single market' as embracing virtually every aspect of EU business. Therefore, it proves difficult, in practice, to distinguish between measures introduced to improve the transparency of the SIM and legislation designed to create a minimum framework of social and labour rights, and or promote federal economic governance. The removal of barriers to trade and of obstacles to the free movement of people can, therefore, be viewed as a convenient excuse to centralise more powers at EU level.

Table 3.15 summarises the changes made at Nice to the weighting of votes in the Council of Ministers and in the European Parliament. The British government has repeatedly claimed that these changes increased the UK's influence within both institutions. Table 3.15 proves the falsity of such claims; on the contrary, British influence is on the wane. On the Council of Ministers, Britain's share of votes will fall from 10 of 87 (11.5 per cent) to 29 of 345 (8.4 per cent). In the European Parliament, Britain's proportion will decline from 87 of 626 (13.9 per cent) to 74 of 732 (10.1 per cent). Furthermore, Britain will lose a Commissioner; each member state will appoint one Commissioner until the total reaches 27.

The voting system introduced at Nice especially benefits Germany. 'Double majority' voting requires two conditions to be met before a decision is adopted:

1. A proposal must garner 238 from 345 or 74.78 per cent of the votes in the Council of Ministers.
2. A proposal has also to be backed by countries representing 62 per cent of the EU's population.

Thanks to the second clause, Germany and two other large countries will be able to block anything they oppose, whereas Britain would need more than two other nations in support to prevent unacceptable decisions.

Table 3.15   Weighted votes in the Council of Ministers and seats in European Parliament

	Weighted votes in the Council of Ministers	Seats in the European Parliament
Germany	29 (10)	99 (99)
United Kingdom	29 (10)	72 (87)
France	29 (10)	72 (87)
Italy	29 (10)	72 (87)
Spain	27 (8)	50 (64)
Poland	27	50
Romania	14	33
Netherlands	13 (5)	25 (31)
Belgium	12 (5)	22 (25)
Portugal	12 (4)	22 (25)
Greece	12 (5)	20
Czech Republic	12	20
Hungary	12	20
Sweden	10 (4)	18 (22)
Bulgaria	10	17
Austria	10 (4)	17 (21)
Slovakia	7	13
Denmark	7 (3)	13 (16)
Finland	7 (3)	13 (16)
Ireland	7 (3)	13 (15)
Lithuania	7	12
Latvia	4	8
Slovenia	4	7
Estonia	4	6
Cyprus	4	6
Luxembourg	4 (2)	6 (6)
Malta	3	5
Total	345 (87)	732 (626)

Note: Previous numbers for weighted votes in the Council of Ministers and seats in European Parliament in parenthesis.
Source: Treaty of Nice: Provisional Text approved by Intergovernmental Conference on Institutional Reform (2000).

'Enhanced cooperation' is the fashionable name for a two-speed EU. Jacques Chirac summarised the concept as a 'certain number of countries will have to act together to show the others the way'. A subset of member states that wishes to proceed with further integration will be allowed to do so. Other countries will be 'relegated' from an 'inner' to an 'outer' core. Enhanced cooperation, therefore does the following:

1. Aims at furthering the objectives of the Union, at protecting and servicing its interests, and at reinforcing its process of integration [Clause A (a)]
2. Respects the *acquis communautaire* and measures adopted under the other provisions of the Treaties [Clause A (1)].

These sub-clauses rule out any blocks to further integration that reverse the *acquis communautaire* and confirm beyond doubt that the EU notion of 'flexibility' undermines, rather than protects national democratic accountability. The significance of 'enhanced cooperation' is illustrated by the following clause:

> Authorisation to establish the enhanced cooperation referred to in paragraph one shall be granted by the Council of Ministers acting by a qualified majority on a proposal after consulting the European Parliament [Clause G].

Therefore individual countries possess no veto to prevent other states from proceeding with further integration.

The Charter of Fundamental Rights could be used to intervene in a member's domestic policies, regardless of its official legal status. Certainly, the ECJ has not been afraid to use judicial activism to promote centralisation and there is no obvious reason why its behaviour should alter in the future. The vacuous, legally imprecise language of the Charter will doubtless be interpreted by the ECJ to promote the QMV outcome in the Council of Ministers. The Charter of Rights, which every EU political leader except Tony Blair admits is the basis of the Constitution for an enlarged yet integrated EU, will be 'taken into account' when determining its judgements.

Conclusion

The UK's membership in the EU to date has proved to be rather disappointing to those early pioneers of European integration, both economically (via the balance of trade, the CAP, the CFP, the ERM and the EU budget) and politically (via encroachments on the UK's capacity to maintain an independent policy to reflect its particular circumstances). Moreover, these costs are not simply a one-off payment borne in the past; the majority exert an annual burden that will continue indefinitely and may even intensify over time. For example, the EU Commission has frequently raised the possibility of eliminating the UK's budget rebate, a change which would substantially increase the net cost of EU membership, whilst agricultural protectionism, even after repeated reform attempts, will remain costly to the UK economy and consumer for the foreseeable future. Moreover, the devastating experience of ERM participation casts considerable doubt upon UK membership of another fixed exchange rate system, at least in the near future, and similarly it must caution against a perceptive entry into EMU since a forced exit from this scheme would bear a considerably greater cost. Indeed, even the SIM, the one area where most commentators would have assumed the UK to be a net beneficiary of European integration, produces conflicting evidence, suggesting the necessity for cautious analysis simply to determine whether or not the extension of free trade between EU member states has in fact been beneficial for the UK economy.

Chapter 4

Current EU Trends and Developments

Introduction

Having established that the historical economic cost of EU membership has, most likely, been negative for the UK economy, this chapter examines those current and future trends within European integration that will impact this general evaluation. Thus, even if past costs have been predominant, there would be a strong argument to maintain EU membership if future benefits would appear to become most significant. Thus, this chapter reviews ongoing and future developments in a number of key areas: EU budget, the CAP, regional policy, the SIM, the single currency and enlargement.

Before proceeding to examine these substantive economic issues, Table 4.1 summarises the present and future trends in the major macroeconomic indicators for Britain and the EMU zone in terms of growth, jobs and inflation. Whilst forecasts of economic performance are always open to uncertainty (Baimbridge and Whyman, 1997), the overall direction illustrated by these figures appears undisputable.

Table 4.1   Britain and the EMU zone

	Britain	EMU zone
GDP forecasts:		
2006	2.3	2.1
2007	2.4	1.7
Consumer price forecasts:		
2006	2.0	2.0
2007	1.9	2.0
Unemployment rate	4.7	8.7

Source: The Economist (2006).

Although the differences in GDP growth rates appear negligible, the accumulative nature of economic growth is crucial, whereby even a comparatively small fluctuation in growth rates over a long period will have a significant impact upon the eventual increase in growth. For example, if output rises by 2 per cent per year then GDP will increase just over 7-fold in a century, whilst an annual growth rate of 2.5 per cent will result in nearly a 12-fold rise. Indeed, it has been suggested that the effects of such differences is already evident when considering the prevailing levels of unemployment in Britain and the EMU area, where the rate in latter is almost twice that of the former and is likely to remain stubbornly so.

Moreover, the frequently cited trade-off resulting from strong growth and low unemployment does not appear to present. Indeed, the much vaunted guarantor of price stability for the eurozone in the shape of the European Central Bank, appears to be exerting little influence over this macroeconomic variable even with eurozone interest rates at 2.5 per cent compared to 4.5 per cent in the UK, although its potential for creating a deflationary economic environment is supported.

EU Budget

European finances are much more complicated than the mere size of the budget suggests. While the revenue side restricts the size of the budget due to the balanced budget requirement and the system of own resources that is largely based on member-states' contributions, the EU determines the structure of spending. Compulsory spending (agricultural expenditure) is strongly influenced by the Council and the Commission, and noncompulsory spending (structural funds) is mainly determined by the Parliament (Feld, 2005).

An examination of the EU budget reveals that approximately 45 per cent of the own resources are used to finance the CAP, whilst another 30 per cent are allocated toward structural policies including social, regional and rural development. Thus, approximately 75 percent of the budget is allocated on either protecting one sector from global competition or to reduce economic disparities that exist between the EU's richest and poorest members (Baimbridge *et al.*, 2004).

In analysing the structure of revenue and spending, the question emerges of why a European budget is actually needed. Theoretical guidelines, such as those from the economic theory of federalism, suggest that aside from the provision of the internal market, EU-wide public goods, or a need for coordination at the EU level, may exist. The European Convention suggests further attempts to coordinate these policies, but is far from proposing any dominant competence of the Union. It does not propose far-reaching additional spending competencies of the EU, nor does it say much about additional own resources or coordination of taxation. Rather it only suggests abolishing the distinction between compulsory and noncompulsory spending, and increasing coordination among member-states in cases of tax fraud. Enlargement is also not expected to greatly affect spending or revenue. However, the current tax reforms in Eastern European countries indicate that tax competition in the enlarged Europe will be even more intense than it is today. It remains to be seen whether this will finally lead to additional restrictions of national sovereignty in taxation (Feld, 2005).

The EU budget mainly plays a role in balancing the gains and losses from European integration through intercountry redistribution (Begg, 2000), while the provision of EU-wide public goods is neglected (Blankart and Kirchner, 2004). To remedy this undesirable situation various solutions have been advocated (Buti and Nava, 2003). What are the chances for additional EU resources? The European Commission (1998) discusses several alternatives for EU own taxes. They potentially range from personal or corporate income taxes to ecological taxes or a surcharge on the national VATs (Blankart and Kirchner, 2004; Feld and Kirchgassner, 2004). With respect to the EU influence on national fiscal policies, the efforts of the EU in achieving minimum harmonization in indirect (VAT) and direct (corporate and capital income) taxation have been partly successful in recent years. With respect to corporate and capital income taxation, the first steps of minimum rules have been decided after an intense struggle among member states. However, the political feasibility of such a proposal is strongly affected by the same interest groups that have blocked major reforms in agricultural policy for decades. Prospects for consideration of this budgetary proposal therefore do not look hopeful. Indeed, historically, revenue systems of contributions of member-states do not appear to be stable in quasi-federal states (Feld, 2005).

Common Agricultural Policy

In the context of the ongoing developments in the EU, it seems rather perverse that agriculture should continue to be treated so differently. It is somewhat ironic that while the CAP is seen as a cornerstone of European integration, it is a policy where competing national interests have been longstanding. This has been seen in two ways: first, in how the Council of Ministers has fought to retain power from supranational institutions such as the European Parliament and second, in how the member-states have lined up against each other in the battles over reform as was highlighted by the confrontation between Britain and France in June 2005. This contrast remains evident when examining the experience of the last decade, where on the one hand significant progress has been made in advancing the principles of competition and barrier-free trade under the auspices of the single market, whilst Europeans continue to spend just under half of the EU's budgetary resources subsidising a farming sector which today accounts for merely two per cent of EU(15) GDP. Justifiably, greater support for agriculture was taken from the political standpoint of ensuring food security and continued political stability in the early post-war years, whilst securing a fair standard of living for the rural community (Baimbridge *et al.*, 2004).

A number of potential contradictions were also observed. There is evidence that farmers have had little influence over the shaping of recent CAP reforms. Moreover, ministers of agriculture have been joined, even supplanted, by ministers of finance in negotiating these reforms. Yet, despite this evidence that national agricultural policy communities have been weakening, the level of spending on the CAP has been sustained. Typically, those who block reform are receiving large CAP transfers, together with experiencing reduced variability in their share of CAP spending. Those seeking CAP reform are not always major net contributors to CAP spending, but they are most likely to be net contributors to the EU budget overall. Indeed, as outlined above, given the dominance of CAP spending in the EU budget negotiations over the CAP and its spending have transcended the agricultural arena. Therefore, it is suggested that decision makers might still seek to defend the pattern of transfers established at the outset of the CAP (Ackrill, 2005).

The financial discipline element of the 2003 reform will, however, provide a serious challenge to the budgetary status quo when it becomes operational in 2007, because it presents the very real possibility of member-states having to choose either to make cuts to direct payments or allow a spending limit to be breached. However, the shift in Europe toward capital-intensive technology based industries moves hand in hand with World Trade Organisation (WTO) agreements designed to erode protectionist world agricultural markets and aid the development of poorer countries in an earlier stage of their development cycle. This change in doctrine from mercantilism to globalisation leaves European agriculture in a very different position to that fifty years ago, whilst changes in consumer expectations of agriculture in the twenty-first century have catalysed the beginnings of a reorientation in EU agricultural policy (Baimbridge *et al.*, 2004).

Regional Policy

One of the EU's priority objectives is to ensure equal income standards and economic development between member-states and regions. At the end of the 2002–2006 program period, the EU will have to fully extend its cohesion policy to the 2004 enlargement countries. Given the income gap of the accession countries compared to the EU15 (only 42 per cent of average EU15 per capita GDP in 2001), it becomes clear that enlargement constitutes a major challenge for EU regional policy (Tondl, 2005). The share of cohesion countries, which presently account for one-sixth of the EU population will then constitute one-third of the population. Hence, a significant increase of regional development problems is to be anticipated whilst the entire EU budget will be limited to 1.27 per cent of the Union's GDP. Consequently a debate has begun on the future of regional policies. Since the cohesion problem of the EU is defined in relative terms, it will considerably shift to the east whereby 18 Objective 1 areas will lose their status, 30 will retain it, whilst an additional 36 Objective 1 regions will be located in the new member-states (European Commission, 2003).

However, for areas that will likely lose that status their development problems will still be the same, even when the reference EU average income value of less than 75 per cent to define objective 1 areas will have changed after enlargement. The reluctance of the net budget contributors to provide additional resources also led to fixing a 4 per cent of GDP ceiling for EU regional transfers in the Agenda 2000. Fearing that a proportionate transfer of present regional policy support to significantly poorer Eastern European regions would require additional financial resources, the argument of limited absorption capacity for development support was put forward, followed by the demand to limit support. Indeed, opponents of the regional policy claim that it has largely failed to promote economic development and convergence, that it would counteract market forces and thus would either harm natural economic forces or be ineffective (Midelfart-Knarvik and Overman, 2002). Finally, an important issue is the consistency of other EU policies with the goal pursued by cohesion policy. Several policies counteract the efforts of EU regional policy such as government assistance, corporate tax policies, transport, research and development and labour market policies, may potentially come into conflict with cohesion policies (Tondl, 2002; Molle, 2003).

There is no doubt that regional policy will continue to play a prominent role in overall EU policies in the future. The dramatic cohesion problem in an enlarged EU will clearly maintain the demand for this policy. However, any conversion of regional policy into a significant redistributive policy within a fiscal federalism system at the Union level, as required in the context of monetary union, is out of sight. Moreover, it should be cleat that EU regional policy is no guarantee for development since thus far, it has not met the goal of reducing income disparities (Tondl, 2005).

Single Internal Market

Since the inception of the first treaty over fifty years ago, the principle of a borderless zone for the trade of goods and services and free movement of factors of production has remained at the heart of European thinking. The Single Internal Market (SIM) program was a watershed in the EU's development, and although seen at the time as revolutionary, it was really part of an evolutionary process. Now just over a decade after the 1992 program, it is clear that great strides have been made, although the actual benefits are still less than those projected. Some aspects were given too much significance such as economies of scale, while others such as FDI have risen far than expected (Harrop, 2005).

Whilst further legislation has helped to deepen the ties between member states through the introduction of three pillars of support, the prioritisation of the single market in the first pillar and the ratification and introduction of a single currency demonstrates the continued eagerness of EU policy to forge ahead with the creation of a truly integrated market system. Undoubtedly, remarkable progress has been made, whilst the goal of a single market is still short of being realised. National government expenditure still generates a small proportion of cross-border trade, whilst external trade policy is not yet completely harmonised. Furthermore, discrepancies remain in the tax system across member states and the notion of free labour mobility, whilst true in theory, is minimal in practise. Indeed, it is a mistake to take the SIM for granted, and in May 2003 the Commission published its SIM strategy until 2006 in response to a Commission report that listed 92 barriers encountered by business, and proposed a ten-point plan to improve the situation (Harrop, 2005). These apparent deficiencies are widely recognised as being attributed to the absence of a supra-national EU government and associated budget mechanism. Moreover, the common usage of multiple spoken languages and rich diversity of traditions and customs are certainly admirable pan-European features, but seriously inhibit intra-EU labour migration. Despite these shortcomings, further steps are still being taken to continue the process of integration including liberalisation of national public and financial services sectors, the enforcement of competition policy and tougher rules on State aids (Baimbridge *et al.*, 2004).

Furthermore, while the SIM concentrates on a growth of inter-related developments inside the Union, it is worth recognising its significance regarding the EU's external influence. The SIM was important in the process of enlargement, in leading some of the former European Free Trade Association (EFTA) countries from the European Economic Area (EEA) into the EU in order to have a say in the rule making and maximize their economic benefits. It can be seen therefore that the true importance of the SIM lies in the momentum, which it has provided to the continuing process of integration (Harrop, 2005).

The Single Currency

One of the greatest milestones of political and economic integration has been the creation of the single European currency. Whilst indelibly linked to the ongoing process of greater integration of the single market, the scale and scope of theoretical and applied economic connotations form the next two sections of this book. The ethos of this initiative was the need to increase 'transparency' between member states trade by eliminating transactions costs arising from the usage of national currencies. In eliminating such costs, price transparency between member states would enhance competitive forces, and also reduce risk associated with cross border investments. Furthermore, in clearing a path for Monetary Union under the auspices of the Treaty on European Union (TEU), qualification standards on economic convergence targets for inflation, budgetary discipline and interest rates had a beneficial effect on those countries which had up until that time been rather lax with their fiscal and monetary discipline (Baimbridge *et al*., 2004).

Clearly this undertaking has not been without risks either, particularly given the absence of any EU government or budget mechanism to preside over the system. Furthermore, the removal of national central banks from signatory members and the introduction of rules governing both budgetary and public debt limits under the auspices of the Stability and Growth Pact (SGP) agreed in 1997, has opened up potentially dangerous consequences to members states that fall out of synchronisation with the European business cycle. Indeed, without traditional means of macroeconomic management, many argue that the success of the currency for members in the long term relies at least partly on advances in improving labour market flexibility both within and between member states. The importance of economic alignment within the common currency scheme has, to some extent, been highlighted by current events. Indeed, under the current framework of the SGP, member states with a deficit of over three per cent of GDP are accountable to pay an interest free deposit of 0.5 per cent of national GDP to the European Commission, returnable only if the offending member rectifies the problem within two years. It is unfortunate for the architects of the SGP that the two biggest economies within the eurozone, France and Germany, have breached this fiscal condition citing the need to stimulate sluggish economic growth. This is unlikely to bode well with smaller members in the eurozone who have adhered to the guidelines as it does not appear that any form of discipline under the auspices of the SGP agreement will be administered (Baimbridge *et al*., 2004). In light of these challenges, it may be that flanking policies and the role of new institutions (such as the Eurogroup) might have to be reconsidered as new countries may join EMU. Furthermore, although not immediately likely, it is not unthinkable, that countries will leave the Eurozone (Verdun, 2005).

For participating countries, the euro has resulted in fundamental changes to economic management at both national and EU level. In relation to the former, there has been an unparalleled separation of fiscal and monetary policy. Although member-states retain control over most aspects of taxation and expenditure, this is proscribed by two sets of EU-wide guidelines. The TEU contains the five convergence criteria that include budget deficit and debt-to-GDP ratios, while the SGP imposes financial penalties on breaches of budgetary limits. These twin additional aspects of fiscal management have introduced new dimensions to public administration, while a potential future aspect is the issue of fiscal federalism (Baimbridge, 2005). In the absence of any EU supra-national government, the key driving forces behind the success of the single currency are the convergence guidelines and penalties outlined in the legislature, and the European Central Bank (ECB) in Frankfurt which is charged with the regulation of European monetary policy whilst functioning independently of both European institutions and national governments.

Enlargement

The current enlargement is significant, not because of its scale, but because of its meaning, signalling the start of a new and less divided Europe. The Copenhagen (2002) Council accepted 10 new members for 1 May 2004 and at least two more were approved for membership in 2007 (Schoors and Gobbin, 2005). Their economies are clearly less stable and poorer than the EU average, which possesses consequences for regional and agricultural policy inside the EU. This presents a fundamental challenge to EU policy makers, largely because it involves the costly supra-national policies of structural funding and the CAP. The Central and Eastern European Countries (CEECs) which form the bulk of the accession members, are still in a phase of transition since the fall of communism in the late 1980s and as such their level of development and comparative economic wealth (i.e. per capita income) is considerably lower than even the relatively poorest members of the Union (Greece and Portugal). Secondly, whilst there is slow convergence to the EU average, agriculture's share of national output (and therefore employment) in each of the CEEC remains relatively high (Baimbridge *et al.*, 2004).

As far as agriculture is concerned, this enlargement is indeed very large. Therefore, agriculture became the main bone of contention in the accession negotiations. Eventually, the new members accepted the principle of phasing-in direct income support, provided that they were allowed to increase the phase-in levels with their own money and a maximum 40 per cent from the EU's rural development funds until 2006. Structural policy is also affected by the enlargement, and faces a spectacular transformation. In this respect, the negotiations for the new financial framework for 2007–2013 promise to be very difficult. The zero-sum game of budgetary negotiations ultimately implies that the old poor will need room for the new poor. In addition, the accession has increased the welfare gap between EU's rich and EU's poor, which makes the task of reducing intra-Union inequality ever so challenging (Schoors and Gobbin, 2005).

Combining these factors, these countries will undoubtedly become net recipients from the EU budget, at least in the medium-term. However, this comes in a period where EU paymaster member states are seeking to rationalise contributions, particularly when in need of funds to alleviate national budgetary breaches pertaining to eurozone membership. Reminiscent of previous UK Prime Minister Margaret Thatcher in the 1980s, the Germans and the Dutch are attempting to claw money back from the EU budget, whilst the UK's negotiated rebate looks increasingly under threat. On the other hand, the Germans are also trying to hold onto structural policy revenues for their Länder, whilst the traditional beneficiaries of Spain, Greece, Portugal and Ireland are looking to sustain their advantageous positions[1] (Baimbridge *et al.*, 2004).

A further immediate priority for the EU and the CEEC is the necessity for the latter to successfully adopt the EU's common visa and border regimes, known as the Schengen system. Within most of the EU these borders have already disappeared, which is what will also be required of the new members over the coming years. Moreover, accession members will be expected to have successfully instigated tough new border controls on non-EU members, including previously communist trading partners, a prospect that worries some members.[2] To some extent, pre-accession financial support mechanisms have been provided by the EU, although the ability of these members to align themselves successfully with the economies of the EU will be largely determined by their willingness to embrace continued institutional reform (Baimbridge *et al.*, 2004).

Slightly further a field is the need for accession countries to consolidate their participation in the single market through eventual membership of the single currency as soon as entry criteria are met although it is likely that a transition time period will be required before a number of these countries qualify. However, the TEU criteria appear inadequate since they unduly stress nominal convergence, even to the detriment of real convergence between new members and the EU-15 level. Advocates of the euro will clearly hail an extended eurozone as a major milestone toward an enlarged single market, although given the caveats of the current experience of euro membership for Germany and France, caution must be urged.

Conclusion

This chapter highlighted the overall development of the EU, focusing upon several key policy areas. The scope of the modern EU is so wide-ranging that a single chapter

---

1   Ireland began a phasing-out of the Cohesion Fund from 2004 onwards. Moreover, these countries have a substantial blocking minority of 157 (186 if Italy supports as well) votes out of 321 in the European Parliament that could threaten the net payers of the budget, although the impact of the new members in 2004 will inevitably impact on this.

2   Of the current accession wave, Poland would like to keep ties with the Ukraine; whilst Hungary is keen to maintain relations with ethic Hungarians in Serbia and the Ukraine.

cannot seek to encompass the myriad of topics associated with it.[3] However, given the format of this book in terms of the following two substantive Parts concerning EMU discussing its theoretical and practical aspects, together with examining alternative options for the UK; we choose here to focus upon those areas central to the stability of the EU as a whole and in particular EMU. The latter is the most important economic development within the current EU structure since the advent of the EU itself as a customs union. As the process of integration deepens, so does the level of peril if it were to catastrophically fail. The adoption of a common currency and setting of a single interest rate entwines national economies unlike any other form of economic association, such that the EU has significantly moved away from the situation when economic failure can frequently be quarantined within national boarders.

Hence, the topics examined are similarly entwined in determining the EU's future economic prosperity. The fiscal cornerstone of any modern state is its budget; hence the EU budget is central to both its ambitions in terms of EMU and enlargement. The chapter reviews the well-known shortcomings of the budget and subsequently focus upon two key aspects, the CAP and regional policy. As the disagreement between, principally, Britain and France in mid-2005 illustrated, the CAP still possesses the power to create seismic divisions amongst the member states. The proportion of the relatively small (federal) budget taken-up by agriculture still remains massively skewed in terms of its contribution to EU GDP and its share of the labour force. However, the 2004 enlargement of 10 new member states with others to follow will potentially rekindle this debate given the role of agricultural production within these economies. An alternative source of structural funds is offered by the enhanced use of regional policy, which amongst other aspects can be used to wean regions and countries off declining sectors such as agriculture. Moreover, given its primary goal of evening-out income disparities, its role is again likely to be influenced by the ongoing enlargement process and the simultaneous requirement to ensure that these countries are able to cope with compulsory EMU membership.

The microeconomic and macroeconomic aspects of the EU becoming a single economy were next reviewed. Although the SIM has now been established for more than a decade, the entrance of new member states and broadening of EU competences has resulted in a perpetual expansion of its remit. Moreover, much of the EU's ambitious Lisbon Agenda in terms of developing a 'knowledge based' economy has its key underpinnings within the SIM. However, it is EMU as previously discussed which forms the fulcrum of these economic aspects of the EU. Although its eventual implementation proved successful, the real test for EMU is yet to come as the member states move through the economic cycle. The evidence to date, with the

---

3   For an indication of see van der Hoek (2005) which analyses, *inter alia*, the following: European Council and the Council of the European Union; the European Commission; the European Parliament; judicial, controlling, and advisory institutions; the EU budget; Single Internal Market; the Common Foreign and Security Policy; the Common Agricultural Policy; energy policy; environmental policy; transport policy; regional policy; social policy; development policy; enlargement; Economic and Monetary Union; the European Central Bank.

jettisoning of the much-heralded SGP and threats from coalition parties in Italy to leave, are disturbing precursors for its long-term stability. Indeed, it precisely these issues, the theoretical underpinnings and practical implications that we explore in more detail in he following sections.

Finally, in terms of current EU developments, we briefly reviewed the issue of enlargement. This is an area of the EU that has largely gone unnoticed by observers given the random and periodic nature of its occurrence. Moreover, circumstances for the three previous rounds of enlargement in 1973 (Denmark, Ireland and the UK), the 1980s (Greece, Portugal and Spain) and 1996 (Austria, Finland and Sweden), have now substantially changed. In particular, two key differences are that EU's scope has increased beyond comprehension and the nature of the accession countries. The major aspects of the former are outlined above, whilst the latter is discussed in Baimbridge *et al.* (2008) and Baimbridge and Philippidis (2008).

PART II
EMU: Theoretical Considerations

Chapter 5

An Overview of European Monetary Integration

Introduction

The advent of a single currency covering the majority of European Union (EU) member states was a momentous event that will have profound consequences for people across the Continent and beyond. The euro has become the currency in which individual citizens are paid and denote the price of all goods, services and labour across the whole Economic and Monetary Union (EMU) zone. Thus, a coin minted in France is legal tender in Germany, Italy and Belgium, creating a greater transparency of transactions in the process. More importantly, monetary union required the transfer of monetary and exchange rate policy from each participating nation state to a central authority, in this case the European Central Bank (ECB) based in Frankfurt, which operates a uniform monetary policy for the entire single currency region. Therefore, Finland, Spain and the Netherlands each have an identical interest rate, set by the ECB for the benefit of the participating nations as a whole. In addition, to ensure that divergent fiscal policy does not destabilise the currency union, individual countries are subject to commonly accepted constraints upon their budget deficits that, if they were to rise above a target rate of between 1 and 3 per cent, theoretically results in the country being fined by the EU. Thus, discretionary national macroeconomic management has been largely superseded by rule-based economic co-ordination, intended to sustain monetary union whilst creating ever-closer economic union between participating member states. Consequently, methods of economic management and democratic accountability have been fundamentally altered.

Exchange Rates, Competitiveness and International Trade

In order to fully understand what is involved by joining the single currency, we must first establish why the exchange rate is an important macroeconomic policy instrument. The exchange rate acts as a price like any other; it is the price of one country's currency when translated into the currency of another for the purposes of international trade and financial movements. If the demand for sterling exceeds supply, the price rises (sterling appreciates in value) alternatively, If the supply of sterling exceeds demand, the price falls (sterling depreciates) and is worth less foreign currency. An appreciation of sterling benefits British citizens wishing to take a foreign holiday and those purchasing cheaper imports, but disadvantages those whose jobs depend upon British exports, the price of which is made more expensive when valued in foreign currency. Consequently, changes in the value of one currency in terms of another can exert a decisive impact upon prices, the balance of payments and employment.

Supporters of a single currency have therefore argued that, by permanently fixing European exchange rates, uncertainty would be reduced, thereby stimulating trade between EU countries and in the process facilitating investment together with an expansion in output and employment. This apparently plausible argument is, however, based upon a number of questionable assumptions. For example, whilst it is undoubtedly true that a relatively stable environment encourages international trade and investment, the experience of the past quarter of a century has demonstrated that a dramatic increase in internationalisation can occur without the 'assistance' of a fixed exchange rate regime. Indeed, history also demonstrates that an exchange rate regime which is too rigid, over a long period of time, will inevitably collapse because it prevents individual economies adjusting to the divergent impact upon production and employment structures caused by external shocks and changes in the pattern of demand for specific product ranges.

Alternative Exchanges Regimes in History (1870–)

EMU is the latest experiment in designing an international monetary system, although it has been on the drawing board of the architects for EU integration even prior to Treaties of Rome in 1957.[1] International monetary systems are broadly defined as the set of conventions, rules, procedures and institutions that govern the conduct of financial relations between nations. Their need derives from the inherent interdependence of open national economies and different systems are designed to support specific forms of trade and economic development (Foreman-Peck, 1995). However, the design of international monetary systems has a considerable influence upon the ability of national economies to achieve their goals of maintaining internal and external balance. The six principal systems operating between the major industrialised nations since 1870 have been: the Classical gold standard (1870–1914), the modified gold standard (1925–1931), free floating (1931–1939), Bretton Woods (1944–1971/2), free and managed floating (1972–) and EMU (1999–).

One of the most debated issues in international economics concerns the choice of exchange rate regime and the 'pros' and 'cons' of fixed versus flexible or floating exchange rates. In practice neither extreme has ever really existed, but it remains useful to use these ideal types as the basis for drawing some positive and normative conclusions of relevance when choosing a hybrid system. In this sense, the debate over fixed versus flexible exchange rates is analogous to that between perfect competition and monopoly in the economic analysis of market structures.

---

1   See Verdun (2004) for an in-depth review of the origins of EMU. For an overview of the historical precedents of monetary unions see Kaergard and Henriksen (2003) and Barrell and to Velde (2003).

Fixed -- Floating							
Single	Classical	Gold	Adjustable	Sliding	Crawling	Target ERs	Managed
Currency	Gold	Exchange	Peg	Parities	Peg		Floating
(EMU)	Standard	Standard	R +/- 1%	(ERM			1972-1990
	1870-1914	1926-1931	1944-1972	1990-92)			& 1992-

Figure 5.1   UK membership of exchange rate systems

Figure 5.1 depicts the spectrum of exchange rate regimes. It is interesting to note that since the industrial revolution there has been a movement away from fixed towards more flexible exchange rate regimes for the industrialised world. This trend, however, now appears to be in reverse for the membership of the European Union (EU). The European Exchange Rate Mechanism (ERM) of the European Monetary System (EMS) was a distinct shift back to less flexible exchange rates between the participating countries. Moreover, the continuation along this path to Economic and Monetary Union (EMU) entailed the disappearance of exchange rates between EMU members altogether as a single currency (the euro) is adopted for use.

In its present form, the proposed EMU is without precedent in the history of the civilised world. There has never been an economic and monetary union between a group of countries without a simultaneous movement towards political union, although a number of attempts have been undertaken to secure the greater predictability that a fixed exchange rate regime can provide, the aim being to reduce exchange rate risk and hence promote trade, investment and ultimately economic growth. The most successful fixed rate regimes, the Classical Gold Standard and Bretton Woods, each helped to establish an international economic environment that facilitated decades of economic expansion, before a combination of political and economic factors forced their ultimate termination. However, a badly constructed fixed exchange rate system, such as the 1920s return to the Gold Standard on pre-First World War parities or the UK's experience of ERM membership at too high a parity, has been associated with economic recession, bankruptcies, house price collapses and mass unemployment. Consequently, whilst a properly constructed system can be a benefit to participating countries, a badly designed regime can cause untold damage to its members. The importance of this point is reinforced by the fact that EMU membership is intended to be an irrevocable act, with the TEU deliberately failing to specify a means by which a member state might exit the arrangement in the future. It is intended to be a one-way shift towards further economic integration. Consequently, even greater emphasis is placed upon the estimated balance of costs and benefits by which a country decides whether or not to participate in this unique currency arrangement.

The implications that membership would exert upon the UK economy signify that British reaction to the single currency is likely to be the most important and far-reaching economic and political decision of the present generation. Assuming that present political promises are not subject to modification over time, the ultimate decision as to whether the UK joins EMU is likely to be subject to a democratic referendum. In view of the importance for our own future prosperity, a national debate focusing upon the relative advantages and disadvantages of EMU membership must be serviced by material that is both easy to understand and which takes an unbiased stance on the issue. The problem currently facing an individual eager to understand more about this vital topic is that most of the literature tends to present only one side of the argument. Whilst an experienced scholar of the subject may have no difficulty in reading between the lines in such circumstances, it can be frustrating to those less familiar with the material. This book therefore endeavours to examine both pros and cons of the single currency.

Arguments Regarding Fixed v. Floating Exchange Rates

The main issue of debate concerning exchange rate regime regards the case for or against greater flexibility. In other words the question is: where over this spectrum lies the 'ideal' exchange rate mechanism? Unfortunately, there is no simple or conclusive answer to this problem, with each set of arguments possessing their own merits. Moreover, in the dynamic modern world of ever-greater globalisation, the 'ideal' exchange rate regime can change over time depending upon the domestic economic circumstances of the country involved and the global economic environment in which it finds itself. Most policymakers would agree that in general, the 'ideal' situation is for the exchange rate to possess short-term stability, but long-term flexibility. This offers the best possible environment for business, investment and trade that prefers stability, whilst not locking the country into an exchange rate position which may prove harmful in the long-run as national, regional and global economic circumstances change over time.

Hence, a key aspect of such international monetary arrangements is the choice of exchange rate regime, which centres on the issue of flexibility (Ghosh *et al.*, 2002; Sarno and Taylor, 2002). The case for greater flexibility can be summarised by the following arguments:

1. Perhaps the most popular argument in favour of floating exchange rates can be summed up by the expression, 'the market knows best'. 'Best' here implies that a competitive foreign exchange market would be a more efficient means of achieving balance of payments equilibrium and adjustments of the exchange rate over time. However, it may also reflect normative preferences that market mechanisms are more desirable than leaving decisions to government officials and/or monetary authorities.

2. A second argument notes that exchange rates always adjust to ensure continuous equilibrium between the demand and supply of the currency. Thus, an efficient market clearing mechanism quickly eliminates temporary disequilibrium positions, based upon the current account theory. Excess demand for a currency leads to its appreciation, thereby making imports cheaper and exports more expensive, and consequently reduces the excess demand for the currency as imports rise and exports fall. Similarly, excess

supply of a currency leads to its fall in value, making exports cheaper and imports more expensive, and therefore stimulating demand for the currency through higher exports and lower imports. No one expects the adjustment process to be quite as smooth as this. However, if arbitrage and speculation are stabilising, it provides an efficient and automatic solution to the balance of payments problems.

3. Floating exchange rates enable countries to operate independent monetary policies. Floating is, according to this viewpoint, essential to restore monetary autonomy for each country, which would otherwise be constrained by an arbitrary exchange rate target, thereby allowing it to determine its own employment and inflation rates. Under fixed systems, the need to maintain long-term competitiveness requires a country to achieve essentially similar inflation rates to other countries, thereby restricting it from pursuing markedly different economic policies. Under fixed exchange rate regimes, monetary policy is focused upon the maintenance of the exchange rate parity and is therefore not available for other macroeconomic goals. This economic argument is also sometimes expanded to claim that this element of fixed exchange rates disempowers democracy since democratic decisions to pursue an economic strategy aimed at securing full employment, for example, would be de-railed if inflation remained higher than elsewhere. A counter argument asserts that, in a world of global financial capital flows and international money markets, monetary autonomy does not exist. This view holds that interest rates must move towards a world norm, which negates this criticism of fixed exchange rates to the extent that it is an accurate description of economic reality.

4. Floating rates may also partially insulate the domestic economy from foreign price shocks (i.e. inflation caused by the USA Vietnam war or raw material price rises such as the 1970s OPEC oil price shocks). If there is an increase in foreign prices under floating exchange rates, provided the exchange rate moves roughly in line with the fundamental balance of the economy (arguably expressed by the purchasing power parity (PPP) relation), the domestic exchange rate would appreciate to prevent the importation of foreign inflation. Under a fixed exchange rate, the same scenario would leave the exchange rate over-competitive, thereby leading to increased demand for exports and stimulating domestic demand. Assuming the economy was already operating at full employment, this would cause inflation unless countered by compensatory fiscal or monetary measures. The more difficult scenario under fixed exchange rates is if the domestic exchange rate becomes uncompetitive. Instead of allowing a currency to depreciate, price and wage downward flexibility would be required to ensure a real depreciation. This is a scenario that is difficult to achieve in the short term because of wage and price stickiness, and would therefore be likely to require deflation and high unemployment. Under floating exchange rates some of this adjustment can be borne by changes in relative prices if the fall in the value of the currency allows expenditure switching to take place. This helps to cushion the country from deflationary pressures by causing the rest of the world to share some of the burden. Consequently, floating rates are deemed to be more conducive

to economic stability because of their superior ability to adjust to external shocks and relative changes in domestic prices.

5. It is argued that floating exchanges rates releases the balance of payments constraint on growth of a country's economy – i.e. achieving both internal and external balance simultaneously. The assumed advantage is that flexible exchange rates allow the government to 'forget' balance of payments problems, as it will automatically adjust itself. In practice flexible exchange rates have not eliminated the balance of payments constraint as governments do not forget that deficits exist, it only makes external and internal economic management slightly easier. However, supporters of flexible exchange rates would argue that totally freely floating exchange rates have been given their chance.

6. Economies on foreign exchange reserves could be achieved if the foreign exchange market works efficiently under flexible exchange rates as governments would not need to hold official reserves of foreign exchange. Official 'accommodating transactions' are not required, as the exchange rate 'cures' the balance of payments deficit by falling in value in the foreign exchange markets. Thus, the opportunity cost of holding foreign exchange reserves would be lower, thereby releasing considerable resources to finance alternative objectives – either stimulating consumption or investment in public and private sectors, or to reduce domestic money supply and therefore inflationary pressure. This is especially important to less developed countries, which may find that the necessity of holding extra reserves to cushion swings in the balance of payments high in terms of the development opportunities forgone by not being able to use these reserves to purchase scarce inputs from abroad. However, in reality, currency floating does not work perfectly; so governments still need to intervene to push the exchange rate in the required direction even if they are committed to floating. Nevertheless, even managed floating would probably require smaller foreign exchange reserves than a fixed exchange rate.

These arguments were powerful enough to tip the balance in favour of greater exchange rate flexibility in the 1970s and 1980s, after a period of almost continuous fixed rates before the First World War and following the Second World War. Nevertheless, there are some counter-arguments that are vociferously presented by those who believe that too much flexibility has been permitted and that a return to greater fixity would be appropriate.

In contrast, the case against greater flexibility is summarised by the following arguments:

1. In the first case it is suggested that floating rates generate wider fluctuations in exchange rates, which increases uncertainty, leading to a contraction in volume of international trade. Thus, fixed exchange rates should minimise uncertainty and therefore provide the optimum environment for international trade and productive investment. Small companies, in particular, will minimise their exposure to exchange rate variations by either adding a premium to their prices to hedge against this risk, thereby reducing potential export sales,

or concentrating upon domestic sales instead of expanding internationally. Creating a relatively stable trading environment will therefore stimulate international trade and investment. However, this argument is based upon the assumption that greater fluctuations in exchange value equate with greater uncertainty that will, in turn, depress trade flows. This is not, however, necessarily the case. Instability, in the greater sense of greater fluctuations in rates, is not the same thing as uncertainty since regularly reversing fluctuations can be quite predictable. Moreover, fixed rates have also been frequently changed in practice and have often fluctuated quite strongly between certain limits. These changes could have been similarly off-putting for traders. Secondly, the transactors involved would have to be *risk averse* for the negative economic effects to occur, where traders are unwilling or unable to use forward markets to hedge the risks involved. Only if traders expect future exchange rate movements to be unpredictable, and are put off by the risks of fluctuations, then there will be adverse effects on the volume of trade.

2. A second argument against floating concerns its association with destabilising speculation. Speculation can be a stabilising influence upon exchange rates if speculators are able to calculate currency deviations from purchasing power parity rates and consequently speculate that they will return towards this long-term underlying rate. If, however, they guess wrongly or are unable to accurately assess the currency value most accurately expressing the underlying international competitive strength, then speculation will be destabilising and the currency will fluctuate more than it would have done otherwise. The unjustified appreciation of sterling in the first half of the 1980s, which helped to destroy large swathes of manufacturing industry, and the 1980–1985 rise in the price of the US dollar, were both damaging for the economies concerned. However, it must be stressed that speculation can be rife under fixed exchange rates if it is abundantly clear that the economy is suffering from 'fundamental disequilibrium' and that devaluation is imminent. Such was the situation before the devaluation of sterling in 1967 because of the one-way option to sell sterling just before devaluation and then buying it back after the change in parity. A more recent example concerns sterling's forced exit from the ERM, when speculators believed (rightly) that it was over-valued. These speculators were able to sell at the guaranteed fixed rate (since sterling had fallen to the lowest allowable value within its band) on the basis that, were they to be wrong, they could re-purchase the currency in the future at approximately the same rate, having to pay only the small commission charges that are charged for large volume transactions.

3. Flexibility of the exchange rates is claimed to result in greater inflationary pressures on the domestic economy. If the value of the currency falls, this raises import prices and may result in 'cost-push' inflation, whilst an appreciation of the currency is unlikely to be passed on in the form of lower prices. Thus, there is an in-built 'ratchet' effect under flexible exchange rates. Furthermore,

'demand-pull' inflation is also possible if the economy is unable to respond rapidly (i.e. too inelastic supply) if a depreciation of the currency increases exporters' incomes.

4. Fixed rates may provide a greater degree of discipline upon government macroeconomic policies than a floating regime is unable to exert. If a balance of payments deficit occurs under fixed exchange rates, a country must either be borrowing or running down reserves, thereby making the deficit immediately visible and leading to prompt corrective action. A flexible regime enables the authorities to delay corrective measures since currency depreciation may mask the worst effect of this process. However, the country may suffer inflationary consequences as a result. Monetarists argue that as the currency depreciates the price level will rise and so is a clear signal to governments to respond by raising interest rates.

5. Fixed rates, by their nature, depend upon a degree of international co-operation and co-ordination between countries that is typically lacking under alternative floating regimes. At a minimum, fixed exchange rate regimes require agreement to avoid damaging competitive devaluation's undermining the exchange rate arrangement, such as occurred in the 1930s, and negotiate rules preventing realignment apart from explicitly sanctioned scenarios such as fundamental disequilibrium. At best, fixed exchange rate regimes could facilitate macroeconomic co-ordination between participating nations, such as the G7 efforts in the late 1970s and the EU member states under the EMS regime. Co-ordinated reflation or deflation could minimise leakages and thereby enhance the success of the initiative.

6. One final argument for fixed rates is that, if an economy is fairly rigid in the sense that resources are relatively immobile, then changes in the foreign exchange market may not result in the necessary changes in trade flows for the balance of payments to be in a position of equilibrium. Devaluation to (stimulate export demand) requires producers to take advantage of their new competitive position by reducing prices abroad and increase output. However, they may choose to maintain prices and reap higher profits, which blunts devaluation as a means of reducing unemployment. Alternatively, variation in exchange rates may be an attempt to use market prices to signal the need for one sector of the economy to expand relative to others. However, sticky prices and wages, particularly the latter, may frustrate this mechanism. This is largely a reiteration of the structuralist school of thought, which has relatively little faith in market clearing. A counter argument asserts that exchange rate adjustments can be effective, with those made by Britain in 1931, 1949 and 1992 having boosted exports, growth and production without triggering an inflationary spiral.

Pros and Cons of a Single Currency

As indicated by Figure 5.1, EMU represents an extremely fixed form of exchange rate regime and therefore possess many of the characteristics relating to the above general arguments in relation to the regime debate. However, there are important aspects of the EMU process that signal its uniqueness given the specific nature of EMU in relation to a focused group of developed countries, its detailed timetable for implementation, the addition of a new institutional framework around the European Central Bank (ECB) and later rules, in the form of the Stability and Growth Pact (SGP) to prevent fiscal profligacy.

If the advocates of membership are correct, joining the single currency could unleash economic potential which would increase economic growth and investment throughout the EMU zone, achieve low and stable inflation, and build a strong European economy to the envy of the rest of the world. Some of the main economic and political benefits claimed for EMU entry are:

1. Greater nominal exchange rate stability will occur, which reduces the risk associated with fluctuating exchange rates and is therefore assumed to encourage greater trade and investment, which, in turn, should result in higher growth and employment in the longer run.

2. A reduction in transaction costs should occur since firms exporting or importing goods and services to another participating country will no longer have to exchange currency to complete the sale, thereby saving upon commission charges. Whilst less onerous for large companies than tourists changing small amounts of foreign currency, the removal of this small but significant charge upon international trade should encourage exports and thereby stimulate economic growth. Even a small annual boost to economic activity may become significant if its effects are cumulative over time.

3. Price transparency should increase, because goods, services and labour are priced in the same currency, facilitating traders to make cheaper purchases and increase competition across the eurozone, thereby exerting a downward pressure upon prices to the benefit of European consumers. It is further argued that this price transparency is a precondition to the final completion of the single market.

4. The ECB is charged with ensuring price stability above all alternative economic goals and therefore many proponents of EMU entry argue that inflation is likely to be lower for those countries with the single currency, particularly in the longer run, and accordingly interest rates should be lower, thereby boosting investment and economic growth.

5. Creation of the euro would establish a major world currency capable of rivalling the US dollar and Japanese Yen, which could confer certain economic advantages as well as providing political prestige based upon the EU's combined economic strength and greater world political influence. This might, or might not, involve closer political integration between EU member states, which would rival the USA in terms of population and wealth.

6. Advocates of EMU participation argue that failure to join will leave the UK vulnerable and incapable of influencing the monetary policy of the EMU-zone from the outside. Potential threats are suggested to include the risk of losing markets due to some sort of 'unofficial' protectionism preventing the free passage of UK goods and services across the rest of the EU, the risk of

losing political influence within the EU and a risk to the position of the City
of London with the ECB strengthening the prestige of the Frankfurt financial
market.

7. Arguments that membership of EMU reduces national sovereignty are
    rejected on the grounds that sovereignty is not absolute any more, due to
    the globalisation of financial markets and voluntary limitations imposed by
    international treaties such as membership of NATO, the Geneva Convention,
    the United Nations and the World Trade Organisation. Sovereignty is not
    given away because nations are still able to influence decision-making through
    the European Council, but as one voice amongst fifteen. Thus, sovereignty
    is shared, or pooled, within the EU, with decision-making subject to the
    collective viewpoint of participating member states.

8. Advocates of further European integration often point out that many critics
    of monetary integration are content to support EU membership in general
    and in particular the SIM, despite the fact that both reduce UK national
    independence to a greater degree than EMU may require. The Treaty of Rome
    required the freedom of movement of labour and capital, thereby undermining
    the potential for isolating individual economies from international financial
    markets, a move exacerbated by the Single European Act (SEA) which
    required the abolition of exchange controls and gave the European Court of
    Justice jurisdiction over UK law where a contradiction occurs. This apparent
    inconsistency amongst many single currency critics may undermine their
    arguments or require them to reassess continued EU membership, a policy
    which appears to be less popular than opposition to EMU.

9. Finally, the argument which caused the majority of UK trade unions to accept
    EMU entry is based upon their desire to achieve the European 'social model'.
    The recent period of Conservative government convinced many trade union
    leaders that locking the UK economy into a European model, which embraces
    a social dimension intended to moderate the worst excesses of the competitive
    pressures unleashed by the SIM and EMU, is better than the *laissez-faire*
    alternative variously supported by Labour and Conservative leaderships.
    The conditionality of this support distinguishes trade unionists from other
    advocates of EMU, because of their concern that the social dimension may be
    abandoned in favour of fiscal rectitude.

However, many critics of the single currency argue that the costs of entry are in
fact potentially far larger and specifically problematic for the UK, so that it is in
the British economic interest to remain outside the currency union. The principal
arguments advanced by those critical towards EMU, include:

1. The loss of control over monetary policy and of influence over the exchange
    rate weakens national economic management, which is further constrained by
    the restraints upon fiscal policy resulting from the Maastricht Convergence
    Criteria (MCC) and SGP rules on government borrowing. This combination

reduces the potential capacity of a country to respond to internal or external shocks, exacerbating the danger of national destabilisation.

2. The lack of prior cyclical and structural convergence amongst all participating member states will create strains within EMU. Consequently, unsynchronised business cycles and/or structural differences magnify the effects of asymmetric external shocks (i.e. oil price rises), whilst a unified monetary policy will be unable to meet satisfactorily the needs of all economies, concentrating upon the 'average' member state as it is likely to do. Thus, incorrectly set interest rates may damage individual economies, increasing their initial misfortunes rather than moderating them (see Chapters 6 and 9).

3. The 'generous' interpretation of the MCC in order to ensure as many countries as possible participated in EMU implies that the majority of participants must continue to deflate their economies by raising taxes or cutting government spending in order to meet the rigid financial criteria established by the MCC and SGP. The combination of these measures will result in higher unemployment and slower growth within the single currency zone (see Chapter 6).

4. The absence of any substantial fiscal redistribution mechanism, which could stabilise EMU by transferring resources from favoured to weaker regions, means that less competitive areas may suffer declining incomes and persistent mass unemployment, thereby increasing inequality and social tension across the single currency area (see Chapter 9).

5. Many of the economic objectives claimed by single currency advocates could be achieved through effective national economic management, such as price stability, high economic growth and full employment. Moreover, since the ECB will include Mediterranean countries as well as Germany, it is unlikely that it will initially possess the anti-inflation credibility that the Bundesbank enjoyed, meaning that the euro might be a weak currency (see Chapter 15).

6. The costs of transition to the new currency may be in the region of £18.5 billion, thereby cautioning against participation unless the benefits can be demonstrated to be substantially higher over time.

7. The UK private financial sector is more sensitive to changes in interest rates since a higher proportion of mortgage debt is denominated in flexible rather than fixed interest rate stock. Consequently, were the ECB to vary interest rates in order to stimulate or restrain average EMU economic activity, the UK would bear a disproportionate brunt of the corrective measures, causing the economy to diverge further from the EMU average. Thus, a uniform monetary policy would be likely to create fluctuating boom-bust cycles in the UK economy rather than a smooth and sustainable rate of economic development.

8. The UK has a particular competitive advantage in high technology, aeronautical and pharmaceutical sectors which, together with oil production, are typically priced in US dollars and compete principally with US and Japanese companies even when exporting to other EU member states. Thus, the sterling-dollar exchange rate will remain far more important to this key element of British manufacturing than sterling-euro. Hence participation in the *euro* might increase exchange rate volatility for a crucial sector of the UK economy.

9. Opponents of EMU dismiss the threat of loss of markets through protectionist measures enacted by single currency members against the UK since these would flout the various EU treaties (Rome, SIM, TEU) and WTO rules.
10. Critics of European integration generally reject the view that sovereignty can be pooled, suggesting that it refers to a national authority using every means at its disposal to achieve its objectives, within the constraints imposed by international markets and treaty obligations. Thus, sovereignty can be exercised *either* by national government *or* by the EU, but not by both. EMU would result in the loss of economic sovereignty to the ECB, with national authorities losing autonomy.
11. The ECB is undemocratic because it is deliberately insulated from all political influence; the authors of the TEU believed that such insulation would enhance its ability to secure price stability (see Chapter 7). Thus, electors would no longer be able to influence monetary and exchange rate policies, whilst fiscal policy is also tightly constrained through the SGP. These policies deeply affect individual citizens' lives, from setting the cost of their mortgage to the possibility of losing their job.
12. One final criticism is that, rather than EMU creating a European super-state, it is in fact designed to 'roll back' the state and reduce its ability to regulate the actions of the owners of private capital and the international financial markets in the interests of their citizens. Increased constraints placed upon government economic autonomy reduce the choices available through the democratic process, whilst limiting the ability of one country to pursue a significantly un-orthodox economic strategy intended to meet nation-specific goals.

Potential Cost-Benefits for the UK

Table 5.1 seeks to quantify the potential costs and benefits of EMU membership for the UK. The EU Commission, unsurprisingly, concludes that EMU would be largely positive, stimulating investment through lower interest rates and exchange rate certainty, thereby generating higher economic growth and employment. However, our estimates of its likely impact of UK participation in EMU would be overwhelmingly negative. The MCC would undermine the economy whilst it, and the expansion of the EU budget, would place a substantial burden upon British taxpayers. The economy would suffer more asymmetric shocks, which the operation of ECB monetary policy would exacerbate. Economic growth would be stymied, unemployment would rise dramatically and the disaster of UK participation in the ERM would be repeated, but this time there would be no easy escape!

Table 5.1   Estimated costs and benefits of EMU

	EU Commission estimates	Our estimates
BENEFITS		
Transaction costs	0.4 per cent GNP p.a.	Costs for business are currently as low as 0.05 per cent for transactions exceeding $5 million.
Information costs	0.3 per cent GNP p.a.	Lower UK intra-EU trade implies a lower cost saving of perhaps 0.15 per cent GNP p.a.
Exchange rate stability dynamics	0.7–1 per cent GNP p.a.	Hallett and Vines (1993) estimated the dynamic effect might be as low as 0.3 per cent of GNP per annum across the whole EMU zone. Moreover, since the majority of UK trade is outside the EU, a ratio around twice the average of 'core' EU member states, any such dynamic effects are likely to be around only half the estimated amount. A generous estimate would thus be in the range 0.15–0.5 per cent GNP p.a.
Net benefits	1.4–1.7 per cent GNP p.a.	0.35–0.7 per cent GNP per annum. To put this in context, whilst a worthwhile gain, it is smaller than the typical region of error allowed for in all macroeconomic forecasts, so even a minuscule shock could overturn such benefits.
COSTS		
Maastricht Convergence Criteria (MCC)	Marginal (unsubstantiated) costs, certainly less than the estimated 1.4–1.7 per cent GNP p.a. benefits EMU is supposed to generate.	The UK government finances may require tax increases or public expenditure cuts worth between £38 and 47 billion, equivalent to 4–5 per cent GDP, in order that the MCC can be met at the bottom of the economic cycle as well as during boom years. Moreover, the estimated effects for total compliance with the MCC across the EU are an additional 10 million unemployed or an annual reduction in average EU GDP of some 2.6 per cent per year until after the turn of the century.
External shocks	Mostly symmetric, therefore monetary policy beneficial for all participating countries	Approximately 85 per cent of the duration or content of external shocks will affect the UK asymmetrically when compared to Germany and most other potential 'core' EMU participants. Consequently, monetary policy will be destabilising for the UK, in most instances.
Wage flexibility	No discussion – assumed not to be problematic	Nominal and real wage rigidities are problematic; implying that reliance upon market forces is insufficient to achieve adjustment in the face of external shocks.
Labour mobility	No discussion – assumed not to be problematic	Low rates of labour mobility similarly do not provide an alternative method of reducing areas of high unemployment.
Fiscal policy	The MacDougall Report (1977) stated that the EU budget needs to rise to between 5 and 7 per cent of Community GDP	EU budget needs to rise to the average of 20–25 per cent of GDP in existing federal states, implying an additional transfer of between £109.3 and £138.1 billion, which represents in the region of 15.4 per cent to 19.5 per cent of total UK 1995/96 GDP. Even if transferred over a decade, it would effectively eliminate almost the entire UK trend growth rate for the whole period, leading to economic stagnation and rising unemployment cumulatively far worse than the 1980–81 and 1990–92 recessions put together. The only alternative would be to transfer approximately half of the current UK national budget over to EU control, effectively acknowledging the existence of a new European super-state through the back door.

Source: Baimbridge *et al.* (1997).

Thus, critics of EMU claim that Britain's fundamental structural differences to most continental European economies would preclude an easy 'marriage'. Instead it would expose the UK to monetary policies unsuitable to its circumstances and to participation in a depressed 'club', constantly reducing public expenditure to meet the rigid fiscal rules imposed by the MCC and the SGP. On the most optimistic scenario, EMU could re-create a golden era similar to the original Gold Standard of the nineteenth century or post-war Bretton Woods, when members shared decades of economic growth and relative price stability. However, at worst, it would generate the conditions pertaining in the 1930s depression, as adherence to a fixed exchange rate unsuitable to the economic realities of individual countries compounds the misery of mass unemployment.

Conclusion

This chapter presented the background to the thorny issue of EMU, which is a feature that frequently absent from comparable texts. The process of EMU is, for example, merely a step along a theoretical road in terms of exchange rate regimes. Although its practical consequences in terms of both economic and political national sovereignty are substantial and therefore these practical implications require deep analysis, the adoption of any exchange rate regime is not a decision for any country to take lightly. Hence, the first part of this chapter reviewed the development of adopted exchange rate regimes by Britain since the Gold Standard of the 19th century and in particular summarises the arguments concerning the polar extremes of fixed and floating systems. The lessons to be learnt from this historical experience are that the 'holy grail' of an ideal exchange rate system is an elusive aspiration for policy makers. The key to understanding exchange rate regimes is to realise their inherently temporary nature relative to the level of economic development experienced by the country in question, its main trading partners, together with the overall global trend in international monetary systems. Hence, the need for countries to maintain a degree of 'philosophical' flexibility given that an alternative regime might prove optimal as economic circumstances.

Looking towards the prospect of EMU itself, a similar cost-benefit calculation is required by potential participating member states. We summarise the principal advantages and disadvantages of joining a single currency system, which is in essence the ultimate form of fixed exchange rates. There are, however, several complications to what appears a simple trade-off optimisation problem. Firstly, the various cost and benefits need to be assessed within the context of both the potential partner country and in relation to the already established monetary union, or the other prospective members. Each economy is unique in its blend of sectoral strengths and weaknesses and comparative advantage etc, therefore the national interest will be distinctively different for each potential participant. Secondly, there is no set rule in which to weigh the relative merits of the arguments associated with membership of a monetary union. Again the above consideration of relative strengths and weaknesses need to be taken into account. Finally, it must be remembered that although we are focusing upon the economic aspects of the relationship between Britain and the EU, as discussed in Chapter 2, the political relationship is at least, if not more, crucial. Indeed, as has been witnessed by the vacillations of both Conservative and Labour governments, EMU membership is essentially a political issue. Thus, the final arbiter of decision-making will be via a political process rather than an economic one.

Chapter 6

EMU Convergence

Introduction

Most academic social science literature either accepts that closer EU integration is desirable, or more usually, given the political will of EU leaders, that it is inevitable. Therefore economists, political scientists and sociologists frequently devote their research to the dynamics of EMU, the political institutions fostering 'ever closer union' and the social implications of these momentous changes. However, whilst such detailed analyses generate important policy proposals, they tend by their weight to obscure the crucial strategic issue: is EMU beneficial or not for the EU *as a whole*? The purpose of this chapter is to analyse this issue. More specifically, it seeks to evaluate the criteria that have been advanced by different authorities to assess whether or not membership of the single currency would prove beneficial.

Over the last 20 years, economists have studied the potential impact of monetary union between countries under the rubric of optimum currency area theory. It concludes that a single currency boosts participants' living standards when they possess similar economic structures and international trading patterns, but proves detrimental where these diverge. The danger of locking a country's currency within an international regime ill-suited to meeting domestic and external economic goals is illustrated by British mass unemployment under the Gold Standard of the 1920s and, to a lesser extent, the 1990–92 recession worsened by sterling's over-valuation within the ERM. Consequently, to avoid making a potentially costly mistake, especially since single currency membership is intended to be permanent and irrevocable with no exit clause negotiated in the TEU, there is an obvious need for a series of measurements to determine whether an individual economy is prepared for the demands of membership (EC Commission, 1992). These indicators must incontrovertibly demonstrate the existence of prior, sustainable 'real' convergence between participating economies, before the formation of a single currency between these countries is in their economic interests. However, despite the critical importance of such indicators in establishing whether or not membership of EMU is 'good' or 'bad' for a particular country, their construction has been paid relatively scant attention.

Indeed, the convergence criteria contained within the TEU are more concerned with examining transitory *cyclical* movements in *financial* indicators, rather than concentrating upon *structural* convergence in the real economy (EC Commission, 1992). Thus the only questions asked are those concerning the levels of price inflation, interest rates, exchange rate stability, public debt and annual budget deficits. The TEU focused upon 'nominal' convergence, measured by reference values (e.g. 60 per cent debt; 3 per cent deficit) that largely reflect historical levels of debt and deficit in the 'core' EU countries. Their relevance to future conditions is unclear. In contrast, the TEU contained no similar tests to compare the wealth of the different countries, their unemployment, productivity and growth rates, nor the sectoral composition of economic activity. Perhaps this is not entirely surprising as the EMU project was designed by a committee dominated by central bankers, whose particular concern was to devise rules restraining potentially profligate national governments from destabilising the monetary system. However, whilst these matters are important, it is problematic that EMU is designed to proceed from such a narrow, theoretically questionable foundation. Such concerns are magnified by the fact that EMU possesses no historical precedents. No monetary union has existed independently of political union and no independent country has ever unilaterally abandoned its own currency (Goodhart, 1995). EMU is therefore a 'leap in the dark' that has potentially destructive implications if its participants are not sufficiently converged prior to its establishment (Eichengreen, 1992 and 1993).

The October 1997 statement by the Chancellor of the Exchequer sought to clarify the UK Government's approach to EMU, with the detailed argument laid out in the accompanying Treasury document: *UK Membership of the Single Currency: An Assessment of the Five Economic Tests* (HM Treasury, 1997). However, both the speech and the report are ambiguous. The latter is designed to provide an objective assessment of the advantages and disadvantages of joining a single currency, but it frequently displays a bias in favour of participation unsupported by its own research. A recurrent assertion is that 'participation in EMU will be beneficial', although little evidence is produced, with the balance often implying the reverse.

Therefore the Treasury document is an uneasy blend of assumptions and analysis, prompting doubts concerning the five economic tests created as the guidelines for UK entry into a single currency. Furthermore, their choice is neither explained nor related to contemporary economic theory. Hence, this chapter seeks to examine the criteria and tests advanced to support EMU membership, together with analysing the potential impact upon the UK following the adoption of a single currency by other EU member states.

Attainment of the TEU Convergence Criteria

The identification of those individual EU member states that have demonstrated their suitability for single currency membership is officially determined by their attainment of the five Maastricht convergence criteria (MCC) established in the TEU. These are:

1. Each country's rate of inflation must be no more than 1.5 per cent above the average of the lowest three inflation rates in the EMS,
2. Its long-term interest rates must be within 2 per cent of the same three countries chosen for the previous condition,
3. It must have been a member of the narrow band of fluctuation of the ERM for at least two years without a realignment,
4. Its budget deficit must not be regarded as 'excessive' by the European Council,

'excessive' being defined as deficits greater than 3 per cent of GDP for reasons other than those of a 'temporary' or 'exceptional' nature,

5. Its national debt must not be 'excessive', defined as above 60 per cent of GDP and not declining at a 'satisfactory' pace.

Thus, the convergence criteria are denominated exclusively in terms of 'nominal' rather than 'real' convergence targets. Nominal values as represented here concentrate upon specific financial ratios rather than measurements of productivity and output growth, changes in the level of employment and other indicators from the real economy.

The initial two criteria have a clear rationale with respect to the establishment of a single currency area based upon the achievement of prior cyclical convergence. The similarity of inflation rates denotes a low probability of a sudden loss of competitiveness inside a single currency that might lead to unemployment blackspots and a growing inequality at the heart of the monetary union. Moreover, comparable interest rates indicate a relatively straightforward transition to a common monetary policy that does not require dramatic changes in the national strategies formally pursued by the nation states. However, whilst these two convergence criteria are theoretically sound, the latter three have generated both analytical and empirical controversy.

The third MCC, the 'normal' fluctuation bands, was interpreted until 1992 as the relatively narrow margins of +/- 2.25 per cent around the central parity that then operated for most ERM currencies. However, following the 1992–93 exchange rate crises, the bands were widened to +/- 15 per cent for an indefinite period in order to reduce the speculative pressure upon the ERM, whilst Italy and the UK were forced to withdraw from the system entirely. As a result, the third convergence criteria was relaxed in order to adapt to this new reality, so that member states only had to achieve the looser measure of currency stability required by the ERM (Aglietta and Uctum, 1996). However, the re-definition significantly reduced this indicator's utility, because the looser arrangement allowed for a currency to fluctuate by a potential of 30 per cent and still be considered stable. During any period other than an economic crisis or massive competitive misalignment, it would be unlikely that a currency would threaten to breach such a lax target, so that the criteria becomes increasingly difficult to defend. Indeed, at their June 1996 meeting EU Finance Ministers agreed to ignore the ERM membership precondition entirely. The decision was particularly fortuitous, since a significant number of countries still failed to meet such modest standards. The UK and Sweden have not rejoined the ERM, whilst Spain and Ireland realigned their central parity rates; thus they failed to meet the original principle of successively reducing exchange rate fluctuations, whilst preventing realignments prior to the establishment of a single currency in order to minimise adjustment costs.

The inclusion of the final two targets as means to establish the compatibility of potential participants within a monetary union raises further problems. The justifications for their use are, firstly, that they would result in a stable debt ratio in a steady-state economy with 2 per cent inflation and 3 per cent real growth (Trades Union Congress, 1993); and secondly, advocacy of the 'golden-rule' that current government expenditure and revenue should be equated, together with an estimate that EU public investment approximately averaged 3 per cent over the period 1974–91, indicates adoption of the convergence criteria (Buiter *et al.*, 1993). However, the first justification fails to provide a convincing case for the specific values chosen for maximum government borrowing as a proportion of GDP, since the fiscal reference values are compatible with any combination of inflation and growth which sum to 5 per cent per annum. Moreover, there is no evidence that attainment of these criteria would result in a steady-state economy (Arestis and Sawyer, 1996). Consequently the justification for the last two convergence criteria is far from secure and the case for their reliability must rest upon the second justification. However, it appears to be based upon the simplifying and unlikely assumption of zero inflation, otherwise inflation accounting must be included into the calculation. The 60 per cent national debt criterion is of doubtful use in any case, because it is primarily a consequence of the *prior* accretion of debt, reflecting past fiscal activities rather than current policy (Goodhart, 1992). Whilst it is important to avoid a country joining a monetary union so over-burdened by the results of poor previous macroeconomic management that it is susceptible to current repayment crises, the adoption of a 60 per cent maximum figure appears somewhat arbitrary and unnecessarily harsh.

Despite the problematic nature of the convergence criteria, the architects of EMU believed that their attainment would indicate the compatibility of potential participants, together with providing a guide to their subsequent maintenance in both favourable and unfavourable economic conditions (Baimbridge, 1997). The prerequisite of prior convergence is significant over each stage of the economic cycle, if EMU is to prove robust against symmetric and asymmetric shocks (Eichengreen, 1992; Bayoumi and Eichengreen, 1993). However, examining the extent to which EU member states have actually met the convergence criteria over the period 1992–2002 following the signing of the TEU encapsulates both a recession and recovery makes difficult reading for supporters of European monetary integration. Only in 1998, the crucial year prior to the irrevocable fixing of national exchange rates did compliance with the convergence criteria begin to approach that necessary for a sustainable monetary union. Even then, however, only six EU member states achieved strict adherence to all five convergence criteria.

Table 6.1 shows that attainment of all five criteria was fulfilled on only 29 out of a possible 165 occasions over the 1992–2002 period. A record of achievement of approximately 18 per cent is a particularly poor reflection of the prior convergence of the EU economies, as measured by the convergence criteria, particularly manifested in the period preceding EMU, when member states retained considerable control over their economies. Indeed, only Luxembourg, a country atypical of other EU members' economies in terms of its size, industrial base, and the fact that it does not possess its own central bank (allowing Belgium to operate its monetary policy) appears able to consistently meet the 5 criteria. Of the remaining fourteen EU member states, only seven have ever secured total compliance with the convergence indicators with key euro zone countries such as Austria, Belgium, Italy and Greece failing to achieve all five criteria. Moreover, the number attaining all five convergence criteria peaked in the period 1998–2001, but thereafter declined (at least temporarily, before policy instruments were used to force a greater degree of convergence) thereby illustrating the difficulties in maintaining political willpower after the commencement of EMU and adherence in light of an economic slowdown. Whilst the Stability and Growth Pact (SGP) was designed to reinforce the former, the latter is a consequence of the convergence criteria's inherent design faults and questionable *a priori* convergence between EMU candidates.

Table 6.1 provides an additional measure of the ability of each EU member state to participate in monetary union, through examining the average number of criteria met in a given year and by a given country. This examination indicates that only Luxembourg, Denmark, France, Germany, Belgium, the Netherlands and Ireland come close to satisfying the convergence indicators on a permanent basis; although even their record raises significant doubts about their long term ability to achieve the convergence criteria. Thus the available evidence provides little support for the ability of member states to both achieve, and maintain, the stipulated convergence criteria for more than momentary periods. To the extent that the convergence criteria satisfactorily indicate 'fitness' of entry for EMU, the failure of EU member states to consistently meet these criteria raises the prospect of the single currency becoming unsustainable in the medium- to long-term.

The inclusion of standard deviation (SD) figures for each EU country illustrates the degree of variability in their attainment of the five convergence criteria over the 1992–2002 period. As previously identified, Luxembourg was the best performing member state in this regard closely followed by France, Ireland, Belgium, Germany and the Netherlands. However, the more disturbing finding is the significant level of variability of countries such as Finland, Spain, Greece, Portugal and Italy where the SD figure exceeds either 1 or 2 convergence criteria. Although their movement towards fuller compliance in more recent years offsets this, such historical instability regarding the adherence of the convergence criteria highlights the potentially fragile nature of the euro project as presently conceived.

The conclusions reached from the examination of Table 6.1 diverge significantly with the examination of the progress towards convergence and sustainability of the monetary union completed by the EU Commission (1998). Indeed, the Commission concluded that eleven EU member states have 'achieved a high degree of sustainable convergence', with the UK, Sweden and Denmark utilising their opt-outs from membership and only Greece deemed incompatible with EMU. However, its conclusion conflicts with the economic data; for example, Belgium, Germany, Greece, Spain, Italy, the Netherlands, Austria and Sweden all possessed a government debt ratio exceeding 60 per cent in 1999. Even assuming that the economic climate is favourable to reducing previous debt burdens, it is most improbable that Italy and Belgium will be able to meet this criteria since both have government debt ratios in excess of twice the convergence criteria limit. Indeed, their government debt share of GDP is significantly higher than that of Greece, although Italy and Belgium were passed as 'fit' for monetary union membership whereas Greece was initially rejected.

Table 6.1   The number of convergence criteria achieved by EU member states

Country	1992	1993	1994	1995	1996	1997	1998	1999	2000	2001	2002	Ave	SD
Luxembourg	5	4	5	5	5	5	5	5	4	5	5	5	0.4
Denmark*	4	3	3	4	4	4	5	5	5	5	5	4	0.8
France	4	4	4	4	4	5	5	5	5	5	4	4	0.5
Germany	4	3	5	4	3	4	4	4	4	4	3	4	06
Ireland	4	3	3	4	4	4	5	4	4	4	4	4	0.5
Belgium	3	3	3	3	3	4	4	4	4	4	4	4	0.5
Netherlands	3	3	3	3	4	4	4	4	5	4	4	4	0.6
Austria	3	2	3	3	3	4	4	4	4	4	4	3	0.7
Britain*	2	2	3	3	2	4	4	4	4	4	4	3	0.9
Finland	1	1	2	2	3	4	5	5	4	5	5	3	1.6
Sweden*	2	1	1	1	2	3	3	3	4	4	4	3	1.2
Spain	1	1	1	1	1	4	4	3	3	5	4	3	1.6
Portugal	0	0	0	0	1	4	5	4	5	3	4	2	2.2
Italy	0	0	0	0	0	3	4	4	4	4	4	2	2.0
Greece	0	0	0	0	0	0	2	4	3	3	3	1	1.6
Number of member states meeting all convergence criteria	1	0	2	1	1	2	6	4	4	5	3	2	1.9

*Member states exercising their opt-out from the single currency.
Source: Baimbridge (2005).

The variance between the historical evidence that a large number of EU member states will not consistently meet the convergence criteria by the establishment of EMU, and that their participation in the monetary union has already been endorsed by the Commission, may indicate that the decision as to which countries qualify has been taken on political rather than economic grounds. The problem with undermining a rigorous interpretation of the convergence criteria is that, to the extent that they reflect necessary prerequisites for a sustainable EMU, failure to comply could create a potentially weakened single currency which will suffer from a higher degree of inherent tension than would otherwise have been the case. The experience of those countries that narrowly comply with the convergence criteria for only a minority of the period since the TEU was adopted, suggests that they are not permanently converged, but only achieve the necessary conditions in the most favourable economic circumstances. The implication is that, once a recession occurs, the majority of EMU participants will demonstrate a significant divergence from the established criteria, thereby increasing the potential for destabilisation at the heart of the single currency.

The UK Treasury Tests

In view of the rather limited and theoretically suspect set of indicators established by the TEU, the British Government adopted additional criteria (HM Treasury, 1997) which are claimed to be criteria for the decision whether EMU membership would be beneficial for Britain. However, their validity is open to critical assessment (Baimbridge *et al.*, 1999). The five supplementary tests are:

(i) *Whether there can be sustainable convergence between Britain and the economies of a single currency.* In a dynamic global economy, it appears increasingly unlikely that the economies of countries can converge. Even if they did, differential productivity, technology and demand changes, together with the discovery of new process and commodities, will inevitably re-establish 'divergence'. Another difficulty is that the Treasury document slips between, and never precisely defines, two different interpretations of convergence. First *cyclical*, the belief that a single currency is only beneficial when the trade cycles of its members are synchronised, and second *structural*, the belief that a single currency is only beneficial when the national participants possess homogenous economic structures and international trading patterns. Although the two are inter-related, a determined government could potentially achieve 'cyclical convergence' over consecutive five-year parliaments through appropriate fiscal and monetary policy changes. In contrast, the more fundamental 'structural convergence' would require a focused longer-term strategy, potentially over generations (Burkitt *et al.*, 1992). No government, nor the EU Commission, has ever devised, let alone implemented, such a complex programme and none appears to be immediately forthcoming. Moreover, if all EU economies achieved the easier target of synchronising the business cycle, the effect may be destabilising by its inducement of world inflations and recessions on a greater magnitude than previously experienced.

(ii) *Whether there is sufficient flexibility to cope with economic change.* A single currency cedes control over exchange rates and monetary policy. Therefore, without flexibility, future economic shocks are likely to impact negatively upon employment. Whilst the Treasury paper addresses significant dimensions of flexibility capable of national solutions, such as skills and long-term unemployment, it fails to confront directly the crucial issues for a single currency, *i.e.* labour mobility and price-wage flexibility *across* the EMU zone. It is precisely the absence of significant international labour mobility, restricted by language and cultural factors, together with the risk that wage differential transparency, enhanced by a single currency, will give rise to demands for wage equalisation between countries irrespective of productivity, thereby increasing wage rigidities.

(iii) *The effect on investment* and (v) *whether it is good for employment.* For both of these tests, the Treasury argues that the single currency possesses the potential to enhance investment, employment and growth, but these benefits would only accrue if sufficient convergence and flexibility exist. However, the argument ignores the crucial role of British overseas investment, approximately 80 per cent of whose destination is outside the EU (Jamieson, 1995), the potentially deflationary impact of the MCC and subsequent adherence to the Growth and Stability Pact (Pennant-Rea, 1997), together with the establishment of price stability as the sole legal objective of the ECB. Indeed, Bill Martin of United Bank Securities estimated that already 'EMU aspirants' suffered a deflation around 4.5 per cent of GDP during the 1990s by pursuing the MCC. Moreover, it appears that the Treasury fails to appreciate the enormity of any effective convergence and flexibility strategy. Tables 1.1 and 1.2 in the document show that the British and German economies have in fact steadily diverged; indeed since 1981 a negative correlation exists between their growth rates.

(iv) *The impact on our financial services industry.* A frequently cited danger for Britain remaining outside EMU is that posed to the City of London, which is one of three major world financial centres. International financial services in Britain employ around 150,000 people, generating £10–£15 billion in annual invisible exports (Taylor, 1995). It is often asserted that, if the UK exercises its opt-out, London could lose its pre-eminence to Frankfurt or Paris, because euro trading will be focused in the EMU area. However, international business within each time zone tends to gravitate towards a single location, this centralisation being propelled by a preference for deep, liquid markets, accommodating legal and tax frameworks, skilled labour and a cluster of supporting services including accountancy, law, software and telecommunications. The City possesses all these attributes, which any EU competitor would find hard to emulate. Hence, providing that complacency is avoided, the existence of such advantages should ensure the City's dominance even if Britain remains outside EMU.

When analysing EMU's consequences for the City of London, it is crucial to distinguish between its role as the premier European financial centre and its position in the world financial markets. The immediate effect of EMU will be a loss of intra-EU foreign exchange transactions, which can be compensated by an increased volume of euro dealing that will concentrate in London just as French franc-US dollar business does currently. Greater dollar and yen trading against the euro would also offset it. A greater threat arises from the official bond market that will inevitably emerge from EMU, which the relevant authority will seek to retain inside the single currency area. However, without effective exchange controls, it will prove impossible to prevent global trading, so that a bond market will inevitably develop in London. Thus, so long as the City retains its competitive advantage, its European pre-eminence will remain even with Britain outside the EMU. Indeed, this constitutes an attraction as London falls outside the potentially restrictive arrangements required to sustain the euro. Moreover, the City's international position in global markets, where business is growing fastest, would be jeopardised if EMU led to fiscal and political union, since it would become subject to greater regulation leading to its diminution to the benefit of New York and Tokyo. The conclusion therefore appears to be that a Britain outside EMU can provide a bridge between the USA and Europe so that the City of London's status, where the dollar and the euro financial systems have their interface, is preserved (Baimbridge *et al.*, 1997).

In summary, the five tests selected by the UK Government undoubtedly extend the rather limited usefulness of the convergence criteria and highlight a number of important issues for further analysis. However, they ultimately fail to meet the same requirements, namely the absence of a justification for reliance upon this specific set of indicators and the rejection of others (Baimbridge *et al.*, 1998). Moreover, the 'vague' nature of judging compliance with the 'five tests' impairs the clear and unambiguous establishment that a country is either well suited for EMU membership, or alternatively that its inclusion would weaken the union and hamper the effectiveness of its stabilisation policy mechanism. Consequently, a more extensive set of criteria is required in order to establish whether EU member states are ready to join EMU.

EMU and Optimum Currency Area Theory

The debate surrounding the prospects for a single EU currency has begun to focus upon the prior necessity for structural economic convergence, which is wider than simply meeting the MCC or the Treasury tests. These criteria may be largely necessary for a successful and sustainable EMU, but they are not sufficient to fulfil this objective. Therefore a need exists to develop a more comprehensive set of criteria to complement the convergence criteria. To do so, it is necessary to examine that section of economic theory that discusses the optimality of monetary unions and exchange rate arrangements, namely the theory of optimum currency areas (De Grauwe, 1994; Corden, 2003). This extensive literature points to a number of distinct, yet inter-related characteristics that are likely to determine the probable consequences of monetary union. Nine elements are discussed here that are integral to the establishment of an additional set of convergence criteria:

(i) *Degree of factor mobility*. Countries between which there is a high degree of factor mobility are viewed as better candidates for monetary integration, since it provides a substitute for exchange rate flexibility in promoting external adjustment (Mundell, 1961; Ingram, 1962). However, in practice it is unlikely that the EU, with its different cultures, languages and traditions across member states, displays sufficient inter-regional labour mobility to act as a mechanism for payments adjustment. Available evidence suggests that labour mobility within European nation states is one-third the level found in a mature EMU such as the USA, despite the existence of greater regional inequality and unemployment in Europe. This implies that European labour mobility is less responsive to employment and income incentives (OECD, 1986; Eichengreen, 1997). Moreover, these figures relate to labour mobility within individual countries, whereas mobility between countries is likely to be much lower due to language barriers, cultural differences and residual non-recognition of qualifications (Ermisch, 1991; Masson and Taylor, 1993). Furthermore, capital mobility is unlikely to generate sufficient short-term stabilisation due to the time lags involved in the movement of physical capital whilst, due to the transactions costs involved, factor movements are an inefficient means of reacting to transitory regional shocks (von Hagen, 1993; Romer, 1994).

(ii) *Degree of commodities' market integration*. This criterion is concerned with structural convergence and specifically with the requirement that countries should possess similar production structures. Economies exhibiting such symmetry are deemed to be more welfare-efficient candidates for currency area participation than those whose production structures are markedly different (Mundell, 1961). The reason for this belief is that external shocks will tend to impact upon given industries in certain ways, and therefore a group of economies with similar industrial structures should experience similar effects, making it easier for a common monetary and exchange rate policy to mitigate any negative results of the shock. However, in comparison to most EU members, Britain possesses a different industrial structure. For example, it possesses a relatively small agricultural sector, this difference being most noticeable in comparison with Ireland, Denmark and the Mediterranean countries. It would be magnified if Poland, Hungary and the Czech Republic gained full EU membership. In contrast, the UK has a much larger energy industry than other EU countries except the Netherlands, and possesses specific service sector concentration in the financial and media sectors. Thus the UK balance of payments structure depends more heavily on investment earnings than any other EU member economy, to the extent that British direct and portfolio overseas investment earnings totalled £38.5 billion compared to £28.2 billion occurring from exports of finished manufactures.

Britain enjoys a greater reliance upon high technology exports, particularly in the fields of aerospace and pharmaceuticals, where its main competitors are US or Japanese firms, a few of which may be located in continental Europe. Indeed, prices in many of these sectors, such as the oil and high technology markets, are typically denoted in US dollars. EMU might lead to greater exchange rate variability in these areas of UK competitive advantage, since trade in these markets would less affect the euro than sterling is at present. Finally, the UK economy is significantly different from most continental European economies in terms of its reliance upon variable-rate interest borrowing to finance private housing owner-occupation and industrial investment. This makes the UK economy more reactive to changes in short term interest rates than other EU economies, so that the ECB would be likely to vary a common interest rate more than is necessary to stabilise the UK economy, because other EU member states are less responsive to such movements (Weber, 1991; Taylor, 1995; Bank for International Settlements, 1996; Burkitt *et al.*, 1996; Eltis, 1996). It has recently been estimated that the impact of an interest rate change on UK domestic demand after two years is four times the EU average (Pennant-Rea, 1997).

(iii) *Openness and size of the economy.* It is an observed fact that economies where international trade accounts for a high proportion of national income tend to prefer fixed exchange rates, because exchange rate changes in such economies are unlikely to be accompanied by significant effects on real competitiveness. In this sense, the greater the potential for damage to the economy from a fluctuating currency, the more business leaders and employees desire exchange rate stability. If a fluctuating exchange rate affects only an insignificant proportion of the economy, the pressure for such arrangements is lower. Moreover, in open economies frequent exchange rate adjustments diminish the liquidity property of money, since the overall price index varies more than in relatively closed economies (McKinnon, 1963). However, whilst relatively open economies might prefer exchange rate stability, they also require the ability to correct any fundamental misalignment of their currency. Such over- or under-valuation could occur gradually, over time, as the competitiveness and productivity of the economy changes relative to others with whom the country has a fixed exchange rate, or more rapidly as a result of an internal (e.g. wage-price explosion) or external (e.g. oil price rise) shock. Irrespective of the cause, failure to adjust exchange rates to their long term equilibrium value, itself changing over time, prove damaging to the economy in question, unless alternative adjustment mechanisms are sufficient to achieve the same outcome. Most small- or medium-sized industrialised nations fulfil this condition.

(iv) *Degree of commodity diversification.* Highly diversified economies are better candidates for currency areas than less diversified economies, since their diversification provides some insulation against a variety of shocks thereby forestalling the need for frequent changes in the exchange rate (Kenen, 1969). Countries reliant upon a small number of prominent industries react significantly differently to other monetary union participants in the face of changes within those particular markets. This would increase the difficulty of operating a common monetary policy that could stabilise all participants. In general terms, virtually all industrialised member states fulfil this particular criterion, at least prior to the establishment of a single currency. However, the combination of a single market and EMU is likely to generate a degree of specialisation that potentially undermines such insulation. Multinational corporations, in particular, are anticipated to respond to the opening of markets and greater transparency of prices by expanding throughout Europe. Indeed, the creation of large European corporations, intensifying specialisation in fewer, larger concerns better equipped to compete globally, was one principal impetus behind the push towards greater European integration (EC Commission, 1990).

(v) *Fiscal integration and inter-region transfers*. The higher the level of fiscal harmonisation, the greater is the ability to smooth divergent shocks through transfers from low to high unemployment regions. This feature is important for the emerging EMU because, in the absence of national exchange rate variation, wage-price flexibility and/or labour mobility are unlikely to prove sufficiently powerful to adjust economies in the face of asymmetric external shocks. Consequently, budgetary policy can be an important tool to cushion individual countries from shocks (see Chapter 9). Such fiscal flexibility may involve the discretionary strategies associated with 'fine tuning', but can also arise from the operation of automatic stabilisers (Kenen, 1969). It can also occur at the national as well as the federal level. Therefore, despite the constraints placed upon national fiscal policy by the operation of the convergence criteria and the *Stability and Growth Pact*, it is probable that federal policy will expand over time. The current size of the EU budget, at only 1.24 per cent of total EU GDP, appears to preclude the development of any significant inter-regional fiscal transfer system for the foreseeable future (MacDougall, 1992 and 2003). Moreover, its cost may defer meaningful consideration of this potential mechanism to stabilise EMU (Burkitt *et al.*, 1997; Whyman, 1997). However, in the absence of alternative stabilising mechanisms, fiscal integration may be the only practical means of sustaining EMU in the medium and long term, given the likely persistence of asymmetric external shocks.

(vi) *Degree of policy integration*. The fact that monetary union requires the establishment of a common monetary and exchange rate policy, applied across the entire union, means that external shocks which impact upon individual economies in a significantly different manner than for the majority, require different policy instruments in order to restore stability (Ingram, 1969; Haberler, 1970; Tower and Willett, 1970). Fiscal policy variations between member countries can potentially offset nationally-based disequilibria, but the constraints imposed by the convergence criteria effectively limit what can be achieved on a national basis. In any case, the argument for greater macroeconomic policy co-ordination is independent of whether monetary union exists, namely that a more efficient outcome results if all countries affected by a given shock respond in an optimum manner. For example, if the UK suffers a negative shock that reduces its competitiveness and increases unemployment, whilst Germany experiences the opposite effect, an increase in competitiveness and an over-tight labour market, mutual benefit flows from a co-ordinated policy response by both countries. In this case, Germany would raise taxation or reduce government spending in order to prevent inflationary pressure, whilst the UK would reflate its economy. If fiscal federalism existed, part of the resources needed for such reflation could be transferred from Germany to the UK, thereby enhancing the stabilisation of the union between them. However, although the need for an 'economic' as well as monetary union is recognised by the TEU, its only practical applications thus far have been the continuation of EMS membership until monetary union and the SGP.

(vii) *Similarity of inflation rates.* This criterion focuses upon the significance of divergent trends in national inflation rates as a source of balance of payments problems. Diverse price changes impacting upon national competitiveness arise from a variety of potential causes including: differences in national propensities for trade union wage militancy, acute shortages of highly trained employees or differences in investment rates and therefore industrial capacity growth (Haberler, 1970; Fleming, 1971; Magnifico, 1973). The architects of EMU were aware of the danger and included this target as one of the five convergence criteria. Moreover, ERM membership resulted in most EU member states adapting their economic strategies in order to achieve similar inflation rates, particularly during the 1980s when the mechanism was reinterpreted as a means of achieving monetary union through the absence of further realignments. This strategy was partially successful, average EU inflation rates declining from 10.7 per cent during the 1970s to 6.5 per cent in the following decade and further during the 1990s, with the variance between most EU member states declining dramatically during this period. Although these trends were largely in line with international ones outside the ERM, EU member states enjoyed success in reducing both their absolute inflation rates and differentials between them. However, the adjustment of economic policies undertaken by ERM members, in order to reduce inflation differentials, carried the cost of high, persistent unemployment for many countries. Not only was this a high price to pay in terms of economic and social costs to the states and individuals concerned, but also it means that non-ERM countries, such as the UK, are less likely to meet this criterion unless they reduce growth rates and operate tighter fiscal and monetary policies.

(viii) *Price and wage flexibility.* When prices and wages are flexible between regions, adjustment to destabilising shocks is less likely to be associated with unemployment in one region and inflation in another. The need for exchange rate changes is diminished, because wage-price flexibility takes the place of exchange rate variations in maintaining a competitive balance between countries (Friedman, 1953). For example, if the UK suffered an inflationary shock that meant that the prices of its exports suddenly increased by 10 per cent in the absence of an accommodating fall in the exchange rate, only a 10 per cent reduction in UK prices would restore the former competitive equilibrium. This, in turn, would require a fall in wages. However, available evidence indicates that substantial wage-price rigidity persists across Europe, so that market flexibility is unlikely to restore former competitiveness either easily or quickly. As a result, wage-price flexibility cannot prevent the generation of areas blighted by high and persistent unemployment, a fact confirmed by the large literature concerning nominal and real wage rigidity in Europe (Bruno and Sachs, 1985; Eichengreen, 1990, 1993 and 1997; Bini-Smaghi and Vori, 1992; Blanchard and Katz, 1992). If wage-price rigidity prevents an immediate and full restoration of former competitiveness, output will fall and unemployment will rise, until wage reductions, or at least slower wage growth, enhance competitiveness. However, the country in question may suffer from the dual problems of persistent high unemployment and a decline in incomes for its citizens relative to the monetary union as a whole.

(ix) *The need for real exchange rate variability.* The real exchange rate (i.e., adjustment of the nominal exchange rate by the rate of price increases) measures the shifts in a nation's competitiveness. For example, if the nominal exchange rate of sterling against the US dollar declines by 5 per cent, but UK inflation is 5 per cent higher than the American equivalent rate, the real exchange rate remains unchanged as no movement has occurred in relative competitiveness between the two countries. Thus, when a country participates in a monetary union and its nominal exchange rate is fixed at a given value to those of other members, the real exchange rate denotes whether that country (now a region of the monetary union) remains competitive over time. A negative shift in competitiveness will typically cause a deterioration in the balance of payments. However, in the absence of any changes permitted in the nominal exchange rate, a lack of competitiveness could result in areas of high, persistent unemployment. The only available method of reducing the real exchange rate, and thereby restoring competitiveness, is to reduce relative prices. This could be achieved over time if investment in capital and education produced a new competitive edge. However, a more immediate method would be to reduce relative wages, leading to lower income growth than in the remainder of the monetary union. The smallness of countries' real exchange rate movements is a crucial characteristic for determining currency area optimality, because real exchange rate changes are clearly measurable and automatically give the appropriate weights to the economic forces of which they are the result (Vaubel, 1976 and 1978). Given that real exchange rate variability depends upon the absence of real wage rigidity, the comments made for (viii) equally apply in this instance.

The nine optimum currency area criteria, outlined in this chapter, indicate the relative probability of the efficient operation of a single currency. They appear more extensive than either the convergence criteria or the UK Treasury 'tests', both of which constitute an incomplete guide on which to base the decision as to whether the UK should participate in EMU. However, the available evidence gleaned from applying optimum area criteria to the question of potential participation in the EU single currency identifies significant fundamental differences between the UK economy and the majority of nations that are joining the single currency. For example, whilst inflation rates appear to be sufficiently similar at present, there must be some probability that, unless the UK submitted to ERM discipline over the medium term and accepted the significant increase in unemployment that this would imply, differential patterns of inflation will remain over the economic cycle. Neither wage and price flexibility, nor labour mobility is sufficiently extensive to restore competitive equilibrium, when the relative movement of prices negatively affects UK competitiveness and hence real exchange rates. The marked differences in industrial structure leads the UK to respond to external shocks in a markedly different manner from other EU economies, thereby undermining the ability of a common monetary and exchange rate policy to meet the needs of all participating member states. Moreover, the constraints placed upon national economies by the convergence criteria and SGP, in the absence of future policy co-ordination or some form of fiscal federalism, will prevent fiscal policies from moderating either an initial shock or the subsequent destabilisation caused by inappropriate monetary policies operated by the ECB for the monetary union as a whole.

Conclusion

Two key passages from the Chancellor's October 1997 statement were, '*the potential benefits of a single currency are obvious; in terms of trade, transparency of costs and currency stability. Of course, I stress it must be soundly based. But if it works economically, it is, in our view, worth doing*'. And, '*if a single currency would be good for British jobs, business and future prosperity, it is right, in principle to join*'. This approach is dependent upon the existence of a theoretically sound, comprehensive set of criteria that unambiguously indicate that the UK is sufficiently similar to other participating nations so that we would not suffer from the application of common exchange and monetary policies unsuitable to the needs of the British economy. Unfortunately, as this chapter has demonstrated, neither the MCC nor the Government's 'five tests' perform this role. Moreover, using the better guide of optimum currency area theory, it becomes clear that the UK is not an obvious candidate for monetary union without changes that are not justified for any other reason other than a misguided desire to 'be at the heart of Europe' whatever the costs.

The analysis further indicates that the 'favourable circumstances' implied in the Chancellor's statement is unlikely to prevail, because Britain's very different economic structure and international trading pattern simply do not fulfil the conditions for a single EU currency to operate efficiently. Therefore, if the UK loses control over its monetary policy, it will possess a greatly reduced ability to adapt to an inevitably changing environment. Moreover, concerns about EMU relate not only to the adventure itself; for instance, the EU possesses neither the labour mobility nor the US-style federal budget needed to compensate for the loss of the exchange rate as a means of economic adjustment. They also focus upon the deflationary policies to which the TEU committed the EU. Hence, the danger exists that the five Treasury 'tests' may divert attention away from fundamental difficulties that surround the establishment of a single EU currency.

The evidence therefore suggests that, even if other EU members sign up for a single currency, Britain should not. Prioritising sustainable growth and full employment necessitates the rejection of EMU. Moreover, non-participation gleans many benefits and imposes no substantial costs. The advantages of low inflation and high employment can be obtained by pursuing coherent domestic economic policies, whilst arguments that the City of London and the UK's attractiveness for inward investment would be endangered outside the single currency evaporate under scrutiny. Indeed European co-operation may be undermined more effectively by increasing national divergences within an EMU governed through inflexible rules than by the UK and other countries, opting-out. Hence, through an independent yet global strategy, freed from over-concentration on the European continent to the detriment of economic relations with the rest of the world, the UK could achieve an economic performance the envy of EMU participants. Consequently, the single currency 'Emperor' is without clothes!

The decision whether to join EMU must depend upon an analysis of its probable benefits and costs. Economic theory suggests that a monetary union will prove generally beneficial, and be sustainable over time, if the participants are sufficiently converged before they enter. Thus, it is necessary to establish an unambiguous, comprehensive and theoretically sound set of convergence criteria, which can indicate whether such convergence has occurred prior to participation. However, it is questionable whether the MCC satisfactorily perform this role. The convergence criteria present a series of financial tests, of which some are theoretically spurious, whilst the remainder are inadequate to indicate the range of consequences of participation. Consequently, the view advocated in this chapter is that future potential euro members should adopt the more comprehensive guide offered by optimum currency area theory and examine the extent to which they fulfil the elements outlined. A brief examination of available evidence suggests that the Central and East European countries are not obvious candidates for monetary union without undertaking major structural changes, which are likely to take decades to complete (see Chapter 8 for a discussion of this issue).

The decision on whether countries should participate within EMU carries further consequences. The advantages of low inflation and high employment could be obtained by pursuing coherent domestic economic policies (see Chapter 9), whilst European co-operation may be undermined more effectively by increasing national divergences within an EMU governed through inflexible rules than by countries opting-out. Such a situation could lead to the opposite outcome to that envisaged by the proponents of EMU. However, if participation within EMU is considered to be in the national interest, economic theory demonstrates that membership should wait until prior convergence has been achieved; optimum currency area theory provides the tests to establish the validity of convergence. Unless these tests can be attained, monetary union could prove damaging to existing and future EMU countries as a combination of external shocks to the system and a destabilising common monetary policy exacerbate existing differences between economies.

Chapter 7

The ECB and Central Bank Independence

Introduction

The European Central Bank (ECB) is a creation of the TEU, which designed it to be the most independent monetary authority in the world. The ECB's architects sought to insulate it completely from political pressures, both at the national government and at the EMU-zone level. The position of the ECB under the TEU permits no clear accountability to neither national nor federal European institutions. It stipulates that the ECB Council's deliberations remain confidential, whilst the only method of questioning the ECB's policies is through periodic reports to the European Parliament.

The introduction of EMU is one of the most momentous economic events of our generation. Policy makers and economic commentators have concentrated upon criteria denoting initial convergence to trigger membership of the single currency, stringent rules restricting national fiscal policies, and the anticipated benefits which may derive from EMU. However, far less attention has been played to how EMU will operate in practice. In particular, the institutional design of EMU stipulates a central role for an ECB, established independent of government, which is charged with sustaining the stability of the currency zone in the face of asymmetric external shocks. The ECB is the sole body credited with determining the appropriate monetary and exchange rate policy for the entire euro zone and as such its ability to fulfil its stated objectives will be crucial to the eventual success or failure of EMU. Consequently, the paucity of critical analysis of the ability of the ECB to stabilise the euro zone economy, complete with low inflation, full employment, a sustainable balance of payments and good level of economic growth, should be of great concern for all supporters of European integration.

This chapter seeks to compensate for the dearth of current analysis by examining the capability of the ECB to fulfil its designated role. Firstly, it evaluates the design of the ECB selected by the architects of the TEU and reviews the degree of independence attributed to the ECB in comparison to member states national central banks (NCBs). It then summarises the leading conceptual issues and empirical literature in order to examine the merits of establishing the ECB independent from democratic influence. Subsequently, we review the hypothesised relationship between independence and macroeconomic indicators. This is followed by some concluding remarks.

The Design of the ECB

The structure and role of the ECB is detailed in the Articles of the TEU. It is headed by Governing Council comprising the governors of the NCBs, together with members of the Executive Board of the ECB. The latter consists of professional bankers or monetary experts nominated by the member states for a single eight year term of office (Article 109a). All members of the Executive Board and ECB in general, are expected to act independently of 'Community institutions or bodies, from any Government of a Member State or from any other body' (European Communities, 1991). However, the legal framework, institutional arrangements and emerging operating practices of the ECB are increasingly coming under closer scrutinisation and criticism (Buiter, 1999; Howarth and Loedel, 2003). Elsewhere, however, the TEU provides for the Council and Commission to possess non-voting representation at meetings of the ECB's Executive Council, whilst the ECB must present an annual report to the EU's institutions and appear before the relevant committees of the European Parliament when requested (Article 109b).

The crucial operational features of the ECB are that its sole policy objective is the pursuit of price stability. It will also be responsible for defining and implementing the EU's monetary policy, together with supporting the attainment of general economic objectives. This design format is founded upon both theoretical (Kydland and Prescott, 1997; Barro and Gordon, 1983; Alesina, 1989; Alesina and Grilli, 1991) and empirical (Bade and Parkin, 1988; Alesina, 1988 and 1989; Cukierman, 1992; Alesina and Summers, 1993) studies whereby the transfer of monetary policy from governments to an independent central bank is likely to result in lower inflation.

Additionally, the powers and tasks of the ECB are highly significant, with the Bank exclusively responsible for authorising the issuance of bank notes (Article 105a). It is also able to make legally binding and directly applicable regulations on the minimum level of reserves to be held by NCBs, the efficiency of clearing and payment systems and on the supervision of credit institutions. Moreover, where an undertaking fails to comply with an ECB regulation or decision, the Bank will be able to impose a fine (Article 108a). Finally, the ECB is to be consulted by other EU institutions and national authorities and may issue opinions to them on matters within its competences (Article 105).

Table 7.1[1] illustrates the individual features of each of the NCBs together with the ECB, with respect to political independence. It is suggested that the capacity of the monetary authorities to choose the final objectives of policy is primarily determined by three aspects of a monetary regime. Firstly, the procedure for appointing the members of the central bank governing bodies, secondly, the relationship between these bodies and the government and finally, the formal responsibilities of the central bank. In principle, independence to determine ultimate goals may be defined without reference to their contents, but in practice the main virtue claimed for an independent central bank is that they can provide credibility. Hence, independence is frequently identified with autonomy from political interference to pursue the objective of low inflation, so that any institutional feature that enhances its capacity to pursue this goal is hypothesised to increase central bank independence.

---

1   Note: Figures in parentheses indicate the number of board members appointed by each institution. Sources: Adapted from Alesina and Grilli (1991) and EC Commission (1991).

Table 7.1   Summary of political independence of EU central banks and ECB

		Belgium	Denmark	France
Features of political independence – central bank, government and accountability	**Provisions in case of disagreement with government**	Yes – government directives	No	No
	Monetary stability objective	No	Yes	No
	Relation with parliament	Through government	Annual report	Through government
	Relation with government	Approval	Consultation	Approval
Features of political independence – central bank board	**Government representatives**	Government Commissioner (advisory / suspensive rights)	Minister of Trade (supervisory right)	Director Minister of Finance (advisory / suspensive right)
	Reappointment	Yes	Yes	Yes
	Term (years)	Six	Five	Six
	No. of members	3–6	25	10
	Board appointed by	Sovereign (i.e. government)	Parliament (8) Trade Minister (2) Bank Board (15)	Minister of Finance (9) Bank (1)
Features of political independence – central bank governor	**Reappointability**	Yes	No	No
	Term (years)	Five	Indefinite	Indefinite
	Governor appointed by	Sovereign (i.e. government)	Sovereign (i.e. government)	President

		Germany	Greece	Ireland	Italy
Features of political independence – central bank, government and accountability	**Provisions in case of disagreement with government**	Yes – temporary post-position	Yes – arbitration commission	No	Yes – government directives
	Monetary stability objective	Yes	No	Yes	No
	Relation with parliament	Not accountable	N/A	Annual report	On call
	Relation with government	Consultation	Consultation	Consultation	Approval
Features of political independence – central bank board	**Government representatives**	None	Government Commissioner (suspensive right)	Permanent Secretary Minister of Finance	None
	Reappointment	No	Yes	No	Yes
	Term (years)	Eight	Three	Five	Three
	No. of members	8	9	3–8	13
	Board appointed by	President – proposal of government	Shareholders general meeting	Government	Shareholders regional meetings
Features of political independence – central bank governor	**Reappointability**	No	Yes	Yes	No
	Term (years)	Eight	Four	Seven	Indefinite
	Governor appointed by	President – proposal of the government	Government – proposal of the Bank President	President – proposal of the government	Bank Board – proposal of the government

		Netherlands	Portugal	Spain
Features of political independence – central bank, government and accountability	**Provisions in case of disagreement with government**	Yes – government directives	Yes – government directives	No
	Monetary stability objective	Yes	No	Yes
	Relation with parliament	Through government	Through government	Through government
	Relation with government	Consultation	Approval	Approval
Features of political independence – central bank board	**Government representatives**	None	None	None
	Reappointment	Yes	No	No
	Term (years)	Seven	Five	Two
	No. of members	3–5	7–9	10–14
	Board appointed by	Sovereign (i.e. government)	Government	Government (6) Minister of Finance (2) Governor (1–4) Bank (1)
Features of political independence – central bank governor	**Reappointability**	Yes	Yes	Yes
	Term (years)	Seven	Five	Four
	Governor appointed by	Sovereign (i.e. government)	Government	Sovereign – proposal of government

		UK	European Central Bank
Features of political independence – central bank, government and accountability	**Provisions in case of disagreement with government**	No	Explicit conflicts between ECB and governments are possible (Articles 2 and 7)
	Monetary stability objective	No	Primary objective shall be to maintain price stability (Article 2)
	Relation with parliament	Through government	The ECB shall address an annual report on the activities of the ESCB and on monetary policy of both the previous and the current year to the European Parliament, Council and Commission (Article 15)
	Relation with government	Approval	The ECB, nor the NCBs nor the other members of the Council may seek or take instruction from Community institutions, governments of Member States or any other body (Article 7)
Features of political independence – central bank board	**Government representatives**	None	Council of European Communities and/or European Commission representative may attend meetings but cannot vote (Article 15.1)
	Reappointment	No	No (Article 11.2)
	Term (years)	Four	Five-Eight (Articles 11.2 and 14)
	No. of members	16	21
	Board appointed by	Sovereign (i.e. government)	European Council (6) (Article 11.2) National governments (15) (Article 11.2)
Features of political independence – central bank governor	**Reappointability**	Yes	No (Article 11.2)
	Term (years)	Five	Eight (Article 11.2)
	Governor appointed by	Sovereign – proposal of government	European Council (Article 11.2)

Table 7.1 indicates that the architects of the TEU were faced with a wide range of alternative variations of central bank political and economic autonomy from government out of which they created the institutional structure of the ECB. Contemporary examples of operationally independent central banks include the German Bundesbank, the Federal Reserve of the United States of America, the Bank of England and the Reserve Bank of New Zealand. Each has a different degree of autonomy concerning different operational issues. The German Bundesbank is probably the most important of these alternatives as it is perceived to have a track record of delivering consistently low inflation (Marsh, 1992). Faced with a number of alternative models (e.g. US Federal Reserve, Reserve Bank of New Zealand), the designers of the TEU preferred to follow the Bundesbank blueprint when establishing the design of the ECB given that Germany achieved low inflation over the period since 1961 and that those countries which pegged their currencies to the deutschmark, 'imported' a similar inflation performance. Hence, the ECB is anticipated to be as successful in safeguarding low inflation and price stability across the euro zone.

Table 7.2   Political independence of central banks[2]

	Appointments (Governor and Board)			Relationship with government			Constitution		Index of political independence
	1	2	3	4	5	6	7	8	9
Belgium				*					1
Denmark		*				*	*		3
France		*		*					2
Germany		*		*	*	*	*	*	6
Greece			*					*	2
Ireland		*				*	*		3
Italy	*	*	*		*				4
Netherlands		*		*	*	*	*	*	6
Portugal					*				1
Spain				*	*		*		3
UK					*				1
Column total	1	6	2	5	6	4	5	3	
ECB		*		*	*	*	*	*	6

Sources: Adapted from Grilli *et al.* (1991) and EC Commission (1991).

2   Where: [1] governor not appointed by government; [2] governor appointed for >5 years; [3] all the board not appointed by government; [4] board appointed for >5 years; [5] no mandatory participation of government representative on the board; [6] no government approval of monetary policy formulation is required; [7] statutory requirements that central bank pursues monetary stability amongst its goals; [8] legal provisions that strengthen the central bank's position in conflicts with the government are present.

Table 7.3   Economic independence of central banks[3]

	Monetary financing of budget deficit				Monetary instruments				Index of economic independence
	1	2	3	4	5	6	7	8	9
Belgium		*		*	*	*		*	5
Denmark		*			*	*		*	4
France			*		*	*		*	4
Germany	*	*	*	*	*	*	*		7
Greece				*		*			2
Ireland		*	*	*		*			4
Italy				*					1
Netherlands			*	*	*	*			4
Portugal				*		*			2
Spain			*	*			*		3
UK	*	*	*	*		*			5
Column total	2	5	5	10	5	9	2	3	
ECB	*	*	*	*	*	*	*		7

Sources: Adapted from Grilli *et al.* (1991) and EC Commission (1991).

The apolitical status of the ECB can be examined in greater detail in relation to the concepts of economic and political independence. The latter refers to its decisions not being conditional on the approval of government, whilst the former pertains to its ability to operate monetary policy without government undertaking contrary actions. Tables 7.2 and 7.3 indicate the relative nature of political independence concerning the original signatories of the TEU when compared to the ECB with an asterisk indicating possession of a specific feature. Table 7.4 illustrates the comparative position in terms of the political, economic and combined indices of NCBs, following the adoption of the ECB criteria. The comparative figures are calculated by subtracting the value of the ECB indices from those of the EU member states' central banks. This procedure clearly identifies the German Bundesbank as providing the blueprint for the ECB with no required revisions to its independence characteristics. The central bank of the Netherlands is the only other to fall below the overall mean comparison figure of six, whilst Denmark and Ireland coincide with the average. In contrast, those NCBs requiring the largest institutional reforms to meet the TEU requirements were, in ascending magnitude: Belgium, France,

---

3   Where: [1] direct credit facility – not automatic; [2] direct credit facility – market interest rate; [3] direct credit facility – temporary; [4] direct credit facility – limited amount; [5] central bank does not participate in the primary market for public debt; [6] discount rate set by central bank; [7] banking supervision not entrusted to the central bank at all; [8] banking supervision not entrusted to the central bank alone.

Spain, Britain, Italy, Greece and Portugal. It is interesting to note that this division of EU member states mirrors the established concept of 'core' and periphery groups regarding the formation of the single currency area.

Table 7.4 Comparison of central bank independence of EU member states and the ECB

	Present index of political independence	Comparison to political independence of ECB	Present index of economic independence	Comparison to economic independence of ECB	Comparison to combined independence of ECB
Belgium	1	-5	5	-2	-7
Denmark	3	-3	4	-3	-6
France	2	-4	4	-3	-7
Germany	6	0	7	0	0
Greece	2	-4	2	-5	-9
Ireland	3	-3	4	-3	-6
Italy	4	-2	1	-6	-8
Netherlands	6	0	4	-3	-3
Portugal	1	-5	2	-5	-10
Spain	3	-3	3	-4	-7
UK	1	-5	5	-2	-7
Mean	3	-3	4	-3	-6

Source: Derived from Tables 7.2 and 7.3.

Evaluation of Independence

The belief that central banks should be independent from political influence has deep historical roots and featured in the discussions leading to the establishment of many 20th century central banks (Toniolo, 1988). The historical desire to impose limits upon the government's ability to fund itself through seignorage is combined with the orthodox contemporary argument that politicians manipulate monetary policy to win elections, resulting in an excessive concentration upon short-term macroeconomic fine tuning (Swinburne and Castello-Branco, 1991). Consequently it is argued that long-term economic efficiency requires the removal of monetary policy from the sphere of democratically accountable politics, and its delegation to an independent central bank with an effectively designed constitution and internal reward system that impose price stability as the overriding policy objective.

Few institutional reforms recommended by economists have gained such rapid, widespread acceptance as the demand to grant central banks independence from political control. Countries of the North and the South, the post-communist nations of Central and Eastern Europe as well as established capitalist states have all been affected by the debate on the appropriate role and status of the central bank (Posen,

1993). Thus the notion of central bank independence has taken on the character of a panacea, a quick institutional fix, producing desirable macroeconomic results in a wide variety of national contexts.

The conceptual case for central bank independence is primarily based on the view that arrangements raising the credibility of monetary policy will increase its effectiveness in pursuit of price stability. Although this view has long been held, only in recent years has the concept of policy credibility been defined and analysed rigorously (Cukierman, 1986; Blackburn and Christensen, 1989).

The establishment of an independent central bank with strong anti-inflationary preferences is seen as a way for the state to bind its hands against the electoral temptation of inducing unanticipated increases in the price level. As commitment increases credibility, orthodox theory predicts that divergences between the central bank's policies and people's expectations will become smaller. Therefore lower costs and fewer delays are incurred when adjusting to monetary policy shifts. It is from this theoretical perspective of monetarism and rational expectations that the ECB was launched. However, this approach has been challenged. Firstly, if central bank independence increases credibility, it should be associated with greater rigidity in the setting of nominal prices and money wages, reflecting the fact that the bank's promise to keep inflation low is believed. However, studies of OECD countries by Posen (1993 and 1998) indicated that neither effect occurs. Indeed independence not only fails to reduce the cost of disinflation, but rather seems to increase it. Lowering inflation takes as long, and calls for a larger short-term sacrifice of output and jobs on average, in countries with relatively independent central banks as compared to those democratically accountable monetary institutions.

Secondly, most of the contemporary support for central bank independence stems from a partial and frequently historically naive view of West German experience, whereby it is overlooked that any one item that helped to promote rapid post-war German growth, such as the independent Bundesbank, was part of a structural totality defining its role. Accordingly it is unlikely to be effective if transferred by itself to other countries or onto the broader EU stage (Dowd, 1989 and 1994). It may be more appropriate to reverse the fashionable view; the structural conditions that produced the strength of the German economy, allowing it to grow while maintaining a low inflation rate also enabled it to afford the luxury of an independent central bank concentrating on monetary stability. For example, the wage negotiations system in Germany has generally produced a less inflationary outcome than in many other countries over the post-war period, thus not requiring intervention from the Bundesbank. Therefore it must be open to question whether the creation of a more independent central bank is significant in containing inflation, or whether the existence of an independent bank merely reflects a political economy in which price stability is a widely-shared objective, where governments, as well as the central bank, regard low inflation as an over-riding objective (Mitchell, 1993). Consequently, economists accept the possibility of 'reverse causality' as a significant constraint when interpreting the experience of countries with independent central banks.

Moreover, the theoretical case for independence is based on two analytical assumptions that have become generally accepted by economists. Firstly, the vertical long-term Phillips curve, which implies that price stability can be achieved at no long-term cost of unemployment; and secondly, the political business cycle. However, both rest on insecure foundations. The vertical Phillips curve analysis rests upon the concept of a natural rate of unemployment, the frequently changing determinants of which economists remain largely ignorant (Davidson, 1998; Karanassou and Snower, 1998; Madsen, 1998; Nickell, 1998; Phelps and Zoega, 1998). Moreover, several studies indicate that relatively little evidence exists for the occurrence of any systematic political business cycle (Kalecki, 1943; Breton, 1974; Nordhaus, 1975; MacRae, 1977; Wagner, 1977; Frey, 1978; Alesina, 1989).

Fourthly, the empirical evidence concerning central bank independence and lower-than-average inflation, which again drew heavily upon the German Bundesbank, although counter-examples exist, compounds difficulties. For instance, the USA with an independent central bank has not enjoyed such a phenomenon. Moreover, German experience since reunification demonstrated that an independent central bank is unable to guarantee low inflation. However, the persuasive nature of monetarist ideas led to the widespread conviction that low inflation is an important condition for high and sustained growth. Thus its achievement should be the priority for government economic policy. The importance attached to low inflation as the prerequisite for high employment and rapid growth is central to the case for an independent central bank. However, the belief that low or zero inflation produces sustained growth is once again, not supported by the available evidence. Indeed, many studies indicate that no significant relationship exists between low inflation and higher rates of growth, until double-digit rates of price increase occur, which do retard economic development (Thirlwall and Barton, 1971; Brown, 1985; Stanners, 1993). Thus, the consensus of research fails to provide the evidence to support the advantages of prioritising low inflation above all other objectives.

Moreover, economic policy objectives should be sufficiently comprehensive as to include the pursuit of multiple policy targets. However, if responsibility for price stability rests solely with an independent central bank, while others remain with government, economic management potentially becomes more difficult due to the separation of monetary and fiscal policy (Blake and Weale, 1998). Hence, an advantage of a non-independent central bank is that budgetary and monetary measures can complement each other, forging a co-ordinated strategy of economic management. A failure of policy co-ordination was demonstrated in the USA by the shortcomings of the Reagan-Volcker era and within the EU by Germany's problems in the aftermath of reunification. Such policy inconsistency highlights the ambiguous nature of 'independence' itself. Analysis of the role of a central bank confirms that, in a world of external shocks, the case for delegating monetary policy is weak and that a co-ordinated approach is more likely to achieve the electorate's objectives (Rogoff, 1985a, 1985b). Furthermore, if eliminating inflation is all-important and elected politicians cannot be trusted to give it priority, the logical conclusion is that all economic instruments should be taken out of their hands. The assertion often made is that monetary policy is different, because it is a technical operation with a single objective and well-understood, reliable techniques. Such a belief is questionable, since monetary policy impacts upon employment and living standards, as vitally as does fiscal policy. Moreover, periods of high inflation have not occurred wholly, or even mainly, due to lax monetary expansion, whilst there is greater international evidence of fiscal, rather than monetary, policy being manipulated for electoral ends (Alesina, 1989).

When assessing the impact of central bank independence upon price stability, economists have mostly utilised imputed 'degrees of independence' to evaluate the heterogeneous character of central banks. A large body of literature focusing upon single or multi-country time-series studies has been accumulated, with an additional series of studies attempting to rank independence for a cross-section of countries. The majority of this research draws attention to the inherent difficulty of defining, let alone measuring, the concept of independence (Mangano, 1998). The initial method of imputing degrees of independence, based solely on legislature arrangements, found no relationship between inflation performance and independence (Bodart, 1990). The index was refined by subsequent studies, which constructed a measure of central bank independence that reflected both 'political independence' and 'economic independence' (Alesina and Grilli, 1991 and Grilli *et al.*, 1991). The former relates to the ability of the monetary authorities to choose the goals of policy, whilst economic independence is defined by their capacity to choose the instruments with which to pursue policy objectives. The main conclusion from such analyses is that the average rate of inflation, and occasionally its variability, is significantly lower in countries that possess independent central banks.

However, the value of such evidence is problematic, as the authors usually acknowledge, because measurement of 'degrees of independence' possesses serious weaknesses, which cast doubt upon the purported association between central bank independence and the attainment of price stability. The main failings this approach are, firstly, that a limited spread of rankings inevitably restricts sensitivity across a wide number of inherently different countries, which raises difficulties concerning the index's analytical usefulness. Secondly, that many of the studies cover overlapping time periods, opening up the possibility that they have found a result unique to that particular set of data. Therefore it becomes crucial to test a hypothesis on data sets other than those that suggested the hypothesis (Friedman and Schwartz, 1991). Furthermore, the time periods covered by some studies increase concern over the reliability of their findings. For instance, the participation of countries within the EMS could be viewed as a potentially important determinant of inflation rates. Consequently, if all countries in a pegged exchange rate system are compelled to possess the same rate of inflation over the long-run, whatever the various influences are on that rate, the status of NCBs cannot be the main influence. Fourthly, disregard for non-economic factors that shape fiscal and monetary policy choices is a consistent feature of these studies, illustrated by their assumption that electorates always prefer low inflation to the possible trade-off of higher economic growth and employment (Muscatelli, 1998).

However, even after analysing the role of political factors, other potential sources of differences in inflation rates are often neglected. For instance, even if EU countries were subject to the same exogenous shocks in the post-war period, structural differences – labour relations systems, wage indexation mechanisms, vulnerability to raw material price changes, varying preferences for inflation versus unemployment – between them may explain their different reactions. Indeed, the position of the government in the political spectrum and various proxies of social consensus offer some explanation of inflation rates in different countries (Hansson, 1987). Likewise, the size of the public sector appears to be another significant factor (Alesina, 1988). Moreover, lower inflation in Germany and Switzerland could result from the presence of 'guest' workers during periods of economic growth, who absorb part of the unemployment costs of disinflationary policies by having to return to their country of origin when the work is no longer available (Burdekin and Willett, 1990).

In an attempt to compare monetary regimes, many studies focus exclusively on institutional characteristics, disregarding behavioural indicators such as the average rate of growth of the money supply or the level and variability of interest rates. However, new research rarely possesses at first the reliable database it requires. Therefore greater attention should be devoted to improving databases and to recording any national specificity that may exist or has occurred. Moreover, many studies suffer from the omission of indicators not identified as potential explanatory factors, so that influences other than central bank independence may be important, but as yet unidentified, determinants. Finally, a problematical aspect of this research is the statistical analysis of the link between central bank independence and inflation, with most studies relying upon the plotting of graphs. Indeed, Alesina and Summers (1993: 154) admit that 'our empirical procedure is extremely simple. We plot various measures of economic performance covering the entire 1955–1988 period against measures of central bank independence'. Furthermore, the manner in which the determined characteristics of central banks are aggregated to produce the overall index of central bank independence is a major area for concern. Consequently, the index is usually constructed through one of a number of alternative methods, none of which is universally valid. Indeed, despite the occasional econometric testing, the results provide little support for the notion that independent central banks consistently deliver low inflation, whilst the more common approach of the unscientific plotting of a line between inflation and only one other variable (when there are many determinants) constitutes scant evidence upon which to rest the case for central bank independence.

Hence, in view of these potential difficulties associated with the frequently prevailing use of imputed degrees of independence, the chapter now re-examines this issue.

Empirical Analysis of Central Bank Independence

This section examines the issue of central bank independence within those EU member states (excluding Luxembourg which at the time did not possess its own central bank), which were original signatories to the TEU. Although this reduces the number of countries in comparison to several of the previous studies, it offers a logical basis for the subsequent analysis. For example, little analytical precision is gained, when examining the likely impact of the ECB, by including those countries which will never enter EMU (e.g. Australia, Canada, Japan, New Zealand and the USA). Moreover, few previous studies offer a rationale for the countries they include, for instance, whilst focusing upon industrialised economies, they all fail to incorporate every member of such a representative grouping as the OECD.

A further aspect that differentiates this analysis is that it disaggregates central bank independence into its constituent features of political and economic independence. The approach involves dividing these principal features into sixteen individual components, thereby enabling a detailed examination of the separate elements that comprise a central bank's independence alongside an evaluation of the aggregate level analysis pursued in previous research. Finally, in addition to the now traditional comparison of central bank independence and inflation, GDP growth is introduced to evaluate the proposition that independence carries no detrimental consequences for output (Eijffinger *et al.*, 1996).

Table 7.5 shows the correlation results between the series of measures of central bank independence and both the rate of inflation and growth over the period 1961–1994. Analysing a positive hypothetical relationship between central bank independence and inflation, the only statistically significant factors include the '*board being appointed for a period exceeding 5 years*' and the '*absence of prior government approval of monetary policy formulation*'. Likewise, the fact the bank provides a '*direct credit facility at market interest rate*' and '*not participating in the primary market for public debt*', are the sole significant economic characteristics. Hence only four of a possible sixteen features of central bank independence appear to contribute to lowering inflation. Such findings contrast with the blanket contention that an independent central bank is an effective anti-inflationary mechanism.

Although these findings partially support the conclusions of previous studies (Alesina, 1989; Grilli *et al.*, 1991; Alesina and Summers, 1993), there are several important caveats. Firstly, the analysis of the individual features of political and economic independence indicates that only a limited number are statistically significant, raising difficulties concerning the necessity for all such characteristics to be present simultaneously within the ECB. Secondly, the overall index of political independence is insignificant indicating that such criteria proved historically inconsequential to EU member states' inflation rates. Thirdly, although the indices of economic and combined independence are inversely related to inflation, only 66 per cent of the variation of inflation is 'explained'. This appears to offer marginal evidence at best from which to launch such a fundamental institutional reform or to expect it persist over the medium- to long-term, particularly if negative externalities are associated with greater independence.

The second part of this empirical analysis examines the relationship between central bank independence and output to evaluate the orthodox hypothesis that the former constitutes 'a free lunch' (Grilli *et al.*, 1991: 375), because it carries no detrimental consequences for GDP growth. The final column of Table 7.5 shows the correlation results for the individual features and the three overall indices of independence in relation to growth. With respect to political independence, neither the individual factors nor the index are statistically significant, whilst three of the economic independence criteria are significant: '*direct credit facility not automatic*', '*direct credit facility at market interest rate*' and '*central bank does not participate in the primary market for public debt*'. Of particular interest, however, is the negative association between these features and GDP growth, which contradicts the previously established proposition that central bank independence has no 'costs in terms of macroeconomic performance' (Grilli *et al.*, 1991: 375). The implication therefore is that independent central banks exert a negative impact on the rise in their citizens' standards of living and constitutes an ominous background to the actual operation of the ECB.

Table 7.5   Correlation between central bank independence and macro-economic variables for EU member states

Indicator of Central Bank Independence:	Rate of inflation	GDP growth
Indicators of political independence:		
Governor not appointed by government	0.20	0.05
Governor appointed for > 5 years	-0.51	-0.20
All the board not appointed by government	0.52	0.31
Board appointed for > 5 years	-0.63**	-0.13
No mandatory participation of government representative on the board	0.07	-0.10
No government approval of monetary policy formulation is required	-0.55*	-0.23
Statutory requirements that central bank pursues monetary stability amongst its goals	-0.39	-0.01
Legal provisions that strengthen the central bank's position in conflicts with the government are present	-0.20	-0.02
Cumulative Index of Political Independence	**-0.48**	**-0.12**
Indicators of economic independence:		
Direct credit facility – not automatic	-0.34	-0.60**
Direct credit facility – market interest rate	-0.52*	-0.57*
Direct credit facility – temporary	-0.32	-0.15
Direct credit facility – limited amount	-0.13	0.34
Central bank does not participate in primary market for public debt	-0.84***	-0.53*
Discount rate set by central bank	-0.32	-0.31
Banking supervision not entrusted to the central bank at all	-0.16	0.10
Banking supervision not entrusted to the central bank alone	-0.42	-0.35
Cumulative Index of Economic Independence	**-0.81***	**-0.62**
Cumulative Index of Political and Economic Independence	**-0.81***	**-0.45**

*** = $p < 0.01$ ** = $p < 0.5$ * = $p < 0.1$
Source: Baimbridge *et al.* (2002).

Conclusion

The theoretical and empirical evidence surveyed in this chapter suggests that, the creation of an independent central bank is a more finely balanced exercise than is frequently portrayed in particular given national economies which continue to experience varying economic cycles and possess divergent economic structures. Moreover, the interest rate decisions taken by central banks are amongst the most sensitive actions deployed in a modern economy, influencing growth, living standards, the level of unemployment and the cost of credit and mortgages. However, the ECB publishes neither forecasts nor the minutes of its deliberations and its members cannot be removed from office by the European Parliament, the Council of Ministers or even by the European Court.

The ECB's problems arise from its lack of democratic accountability, transparency, democratic legitimacy, arbitrary objectives, questionable economic philosophy and the potential for intermittent conflict with the national governments whose destinies it possesses considerable influence over. An alternative model of a democratically accountable and controlled ECB, operating in co-ordination with a combination of nationally determined fiscal policies, or a newly established federal authority, would prove a more effective and desirable model for EMU.

Chapter 8

Economic Policy within EMU

Introduction

The conduct of economic policy within EMU is considerably different from that outside. Monetary policy (interest rates) are now set by the independent ECB, whilst national governments possess fiscal and supply-side policies. Hence, from an individual country's viewpoint, interest rates are now 'fixed' and will only move if the ECB decides that economic conditions are changing for the euro zone as a whole and not if an individual country or minority of countries suffer an economic shock. Thus, whereas with full monetary sovereignty a country may adjust interest rates to cope with any problem it faces, under EMU the country now has two choices. Firstly, provided that it does not infringe the SGP, it can use fiscal policy to counteract whatever shock has occurred. Secondly, the country can wait for its labour market to alter wages and then prices and thus its overall degree of international competitiveness.

The problem for the eurozone countries is that at the present time there is no large federal fiscal system[1] in place whereby a central government sets taxes and expenditure rules that apply in its constituent states or countries. Hence, fiscal policy is confined to backward-looking automatic stabilisers such that the only channel for a forward-looking policy is through interest rates. Hence, the fiscal framework in EMU increases the burden on monetary policy to react to shocks even before they have fed fully through into output and inflation.

The conduct of economic policy within EMU is considerably different from that previously experienced by EU member states. Monetary policy (interest rates) is now set by the independent ECB, whilst national governments possess fiscal and supply-side policies. Hence, from an individual country's viewpoint, interest rates are now 'fixed' and will only move if the ECB decides that economic conditions are changing for the eurozone as a whole and not if an individual country, or group of countries, suffers an economic shock (McKinnon, 2003; von Hagen, 2003; Wyplosz, 2003). Thus, EMU participating countries now have two choices. Firstly, provided that it does not infringe the convergence criteria/SGP it can use fiscal policy to counteract whatever shock has occurred (Gali and Perotti, 2003). Secondly, the country can

---

1   One common feature of monetary unions is their fiscal federal structures. When a state/country has a slump in growth, it pays less tax to the central government and gets more social security money without any decisions having to be taken. Hence, automatic stabilisers are at work courtesy of federal tax rates and federal rates of social security payments. See Chapter 9.

wait for its labour market to alter wages and then prices and thus its overall degree of international competitiveness.

The IS-LM model was devised in 1937, one year after publication of Keynes' *General Theory*, by the British economist Sir John Hicks to provide a determinate solution to the Keynesian system. It is a model that can be used to show new equilibria for income/output (Y) and the rate of interest (i) after any of the exogenous variables or parameters of the system change. In more recent years it has gone out of fashion, being regarded as too simplistic given that its most basic form assumed that prices were fixed. Thus it was unable to explain and illustrate the high inflation rates of the 1970s, together with the increasing attention applied to the supply-side of the economy (the second policy option outlined above). However, the IS-LM model has regained its relevancy, firstly, given the more stable inflation environment across the EU, partially resulting from cheap labour in China and other emerging economies (The Economist, 2005); and secondly, in relation to the EMU policy debate in that it combines the real (fiscal policy) and financial (monetary policy) sides of the economy in the IS and LM schedules respectively. In any event, the IS-LM approach provides a relatively straightforward means of evaluating the impact of EMU upon economic policy determination and therefore for this reason at least is worthy of initial consideration.

Figure 8.1 illustrates the basic IS-LM model representation that an EMU country faces. The IS function retains its familiar downward sloping nature, however, rather than thinking of it terms of its traditional description of illustrating equilibrium in product markets, we can view it in terms of fiscal policy (FP). This is the aspect of economic policy that national governments retain influence over, albeit within the stipulations of the SGP. In contrast the LM function does not possess its usual upwards-sloping nature since national economies are effectively 'price takers' in relation to the rate of interest, which is determined by the independent ECB (see Chapter 7). Hence the LM or monetary policy (MP) is portrayed as being perfectly elastic (horizontal) and exogenously determined.

Through expansionary or contractionary fiscal policy national governments can manipulate the economy (FP_1) to achieve desired level of national income/output (FP_2), for example, seeking to attain the full employment level of income/output (Y_{FE}). However, as Figure 8.1 indicates the potential scenario facing EMU participants is that the SGP, if applied, could potentially impair the ability of governments to attain full employment through the sole use of fiscal policy (FP_3) with the economy achieving equilibrium at Y_2, thus resulting in a deflationary (unemployment) gap of $Y_2 - Y_{FE}$. Hence, without the ability to adjust interest rates, via the national central bank, to domestic economic conditions, EMU countries are only left with supply-side policies to attain full employment. Although most economists now accept the role of such policies, these are not an immediate remedy for the persistently high levels of unemployment that have been endemic across the Continent of Europe for the past decade.

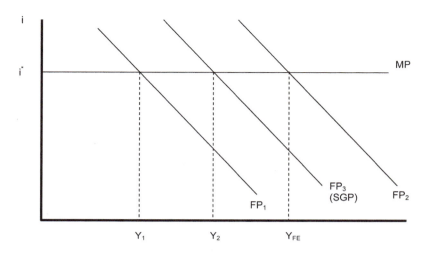

Figure 8.1   Economic policy under EMU

Furthermore, many aspects of supply-side policies are inimical to social model espoused by the majority of EU member states (see Chapter 10). Thus, in an attempt to extricate themselves from this self-inflicted deflationary position, the common reaction has been to blithely ignore the rules of the SGP and expand budget deficits (Germany, Greece and France) and debt-to-GDP ratios (Belgium, Germany, Greece, France, Italy, Austria, Portugal) beyond permitted limits (ECB, 2005). This, however, is not without potential costs in terms of stoking inflationary pressures and diminishing the external value of the euro, the consequence of which is that the ECB will be forced to maintain interest rates higher than is strictly necessary and hence initiating a vicious circle of exacerbating the high rates of unemployment that the breaking of SGP rules sought to address.

Fiscal Policy within EMU

EMU is based on a unique arrangement of public finance relations whereby fiscal policy remains decentralised to EU member states, but is subject to rules to combine discipline and flexibility (Buiter, 2003; Buti *et al.*, 2003). This is provided by the SGP, which complements and tightens the fiscal provisions laid down in the TEU.[2] Buti and van den Noord (2003: 4) argue that the SGP is 'unquestionably the most stringent

---

2   The SGP consists of a Resolution adopted by the European Council in June of 1997, and two Council Regulations adopted in July of 1997. It clarifies the 'excessive deficits' procedure and penalties that were agreed in the TEU. Stark (2001) discusses the rationale for the original German proposal regarding the SGP. For a description its basic features see Buti *et al.* (1998) and Cabral (2001), whilst EU Commission (2000) and Fischer and Giudice (2001) discuss the implementation and operation of the SGP.

supranational commitment technology ever adopted by sovereign governments on a voluntary basis in the attempt to establish and maintain sound public finances'. If fully applied it will have important implications for the behaviour of budgetary authorities in both the short-term (cyclical stabilisation, policy co-ordination) and long-term (sustainability of public finances). It seeks to achieve a balance between constraining national fiscal policy to protect the ECB whilst it established credibility and permitting limited flexibility for counter-cyclical fiscal policy. This was deemed necessary since although ECB policy might be expected to create stable macroeconomic conditions for the euro-zone as a whole it could not be expected to resolve regional cyclical imbalances.[3]

The SGP consists of several central elements (Buti *et al.*, 1998; EU Commission, 2000). Firstly, a commitment to medium-term budgets that are 'close to balance or in surplus' which is interpreted by Canzoneri and Diba (2000) as an implied promise to balance structural (or cyclically adjusted) budgets. Secondly, submission of annual programs specifying medium-term budgetary objectives thereby creating a track record when assessing compliance with the SGP, or convergence criteria in the case of member states who are not in the Euro-zone (EU Commission, 2000). Thirdly, countries that run excessive deficits will be subject to financial penalties and public approbation. Deficits are defined as 'excessive' if they exceed 3 per cent of GDP, unless they occur under 'exceptional' circumstances which is defined as an annual decline in real output of more than 2 per cent of GDP, whilst a decline of 0.75 per cent of GDP might be deemed 'exceptional' if there is additional supporting evidence. The sanctions associated with such deficits are that the member state has to make an interest free deposit of 0.2 per cent of GDP, plus 0.1 per cent of the amount by which its deficit to GDP ratio exceeded 3 per cent. The maximum deposit would be capped at 0.5 per cent of GDP, which is forfeited after two years if the 'excessive deficit' persists. Canzoneri and Diba (2000) estimate that the foregone interest in the first year of sanctions would be in the range of €250–500 million for one of the larger member states.

However, the initial years of EMU have demonstrated little progress towards lower public deficits and debts by participating nations in terms of budgetary consolidation let alone in structural terms. Furthermore, following the omission of the automatic effects of growth on the budget, countries have relaxed their retrenchment efforts in the 1998–2002 period. In particular, the three largest countries of the euro area (Germany, France and Italy) as well as Portugal did not behave according to the SGP. Indeed, although the SGP appears rigid, it fails to address a typical failure of fiscal policy behaviour in Europe, namely the tendency to run expansionary pro-cyclical policies in good times (European Commission, 2000). Whilst an excess over the 3 per cent of GDP deficit ceiling is sanctioned, there is no apparent reward for appropriate budgetary behaviour during cyclical upswings, leading Buti and van den Noord (2003) to argue that the political temptation to 'spend the money when it comes in' may prove irresistible. Hence, the suggestion that the SGP is 'all sticks and no carrots' (Bean, 1998) and may result in a pro-cyclical bias in the conduct of

---

3   See Brunila *et al.* (2001) for an overview of the institutional, legal, theoretical and empirical aspects of the SGP.

budgetary policy since the only carrot is the opportunity for automatic stabilisers to operate during economic downturns. However, Buti and Martinot (2000) argue that if governments retain their historical budgetary culture they will tend to offset the working of the automatic stabilisers for sufficiently large, positive output gaps.

These questionable incentive structures may be further tested during electoral periods. In contrast to the advent of the euro when the incentive to maintain the announced fiscal consolidation path were evident, the situation may be different once in EMU when adherence to the SGP's rules may be politically inefficient (Buti and Giudice, 2002). Resolving such political bias is likely to be problematic. Potential solutions range from the introduction of 'rainy-day' funds permitting countries to set aside revenue in good times (Buti *et al.*, 2003) to the harmonisation of electoral cycles in EMU, which would reduce politically induced distortions and be welfare-enhancing (Sapir and Sekkat, 1999). However, the most likely outcome is the increasing of budgetary surveillance focussing on structural balances and using peer pressure and 'early warnings' to curb fiscal misbehaviour (Viren, 2001; Korkman, 2001; EU Commission, 2002).

In addition to ensuring member states adhere to the rules of the SGP, a further series of difficulties have arisen regarding the convergence criteria reference values for both the deficit and the debt to GDP ratios, whilst none were defined for structural deficits. Subsequently, the SGP added a commitment to structural balance, but the 'excessive deficits' procedure is its only explicit enforcement mechanism. Thus, actual deficits are the focus of the SGP that appear to take primacy over both structural deficits and debt levels (Canzoneri and Diba, 2000). Consequently, it has been suggested that the SGP will become an impediment unless its focus is shifted from constraints on actual deficits and towards constraints on structural deficits, or better yet, constraints on debt levels (Canzoneri and Diba, 2000; Artis and Buti, 2001; Dalsgaard and de Serres, 2001; Rostangno *et al.*, 2001; Missale, 2001). Furthermore, various studies regarding the flexibility built into the 'excessive deficits' procedure suggest that once governments have further reduced structural deficits the 'excessive deficits' procedure should not constrain normal counter-cyclical efforts (EU Commission, 2000). However, at the present time, given the unlikely prospects for achieving structural balance, the current emphasis on the excessive deficits procedure seems misplaced (Balassone and Franco, 2001; Casella, 2001). Moreover, it is unclear how strictly the EU will interpret the provisions in the SGP with it possessing a history of exerting discretion in such decisions.

Even in light of the issues discussed above, potentially the single largest problem for the eurozone is that at the present time there is no substantive federal fiscal system in place whereby a central government sets taxes and expenditure rules that apply in constituent states or countries. Hence, fiscal policy is confined to backward-looking automatic stabilisers confined by convergence criteria/SGP rules, such that the only channel for a forward-looking policy is through interest rates that are now controlled by the independent ECB.

Monetary Policy and Philosophy under EMU

Initially, the TEU left the role of the ECB uncertain, suggesting that it would mainly implement the policies determined by the NCBs by delegating the common monetary policy to the ESCB (von Hagen and Bruckner, 2002). In view of such institutional vagueness a key concern has been how ECB Council members could reach an agreement on a common monetary policy, to what extent that policy would be affected by national circumstances and preferences and how it could be communicated effectively to a very heterogeneous European public (Cecchetti *et al.*, 1999). Initially the European Monetary Institute (EMI) preparatory work narrowed the choice of a monetary policy strategy down to monetary targeting versus inflation targeting (EMI, 1997). However, in October 1998, the Governing Council of the ECB announced that a key aspect of monetary policy strategy being a quantitative definition of price stability. Furthermore, in order to assess risks to price stability, the ECB would make use of two pillars. Firstly, it attributes a prominent role to monetary indicators as signalled by the announcement of a quantitative reference value for the growth of a broad monetary aggregate and secondly, it undertakes a comprehensive analysis of a wide range of other economic and financial variables as indicators of price developments (ECB, 1998, 1999, 2000, 2001; Issing *et al.*, 2001).

In relation to the quantitative definition of price stability it does not give a precise definition. In order to specify this objective more precisely, the Governing Council announced, in October 1998, the quantitative definition of price stability as 'a year-on-year increase in the Harmonised Index of Consumer Prices (HICP) for the euro area of below 2 per cent', which was 'to be maintained over the medium term' (ECB, 1998). Such an announcement is supposed to enhance the transparency of the overall monetary policy framework and provides a clear and measurable benchmark against which to hold the ECB accountable. Furthermore, it gives guidance to expectations of future price developments, thereby helping to stabilise the economy. Consequently, the ECB (2003) argued that this definition of price stability has been conducive to a firm anchoring of inflation expectations in the euro area at levels compatible with the definition, thereby helping to contain the inflationary effects of the substantial price shocks which have occurred. While the announcement of a quantitative numerical value for the price stability objective of the ECB was welcomed, there has been criticism regarding specific features of the definition.

Firstly, regarding the choice of the price measure it has been argued that the ECB should put more emphasis on measures of 'core' or 'underlying' inflation, or even specify its objective in terms of a measure of core inflation (Gros *et al.*, 2001; Alesina *et al.*, 2001). Such measures could help to avoid the risk of monetary policy-makers focusing excessively on temporary price fluctuations. Secondly, that the ECB's quantitative definition may be too ambitious given a positive measurement bias in the HICP that could hamper the adjustment process at low levels of inflation, substantial divergences in inflation rates across countries that imply 'too low' a level of inflation, and possibly frequent deflationary situations and the presence of a zero boundary on nominal interest rates that could hamper the effectiveness of monetary policy in the face of large negative demand shocks and expose the euro area to the risks associated with deflation and deflationary spirals (Fitoussi and Creel, 2002; De Grauwe, 1994). Thirdly, that the ECB's definition is imprecise and asymmetric as it specifies the upper boundary, but leaves the lower boundary undefined. This may result in it being less effective in anchoring inflation expectations and possibly hinder the clarity of explanations of policy moves. Consequently, it has been suggested that the ECB should make its objective more precise, for instance, by officially announcing a lower boundary in the definition or by specifying the objective in terms of a point inflation rate (Svensson, 2002 and 2003; IMF, 2002). Finally, the choice of the specific quantitative objective requires a balance between the costs of inflation and rationales for small positive inflation rates. The costs primarily relate to the misallocation of resources, the inflation tax on real balances, the effects of inflation on income distribution and inflation uncertainty and associated risk premia, menu costs and those costs stemming from the interaction of inflation with the tax system. In contrast, the case for small positive inflation relates to measurement bias in the price index, downward nominal rigidities, sustained inflation differentials and the risk of protracted deflation or a deflationary spiral (Yates, 1998; Wynne and Rodriguez-Palenzuela, 2002; Coenen, 2003a and b; Klaeffing and Lopez-Perez, 2003). Unfortunately, such a review of the costs and benefits of moderate inflation does not allow the optimal rate of inflation to be precisely defined; it indicates the need for an inflation objective embodying a sufficient safety margin against deflation. In response to this criticism the ECB (2003) suggested that inflation objectives above 1 per cent provide sufficient safety margins to ensure against these risks.[4]

In relation to the first pillar, its key characteristic is the announcement of a reference value for the annual growth of M3. Hence, the ECB seeks to communicate the medium-term focus of monetary policy to the public, as it relieves the central bank from responding to short-run fluctuations in financial and other variables (ECB, 2003). Furthermore, by signalling continuity of the Bundesbank's strategy, the ESCB hoped to quickly establish credibility (von Hagen and Bruckner, 2002). However, the role of money and monetary analysis has generated controversy regarding the robustness of the chosen leading indicator's properties with respect to price developments on the grounds that the correlation between money growth and inflation appears to have declined over time in parallel with restored conditions of price stability (Begg *et al.*, 2002). In this context, the necessity for announcing a reference value for money growth has also been queried, together with the usefulness *per se* of a separate 'money' pillar (Svensson, 2003).

In contrast, the second pillar consists of an assessment regarding future price developments (ECB, 1998). Initially, it represented the analysis of short-run price

---

4   This is also in line with the practice followed by all of the central banks of the major developed countries that have specified numerical values for their objectives; all have a midpoint above 1 per cent. For example: the Bank of England: 2½ per cent (RPIX index, approximately 1¾ on average in HICP terms); Sveriges Riksbank: 2±1 per cent (CPI); Norges Bank: 2½±1 per cent (CPI); Bank of Canada: 1–3 per cent (CPI); Bank of Australia: 1–3 per cent (CPI); Reserve Bank of New Zealand: 1–3 per cent (CPI). The Federal Reserve System and the Bank of Japan have not specified a quantitative definition of their price stability objectives. The Swiss National Bank has adopted a definition of price stability that is equivalent to that of the ECB.

developments based on measures of real activity, wage cost, asset prices, fiscal policy indicators, together with indicators of business and consumer confidence (ECB, 1999). However, no framework was specified how these variables would be used to assess price developments, nor their relative weights in such assessments. It is therefore an opaque part to the ESCB's strategy, being void of systematic analysis and fully discretionary (von Hagen and Bruckner, 2002). Furthermore, Gaspar *et al.* (2001) suggest that the analysis is now organized in the form of a macroeconomic projection, although the ECB does not provide confidence intervals for its projections (Gali, 2001).

According to the ECB (2003), the two pillars are used in parallel in monetary policy decision-making. However, there is no indication of what their relative weights are, resulting in an incomprehensible strategy, as Issing *et al.* (2001) partially acknowledge. Although there is nothing that would make the use and revelation of the relative weights of the two pillars impossible, the reason why the ECB has so far denied the public transparency of its strategy is more likely related to the internal decision-making processes (von Hagen and Bruckner, 2002).

Finally, from its ostensively monetarist pre-history the ECB argues that the majority of euro zone's high unemployment originates from structural deficiencies on the supply-side of its member states economies. Consequently, it denies responsibility for increasing aggregate demand to lower unemployment, since no scope exists to reduce unemployment without accelerating inflation. However, if the sole objective of policy is to maintain a constant rate of inflation, wide variations in output and employment may be required. In so far as a potential conflict exists between steady inflation and full employment, the latter should enjoy priority, because of the consequences of market failure in terms of high rates of employment are more serious than those associated with moderate levels of inflation.

The Macroeconomic Framework under EMU

EMU requires the ECB to possess the monopoly power to issue the euro, with existing national central banks becoming mere subsidiaries of this ultimate federal monetary authority. Thus the ECB is in sole charge of monetary policy for all participants in EMU through the establishment of a common interest rate, together with management of the euro's external exchange rate.[5] To fulfil these responsibilities, the ECB is likely to set interest rates according to what the *median* member state requires, implying that there will always be some economies that require higher, or lower interest rates, depending upon their individual circumstances.

The only realistic alternative to varying monetary policy according to the needs of the median participant is for the ECB to prioritise the self-interest of one section of the euro-zone, perhaps by reflecting Germany's pre-occupation with low inflation at the expense of other priorities. Indeed, the TEU commits the ECB to pursue the goal of price stability at the expense of all other economic objectives, which, in any

---

5   EU Commission (1992) lists its founding regulations, whilst Baimbridge *et al.* (1999a) provides a comprehensive critique of the ECB.

case, may be rendered impossible through an over-vigorous pursuit of squeezing the last vestiges of inflation out of the European economy. Such a strategy is supported by economic orthodoxy, which claims that there is no long-term trade-off between inflation and unemployment, so that tightening monetary policy to reduce inflation will not result in persistently high levels of unemployment. However, the fallacy of such an over-simplification of what is a much more complicated relationship was demonstrated by the restrictive monetary policy established by membership of the Exchange Rate Mechanism (ERM), which caused most of Europe to suffer double-digit rates of unemployment over the last decade. It was only sterling's forced exit from the deflationary excesses of the ERM that established the competitive conditions for the UK's recent successful economic record.

The ECB faces another problem in framing monetary policy caused by differences in trade cycles and in the industrial and financial structures of participating countries, which imply that EMU is liable to suffer from *asymmetric* external shocks (Weber, 1991b; de Grauwe and Vanhaverbeke, 1993; Bayoumi and Eichengreen, 1993; Whyman, 1997). For example, an increase in oil prices will exert a beneficial impact upon the energy exporting sectors of the UK and the Netherlands, whilst having a detrimental impact upon all other EU member economies. If the ECB reacts to this variation in the external economic environment according to the needs of the majority, it will enact changes in monetary policy that are contrary to the needs of the UK and the Netherlands. Moreover, differential house-buying patterns between the UK and Ireland compared to continental member states, together with a greater preference for variable rate borrowing in the UK, mean that the rest of the EU is far less responsive to changes in monetary policy (Taylor, 1995; Bank for International Settlements, 1996; Burkitt *et al.*, 1996, 1997; Eltis, 1996). Indeed, simulations performed on the macroeconomic models used by various national central banks indicate that the impact of an interest rate change on UK domestic demand after two years is four times greater than the EU average (Bank for International Settlements, 1994; Pennant-Rea *et al.*, 1997). Consequently, the ECB is again placed in an impossible position since any changes in monetary policy will affect certain countries far more than others, resulting in either an over-tightening or over-loosening of monetary policy for the UK compared with the median EU member country. The end result would be a dramatic increase in the UK economy's volatility as a direct result of the inefficiency of a 'one rate for all' monetary policy in the presence of systematic cyclical and structural differences between different economies.

Empirical studies confirm that supply and demand shocks will prove asymmetric for EMU participants, with 67 per cent of supply shocks and 82 per cent of demand shocks estimated to exert a divisive impact upon the EU economy, whilst the UK economy was found to react differently from those of other member states in no less than 87 out of 100 instances (Weber, 1991a; Bayoumi and Eichengreen, 1993). Comparisons between the UK and Germany produce a compatibility of only 54 per cent, suggesting that UK growth and inflation are moving in the opposite direction to that of Germany almost half of the time. Moreover, Ireland's growth record was related to Germany's on only 9 per cent of occasions, whilst Greek and Portuguese inflation had *no* statistical relationship with Germany (Bayoumi and Eichengreen, 1993). Advocates of EU integration dismiss these findings by arguing that the development of the single market will reduce the frequency and impact of asymmetric shocks as individual economies become increasingly inter-dependent and as large corporations straddle European borders (EC Commission, 1990; Goodhart, 1995). However, it is equally possible that industrial restructuring across Europe will concentrate certain industries in specific locations, such as car manufacture in Germany, thereby exacerbating existing differences (de Grauwe and Vanhaverbeke, 1993). In either case, EMU remains vulnerable to any sizeable asymmetric external shock which will highlight the inability of a single monetary authority to reconcile the different economic needs of individual participants by using only one policy instrument, the common interest rate, whose level is set in the interests of the majority of nations.[6]

The extensive literature concerning nominal and real wage rigidity in Europe undermines faith in price flexibility as an equilibrating mechanism to restore full employment in the aftermath of an asymmetric shock.[7] With labour mobility far lower than experienced in mature monetary unions such as the USA (OECD, 1986; Ermisch, 1991; Eichengreen, 1992; Masson and Taylor, 1993), and capital mobility unlikely to generate sufficient short-term stabilisation due to the time lags and transactions costs involved (von Hagen, 1993; Romer, 1994), fiscal policy is left as the primary stabilising instrument (Kenen, 1969, 1995; Sala-i-Martin and Sachs, 1992; de Grauwe and Vanhaverbeke, 1993; Masson, 1996). However, national fiscal policy is constrained by participation in EMU, due to the requirements of the convergence criteria reinforced by the SGP. Member states are committed by international treaty to prevent budget deficits exceeding 3 per cent of GDP and public debt to extend beyond 60 per cent of GDP, except in particularly deep recessions, defined as occurring when national income declines by more than 0.75 per cent in any given year. Failure to meet these criteria will result in fines being imposed upon the errant nation state, up to 0.5 per cent of GDP, thereby worsening the problematic economic situation which led to rising budget deficits in the first place (EU Commission, 1992; Holland, 1995; Burkitt *et al.*, 1996, 1997; UNCTAD, 1996). Governments may, therefore, be faced with trying to cut public spending or to raise taxes in the middle of a slump, the inevitable result being to deepen the recession, just as pro-cyclical fiscal policy worsened conditions during the 1930s depression.

The alternative is for member states to run a budget surplus of perhaps 5–7 per cent of GDP during favourable economic periods, to avoid surpassing the 3 per cent

---

6　The loss of economic instruments for individual member states due to participation in EMU violates the Tinbergen (1952) rule, which states that if a number of independent policy targets are to be achieved with a number of effective policy instruments, the number of instruments will, in general, need to be at least as great as the number of targets. Consequently, the ability of individual member states to continue to pursue national rather than EU goals will be reduced by the loss of former economic instruments, against the recommendation of Tinbergen.

7　The literature includes: Bruno and Sachs (1985), Carlin and Soskice (1990), Dréze and Bean (1990), Eichengreen (1990), Layard et al (1991), Bini-Smaghi and Vori (1992), Blanchard and Katz (1992), Sala-i-Martin and Sachs (1992), Eichengreen (1993), Goodhart and Smith (1993), Pisani-Ferry *et al.* (1993), Kenen (1995) and Goodhart (1995).

deficit limit during a downturn.[8] A surplus of this magnitude has little economic justification. Moreover, the reduction in EU fiscal deficits from an average of 6.5 per cent of GNP in 1993 to 2.6 per cent in 1998 coincided with a period of mediocre economic growth rates for those EU nations determined to meet the conditions established for entry to the single currency (Ormerod 1999b). Deficit reductions for certain countries, including Portugal, Italy, Spain and Sweden, were equivalent to between 4 to 6 per cent of GNP, thereby imposing a massive constraint upon the ability of the economy to maintain normal growth patterns during this period of fiscal retrenchment. The resulting mass unemployment across the continent, currently nearing 20 million people, is a damning testimony to the higher prioritisation of EMU amongst EU governments than the alternative objectives of full employment and the promotion of economic growth. Nevertheless, to continue to meet the convergence criteria, fiscal restriction must be pursued further, as the average deficit levels are barely sufficient in favourable economic conditions, and must be improved by perhaps 7–9 per cent of national wealth in order to satisfy the SGP in the midst of an economic slow-down. However, further budget cuts or tax rises will only exacerbate the problems of slow growth and rising unemployment already existing. Thus, the annual growth rate of the EU's present membership averaged 4.8 per cent between 1961 and 1970, and slowed to 3.0 per cent between 1971 and 1980, to 2.4 per cent between 1981 and 1990, and to just 1.7 per cent between 1991 and 1998. The EU's growth since 1975 has been an average 0.4 per cent less each year than that of the USA.

A different option involves the expansion of fiscal policy at the federal level, which could act as an inter-regional public insurance scheme to redistribute income to 'adversely shocked' from 'favourably shocked' regions, thus preventing an 'unlucky' area bearing a disproportionate financial burden. However, the current EU budget, equivalent to only 1.24 per cent of EU GDP, is too small to exert a significant stabilising effect upon EMU regions in the advent of an asymmetric external shock (Eichengreen, 1994; Bayoumi and Masson, 1995; EU Commission, 1996). Thus any shift towards fiscal federalism requires an increased flow of resources to a central fiscal authority (see Chapter 9).

EMU is an essentially political strategy based upon false economic assumptions of cyclical and structural convergence. The national interest of the UK requires the implementation of a long-run opt-out from EMU, given that its participation is neither inevitable nor desirable. The central issue therefore becomes, what framework is

---

8   Compliance with the convergence criteria is a long-term commitment to be fulfilled in cyclical troughs as well as peaks. To avoid budget deficits exceeding 3 per cent of GDP in recessions, the surplus during boom years must exceed the total variation in budget balance over the cycle. UK government finances varied from a 5.3 per cent deficit at the depth of the 1980–81 recession to a 3 per cent surplus at the height of the 1988–89 boom. The following deficit exceeded 8 per cent during 1993–94, whilst the Chancellor's current predictions estimate a 2 per cent surplus by early next century. The cyclical variation, 8.3 per cent of GDP during the 1980s rising to between 9–10 per cent presently, indicates that, for deficits to remain above 3 per cent at the low point of the business cycle, the UK budget must be in surplus by a minimum of between 6 to 7½ per cent of GDP, necessitating tax increases or reductions in public expenditure to the extent of £23.3 to £46.1 billion at current prices.

needed for the formation of macroeconomic policy in a Britain outside the single currency on a permanent basis? An initial stage is a national information campaign to acquaint the public and industry with the factual consequences, the opportunities created and the dangers averted by opting-out. It should be supported by a detailed strategy for each British government department, to enable them to identify the trade, financial and investment opportunities arising from the creation of a euro-bloc. For instance, the City of London will gain opportunities to trade in Eurobonds, whilst British manufacturing and service companies will enjoy competitive advantages from being free of the costs of converting to, and implementing, the euro.

Conclusion

This chapter has sought to outline the 'new' shape of economic policymaking within EMU. Although this has evolved from the initial blueprint, the direction is diametrically opposite to what would be beneficial to the UK. For example, the introduction of SGP to reinforce the budgetary aspects of the convergence criteria potentially leads to an unprecedented loss of national autonomy in terms of fiscal policy. However, there is little comfort to be gained from the marked failure of the SGP with numerous member states blithely flouting its provisions since this illustrates the fallacy of the entire Maastricht process in seeking to curtail national well-being for the greater good of the EU. Similarly, in 2003 the ECB undertook a major reassessment of its monetary policy stance given the destabilising effect of the 'one size fit all' interest rate policy upon both domestic EMU economies and in terms of the euro external position upon global capital markets. However, once again the patchwork of remedial policies is far from those necessary to place monetary policy within the sphere of democratic accountability.

This leads us to the question of how economic policymaking could be improved within the eurozone? Two radical, but effective, reforms would be as follows. Firstly, the Council of Ministers tells the Commission that, from the next financial year, member states will finance only those parts of Commission outlays that achieve a zero fraud rating from the European Court of auditors, with all other EU expenditure reverting to national control. At a stroke, such a decision would eliminate about 95 per cent of Commission activity. Gone would be the CAP, the CFP, plus the 'pork barrel' of regional and structural funds. In the last financial year, the auditors approved the accounts on only a derisory 5 per cent of the EU's €98 billion budget. The EU will never accept such a proposal that would compel the Commission to put taxpayers money to efficient and transparent use. However, a British euro-realist government could campaign for it and, when it is inevitably rejected, put it into practice unilaterally.

Secondly, control over economic policy should be repatriated from the ECB and the provisions of SGP to the nation states. On 26 April 2004 the French Finance Minister complained that his job is to deliver economic growth, yet he was unable to do so, because authority over the levers of growth had been given away to the ECB. Given France's record in using the EU to gain advantage, the conclusion that the centralisation of economic policy should be reversed is unavoidable.

PART III
EMU: Practical Considerations

Chapter 9

Fiscal Policy Consequences of EMU

Introduction

The pace of European integration accelerated considerably during the past decade, stimulated by the agreement to form the SIM and enhanced by the process of forming an EMU amongst EU member states. However, whilst the nature of this community of nations significantly changed over this period, many aspects of the EU financial and administrative apparatus failed to evolve to meet these challenges. Whilst detailed consideration has been given to whether individual member states meet the TEU convergence criteria for membership of EMU, the inadequacies of the EU's budgetary arrangements have received far less attention. Nevertheless, the advent of EMU would necessitate a fundamental review of fiscal policy within the EU.

The TEU convergence criteria, combined with the SGP, both reduce national fiscal flexibility whilst the operation of EMU strengthens financial market integration and thereby reduce seigniorage revenues, particularly for the Mediterranean member states. The combination of these factors constrains the ability of participants to stabilise their own economies within an EMU that requires the transfer of monetary and exchange rate instruments to federal rather than national control. If perfect convergence had occurred and could be sustained in the long term, these changes would be of little importance. However, the persistence of asymmetric external shocks requires an alternative stabilising mechanism to be developed to prevent monetary union being undermined by diverse economic and social forces to the extent that it could collapse, as have almost all other similar international monetary arrangements that have not been based upon a firm national identity.[1]

This chapter seeks to complement and extend the existing literature that discusses the evolution of fiscal policy within the context of an emerging EMU (MacDougall, 1977; Lamfalussy, 1989; Goodhart and Hansen, 1990; Wyplotz, 1991 and 1993; Sala-i-Martin and Sachs, 1992; Bayoumi and Masson, 1993; Eichengreen, 1994; Masson, 1996). It outlines the principal economic challenges EMU creates for national and federal fiscal policy, before evaluating the justification for an expansion of the federal budget, or the introduction of an automatic stabiliser mechanism to satisfy these new responsibilities. The chapter concludes by examining the likely

---

1 Examples include the Latin Monetary Union, Scandinavian Currency Union, Gold Standard, Modified Gold Standard and Bretton Woods. The monetary union between Belgium and Luxembourg has not collapsed, although this is perhaps more an example of a small country tying its currency to that of a large, important trading partner, than a model for successful EMU between equal partners.

distributional consequences of budgetary enlargement and the establishment of a semi-automatic stabiliser and how such an expansion in federal EU resources might impact upon all potential participants.

Fiscal Policy Challenges of EMU

External shocks

The variant of EMU agreed in the Treaty on European Union involves the replacement of national currencies with a community currency, whilst monetary policy is transferred to a European Central Bank (ECB) that determines a single interest rate encompassing the whole EMU zone (EU Commission, 1992). National governments must therefore relinquish exchange rate and monetary policy instruments to federal economic authorities. The significance of this reduction in policy tools available to manage individual economies depends upon the extent to which devaluation retains a real effect in the medium-term to long-term, and whether the financial markets within Europe are so closely integrated that independent monetary policy has been rendered impotent. However, should both of these conditions be satisfied, EMU would remain susceptible to destabilisation to the extent that external shocks exert an asymmetric impact upon individual economies. Asymmetric shocks are minimised if monetary union occurs between countries with comparable industrial structures that are, simultaneously, highly diversified. The expectation is that diversification will cause industry-specific shocks to off-set one another whilst broad similarities between economies implies that a given external shock will possess a similar impact and require a matching policy response, which could be satisfactorily accomplished by the ECB or another federal financial authority.

A number of studies have illustrated a number of significant differences between specific EU member states that will require particular consideration were they to participate in the EMU. This has been discussed in the previous chapter, but for present purposes, suffice it to note that:

1. Oil and gas production in the Netherlands and the UK, the manufacturing sector in Germany and the financial and media sectors in the UK are more developed than throughout most of the EU,
2. The propensity for home ownership is different in Ireland and the UK than in continental Europe which, when combined with a higher proportion of variable rate mortgages, causes changes in monetary policy to have a faster and larger impact upon domestic consumption than in the rest of the EU,
3. EMU will exert a proportionately larger impact upon the export earnings of those counties, like the UK, which depend more heavily upon high technology sectors (such as aerospace manufacture and pharmaceuticals) whose goods are typically priced in US dollars,
4. The UK possesses a much greater proportion of corporate and household debt paid at variable rates of interest than the rest of the EU, implying that changes in a

single EU-wide interest rate, controlled by the ECB, will have a more immediate and substantial impact upon the UK economy than other EU member states.

Empirical analysis has ascertained that EU countries were more likely to experience a greater number of primarily asymmetric external shocks than the comparable US economy (Weber, 1991; Bayoumi and Eichengreen, 1993). This problematic conclusion for EMU would have been eased if it had been limited to a 'core' group comprising Germany, France, Belgium, Denmark and the Netherlands, since external shocks had a profoundly more symmetric effect upon this group of countries than the remaining EU member states. Correlation coefficients for this group, measuring 0.58 and 0.31 for supply and demand shocks respectively, compare favourably with the values calculated for US regions. The correlation coefficients of 0.14 and 0.10 for the remaining EU member states demonstrates that their participation in EMU exerts a considerably greater strain upon the ability of the ECB to formulate a monetary and exchange rate policy that is equally appropriate for all countries.[2]

The high degree of external shock asymmetry amongst EU member states highlights the potential cost of EMU in the absence of countervailing forces or government policies. Without the possibility of devaluation, a nation experiencing a loss of competitiveness – for example due to slow productivity growth or a cost-push raw material price shock – would experience rising unemployment unless price flexibility or factor mobility were sufficient to maintain full employment. However, the available evidence from academic studies suggests that neither of these mechanisms can provide more than marginal assistance. The consensus reached by most of the literature on nominal and real wage rigidity in Europe is that between 25 per cent and 75 per cent of price rises are passed onto wages depending upon the country in question, thereby weakening real wage flexibility as an equilibrating mechanism to restore full employment in the aftermath of an asymmetric shock.[3]

Labour mobility within European countries has been estimated to be three times lower than in the USA, despite the existence of greater regional inequality and unemployment in Europe. This implies that EU labour mobility is less responsive to employment and income incentives than the US labour market (OECD, 1986; Eichengreen, 1992), despite evidence that the dispersion of external shocks to labour markets is of a broadly similar frequency and magnitude for Britain, Italy and the US (Eichengreen, 1993b: 155). Moreover, these estimates relate to labour mobility *within* individual countries, whereas mobility *between* countries is likely to be much lower due to language barriers, differences in culture and residual non-recognition of qualifications (Ermisch, 1991: 93–108; Masson and Taylor, 1993; Goodhart and

---

2   Bayoumi and Eichengreen (1993) therefore conclude that there is a strong argument in favour of a two-speed EMU, with the 'core' countries likely to experience relatively little difficulty adapting to a single monetary and exchange rate policy operated by the ECB, whereas non-'core' member states would have far greater difficulties imposed by such a regime.

3   The literature on this point includes: Bruno and Sachs (1985), Carlin and Soskice (1990), Dréze and Bean (1990), Eichengreen (1990), Layard *et al.* (1991), Bini-Smaghi and Vori (1992), Blanchard and Katz (1992), Sala-i-Martin and Sachs (1992), Eichengreen (1993), Goodhart and Smith (1993), Pisani-Ferry *et al.* (1993), Kenen (1995), Goodhart (1995).

Smith, 1993: 422). Thus, it may require substantially higher unemployment and regional inequality to generate labour mobility on the scale required to resolve regional imbalances in the absence of devaluation and wage/price flexibility. This would be equally destabilising for EMU cohesion due to the political implications of large-scale emigration, together with the tensions created by unemployment and relative poverty within a Europe made more transparent through the introduction of a single currency. Indeed, it is possible that, as in Germany after reunification, labour market rigidity will increase as pay differential transparency generates demands for pay equalisation between employees performing equivalent work in different countries, irrespective of productivity equalisation, with potentially damaging effects to competitiveness, output and employment (Doyle, 1989; Horn and Zwiener, 1992; Goodhart, 1995).

Capital mobility can, in principal, substitute for labour mobility in the long-run, as the relocation of productive processes to depressed, inexpensive areas may occur. However, given the time lags involved in the movement of physical, as opposed to financial capital, such movements are likely to reduce long-term regional disparities rather than offset short-term external shocks. The weakness of capital mobility to reduce long-term structural inequalities within existing nation states, together with the insights provided by studies in cumulative causation and endogenous growth theory, caution against over optimistic assumptions of a rapid elimination of unemployment caused by shocks (Myrdal, 1957; Romer, 1994). Moreover, due to the transactions costs involved, factor movements are an inefficient means of reacting to transitory regional shocks (von Hagen, 1993: 278).

One argument that is frequently presented in the literature is that the further economic integration of Europe may reduce the probability of asymmetric shocks, so that existing policy instruments would be sufficient to moderate these disturbances (Emerson *et al.*, 1990: 136). However, the prevalence of regional asymmetric shocks within existing EU nation states may equally indicate that the industrial concentration accompanying economic integration may magnify the frequency and importance of asymmetric shocks (de Grauwe and Vanhaverbeke 1993: 112–125). In view of the divergence of academic opinion on this point, it would be unwise for the architects of EMU to rely upon economic integration to provide a sufficient, permanent reduction in asymmetric shocks in the absence of the introduction of economic instruments designed to ensure the stability of the monetary union.

Fiscal policy assignment

The persistence of asymmetric shocks within an EMU, where monetary and exchange rate policy is determined at the federal level and where price flexibility and labour mobility are insufficient to sustain full employment equilibrium, leaves fiscal policy as the primary stabilising instrument (Kenen, 1969 and 1995: 81; Lamfalussy, 1989; Sala-i-Martin and Sachs, 1992: 198; Masson, 1996: 1002). Critics of the stabilising potential of fiscal policy argue that automatic stabilisers are counter-productive since they reduce the strength of price flexibility and labour mobility (Goodhart and Smith, 1993: 441; van der Ploeg, 1993: 144). A non-accommodative monetary and fiscal stance is claimed to reduce the time lag involved in adjusting to a new equilibrium position as individual economic actors internalise more of the costs of their actions, whilst the operation of EMU may reduce persistent rigidities (Majocchi and Rey, 1993). Furthermore, it is suggested that international policy co-ordination may undermine central bank credibility and cause an unanticipated increase in inflation by weakening the disciplining effects of excessive monetary growth upon the exchange rate (van der Ploeg, 1993: 156). Finally, von Hagen (1993: 265) rejects what he terms the 'parallel unification proposition', namely that currency unification requires fiscal policy unification, although without examining the merits of a policy framework being developed between the extremes of either full fiscal autonomy or complete centralisation at the federal level. However, despite these criticisms, unless the discipline effect of EMU is powerful and immediate, the persistence of price and factor rigidities would appear to necessitate the use of fiscal policy as a stabilising instrument to reduce the incentive for any country to leave the EMU and as an, albeit imperfect, substitute for exchange rate flexibility.

The conclusion that fiscal policy may become the principal instrument to counteract asymmetric external shocks, and therein prevent the destabilisation of EMU, raises the issue of whether it should be deployed at national or federal level. The adoption of the decentralisation theorem or 'layer-cake' concept, whereby functions are performed by the lowest efficient layer of government, accords with the EU's professed belief in subsidiarity and would indicate an initial preference for national fiscal autonomy within EMU (Wheare, 1963; Oates, 1972: 35; Weber, 1991; Bayoumi and Masson, 1995: 268). However, the design and impact of EMU upon member states significantly weakens this conclusion for a number of reasons. Primarily, the constraints imposed by the SGP, necessitating participating member states to maintain budget deficits below and 'excessive' 3 per cent of GDP and government debt below 60 per cent of GDP. This significantly restricts the pursuit of counter-cyclical fiscal policy at the national level (EU Commission, 1992; Holland, 1995; Burkitt *et al.*, 1996 and 1997: 3–6; UNCTAD, 1996; EU Commission, 1997: 12).

Autonomous fiscal policy is further undermined by the operation of the Single Market and the loss of tax revenue for certain member states caused by EMU. The requirement for the abolition of exchange controls, contained within the single market legislation, not only contributed to the currency instability during 1992–3, but also was intended to enhance financial market integration within the EU. However, such integration reduces the ability of member states to borrow cheaply to enable debt-financed fiscal expansion (Courchene, 1993: 152). The potential reduction in fiscal flexibility is compounded for those member states that currently depend upon seigniorage for a significant proportion of their total tax revenue. This relates to the circumstances where the purchasing power of government securities is eroded by inflation, thus providing an inexpensive method to finance public expenditure by, in effect, borrowing at very low real rates of interest. A stable EMU would require a convergence in national inflation rates and, assuming that the European Central Bank achieved the low inflation target established in its founding chapter, seigniorage would be limited to an estimated 0.4 per cent of GDP for all participants. This is particularly significant for Portugal as seigniorage revenues totalled 3.6 per cent of its GDP in 1990, together with Greece (2.3 per cent), Spain (1.9 per cent) and

Italy (1.3 per cent) (Dornbusch, 1988: 26; Emerson *et al.*, 1990; Eichengreen, 1993: 1335–6; Spahn, 1993: 577). Uncorrected, the fiscal drain experienced by certain member states has the potential of triggering fiscal retrenchment independently of the additional requirements imposed by the TEU convergence criteria (Masson, 1996).

The restrictions placed upon national fiscal policy during the transition to, and the subsequent operation of, EMU may, therefore, necessitate the enlargement of federal fiscal expenditure to ensure the stability of the European economy. This conclusion is reinforced by three further considerations. Firstly, governments are constrained from undertaking an optimal level of counter-cyclical stabilisation due to the existence of regional-spillovers or externalities, whereby non-residents derive some benefit from the policy whilst residents must bear the full cost through higher debt or taxation. Factor mobility may also constrain governments from incurring high levels of debt since the risk of higher future taxes may encourage factor relocation to other regions, thus reducing the tax base and providing short-term stability at the price of long-term instability. To the extent that this prisoner's dilemma constrains government fiscal flexibility, the solution requires a co-ordinated stabilisation strategy solution typical of non-co-operative game settings, necessitating either horizontal co-operation amongst member states or centralisation under a federal authority (Musgrave and Musgrave, 1973; Goodhart and Hansen, 1990; Rompuy *et al.*, 1993: 112–3; Masson, 1996).

Secondly, assuming that adverse shocks occur randomly, an inter-regional public insurance scheme can redistribute income from 'favourably shocked' to 'adversely shocked' regions to prevent an 'unlucky' area bearing a disproportionate financial burden. Moral hazard is minimised by ensuring that no incentives exist that encourage potential beneficiaries to manipulate the scheme to their advantage and in so doing to discourage participation from other regions (Wyplotz, 1993: 181; Sala-i-Martin and Sachs, 1992: 198; Courchene, 1993: 134–5; Goodhart and Smith, 1993: 424–5).

Finally, the need to strengthen the cohesion of EMU through redistribution of resources to weaker regions, which reinforces political and social solidarity throughout all participating member states, may entail a significantly enhanced role for federal financial authority. Whilst a detailed discussion of this issue is beyond the bounds of this chapter, it is nevertheless the case that all mature monetary unions exhibit a significant degree of redistribution between wealthy and poorer regions (Bayoumi and Masson, 1995).

Necessary level of stabilisation

The experience of existing federations confirms the necessity for a federal system of fiscal transfers between regions to promote stabilisation and redistribution across the EMU zone. A number of studies have evaluated the ability of fiscal federalism to partially offset the effect of a destabilising external shock, together with its ability to undertake long-term intra-regional redistribution to effect structural regeneration in weaker areas (see Table 9.1). The path-breaking study conducted by Sala-i-Martin and Sachs (1992) claimed that US federal fiscal policy offset approximately 40 per cent of an initial $1 decline in average Gross Regional Product (GRP). However, this was challenged due to its failure to differentiate between the cyclical and structural effects of fiscal policy. Von Hagen (1992) argued that the stabilisation effect of US federal fiscal policy was a mere 10 per cent, whilst Goodhart and Smith (1993) found 14 per cent of an initial reduction in GRP offset by a combination of fiscal transfers and federal taxes. These later studies were criticised, in turn, for underestimating the degree of stabilisation by narrowly focusing upon federal income taxes thereby neglecting other federal taxes. The importance of this omission is clear from the simulation undertaken by Pisani-Ferry *et al.* (1993) where non-income federal taxation generated a greater stabilising influence than income taxation, leading to a 17.1 per cent stabilisation effect for the USA, whilst Bayoumi and Masson (1995) found 30.2 per cent fiscal stabilisation using a similar methodology. The conflicting results produced by these studies impair the formation of a consensus concerning the scale of fiscal federalism necessary to stabilise an EMU. However, the weight of evidence suggests that US fiscal policy produces a stabilising effect between 17 per cent and 30 per cent of an initial external shock.

The generality of the conclusions reached by the literature requires a comparison of the US results with those from additional federations. Accordingly, both Goodhart and Smith (1993) and Bayoumi and Masson (1995) reproduced their analysis using Canadian data and found a significantly larger stabilising effect, calculated at 24 per cent and 17.4 per cent respectively. Furthermore, Pisani-Ferry *et al.* (1993) calculated that Germany achieved 42 per cent stabilisation through the interaction of taxation policy and fiscal transfers. These estimates are largely consistent with the range of results from the USA, although the apparently more pronounced counter-cyclical effectiveness of European fiscal policy cannot be relied upon on the basis of only one study. Further research is therefore necessary to produce more reliable estimates on which an EFTS may rely, whilst additionally ascertaining whether predominantly North American evidence can legitimately be applied to the EU.

Fiscal federalism appears to perform a necessary stabilising function through the counter-cyclical impact of taxation and fiscal transfers, moderating between 17 per cent and 30 per cent of an initial shock for North American federations. It is a reasonable hypothesis to assume that a European EMU federation might prefer a degree of stabilisation at the higher end of this range, as a result of its historically more vigorous pursuit of social solidarity demonstrated through their higher welfare expenditure. This assumption confers with Bayoumi and Masson's (1995) estimate that the average *national* fiscal policy stabilisation across five EU member states[4] currently averages 31 per cent. This level of stabilisation is unlikely to be maintained within EMU, for reasons expounded in the previous section of this chapter, so that fiscal federalism could supplant national initiatives to prevent growing instability. The long-term level of stabilisation required by the EU nations will depend upon whether all member states participate within EMU, in which case diversity will be greater than that found by Bayoumi and Masson (1995), whilst fiscal stabilisation must be correspondingly higher.

---

4   The five countries in question were Germany, France, UK, Netherlands and Belgium.

Table 9.1   Summary of the principal studies estimating the stabilisation and redistribution effect of fiscal transfers and taxation

STUDY	Sala-i-Martin and Sachs (1992)	Von Hagen (1992)	Goodhart and Smith (1993)		Pisani-Ferry *et al.* (1993)	
Country studied	USA, 1970–88	USA, 1981–86	USA, 1981–86	Canada, 1965–88	USA, 1989 data	Germany, 1987 data
Stabilisation / redistribution	No distinction	Stabilisation	Stabilisation	Stabilisation	Stabilisation	Stabilisation
DETAILS	9 regions, all federal taxes	51 states, focused exclusively on the tax side, restricted to federal income taxes	44 states, restricted to federal income taxes	11 provinces, all federal taxes	Simulation	Simulation
Tax	34 (range 22–37)	8	13	15	7.3	8.2
Social insurance						12.5
Transfers	6 (range 1–8)	2	1	9	1.1	0.3
Grants						8.5
TOTAL	40 (range 35–44)	10	14	24	17.1	42.0

Table 9.1   Continued

STUDY	Bayoumi and Masson (1995)				
Country studied	USA, 1969–86		Canada, 1965–88		5 EU countries, 1972–89*
Stabilisation / redistribution	Stabilisation	Redistribution	Stabilisation	Redistribution	Stabilisation
DETAILS	8 regions	8 regions	10 provinces	10 provinces	
Tax	7.3	6.6	3.4	2.4	10
Social insurance	1.3	1.1			
Transfers	14.4	9.9	10.9	15.2	21
Grants	7.2	0.4	3.1	21.6	
TOTAL	30.2	22	17.4	39.0	31

*The five countries in question were Germany, France, UK, Netherlands and Belgium.
Note: Figures denote the fiscal offset (in cents) originating from an initial $1 decline in gross regional product.

The current EU budget, standing at approximately €90.5 billion, equivalent to only 1.24 per cent of EU GDP, is too small to exert a significant stabilising effect upon EMU regions in the advent of an asymmetric external shock (EC Commission, 2004b). Moreover, the structural funds comprise only 36.9 per cent of the 2004 EU budget, with the Common Agricultural Policy support for farmers and rural areas accounting for marginally under half of total central expenditure (EU Commission, 2004a). Indeed, the present budget size limits the EU's ability to enhance member state stabilisation to an estimated paltry 3 per cent, which is clearly inadequate in relation to the stabilisation achieved by mature federations (Eichengreen, 1994: 186; Bayoumi and Masson, 1995: 266). Therefore, a plausible case exists for the enlargement of federal fiscal capability. The question concerns whether this occurs as part of the existing EU budget, thereby facilitating discretionary fiscal policy, or whether a system of automatic stabilisers should be established.

Discretionary or Automatic Stabilisers

The EU Commission's MacDougall Report most notably advanced discretionary fiscal federalism. It suggested that asymmetric shocks could be countered by counter-cyclical grants made to regional or local governments, triggered by regional unemployment or GDP trend indicators, supplemented with an EU unemployment fund which would provide a direct fiscal injection into areas experiencing above average unemployment (MacDougall, 1977).

The latter could be partly financed through individual contributions, although this would require unanimity across all member states concerning the absolute or proportionate payments made by taxpayers and companies to the fund, as well as the level of benefits received by individuals. German reunification experience suggests that such a scheme might increase demands for wage and benefit equalisation throughout the EMU zone, as differentials become more visible irrespective of productivity differences, with resultant negative economic consequences. However, the transfer of certain social insurance programmes to the federal level receives wide support within the literature (Masson and Melitz, 1990; van der Ploeg, 1991; Wyplotz, 1991; Eichengreen, 1992; MacDougall, 1992). The MacDougall Report further advocated the expansion of redistributional transfers to reduce inter-regional differences in capital endowment and productivity.

Discretionary fiscal policy is criticised on two principal grounds. First, the *time inconsistency* problem is essentially a problem of imperfect information, and therefore the more that economic actors can understand about the underlying health of the economy and the motivation of the policymakers, the lower their degree of uncertainty and suspicion that governments seek to manipulate policy for short term advantage. This concept was based upon the work by Lucas (1976), who argued that private sector economic agents understand the intentions of policymakers and therefore changes in policy will lead to changes in private sector behaviour. This increases the difficulty in designing optimal policy on the basis of past experience since the introduction of the new policy innovation would be likely to cause changes in patterns of behaviour.

Lucas' work was subsequently further developed by Kydland and Prescott (1977), whose main concern was that government might try to use their information advantage over other economic actors to try to reduce unemployment through demand stimulation even though they privately knew that this would be unable to achieve its goal without allowing inflation to increase over the expected rate. According to the assumption of a supply-determined equilibrium rate of unemployment (i.e. the natural rate), reflation could only be successful if economic actors mistook a rise in nominal wages for a rise in real wages and therefore actively seek employment; in other words, if economic actors formed adaptive expectations through review of past history and could therefore be surprised for a transitory period of time by unanticipated government action. However, the assumption of rational expectations ensures that wage setters would anticipate that government might undertake such behaviour and therefore economic actors would incorporate the expected higher rate of inflation into their nominal wage demands. Thus, monetary surprise would not occur and employment would remain static at a higher rate of inflation. Hence, policy activism is ineffective.

One solution to this problem could involve the precommitment of the economic authorities to state publicly that they would not attempt to 'surprise' other economic actors with such behaviour. However, Barro and Gordon (1983) argued that this might be difficult to achieve in reality because of the incentive for policy makers to renege on this policy stance in order to mislead economic actors and thereby engineer an increase in employment. Thus, a rule that can be changed relatively easily by government economic authority lacks credibility and therefore fails to solve the time inconsistent problem. It is therefore important for the government to build its reputation and gain credibility in this regard if it lays considerable emphasis upon its policy rules, or alternatively government could establish an economic agency with policy independence, but designated to pursue the policy rules.

A second criticism, however, concerns the existence of time lags inherent within the budgetary and fiscal policy implementation programmes, which result in the mistiming of fiscal boosts and reductions, thereby exacerbating business cycles rather than counteracting their fluctuations (Friedman, 1953; Baumol, 1961; Fisher and Cooper, 1973). This may be caused by informational time lags, given its is costly and requires time to collect and analyse prior to basing policy decisions upon contemporary economic reality. Alternatively, time lags may be caused by institutional operations, since governments typically have only one (or perhaps two) budgets per year, at set times in the calendar, and it is likely that these events will not correspond exactly to the needs of the economy. Parliamentary scrutiny of the proposals and debate leading to eventual approval (or rejection and subsequent renegotiation of budgetary measures) leads to a further time lag. Finally, once approved, implementation may involve an additional time lag, referring to the time duration for fiscal policy to impact upon aggregate demand. As a result, time lags inherent within the policy determination and implementation process may be sufficiently long that fiscal policy becomes pro-cyclical rather than counter-cyclical.

Automatic stabilisers eliminate the implementation lag experienced in democratic countries, where major fiscal decisions are typically presented in an annual budge. Therefore, they reduce the probability of any destabilising impact. Goodhart and Smith (1993: 432) further claim that the transparency of automatic stabilisers enables economic actors to internalise their effects when forming expectations. The conclusion reached, according to this approach, is that fiscal policy should, therefore, be largely passive in nature and be left to automatic stabilisers, operating alongside budgets balanced over the business cycle (Arestis and Sawyer, 2004: 119).

An example of a semi-automatic fiscal policy instrument, designed specifically to stabilise EMU from the impact of external asymmetric shocks, relates to what has become known as a European Federal Transfer Scheme (EFTS). This has the potential to ensure an equitable distribution of the gains and losses resulting from the impact of external shocks to the Euro-zone economy, whilst conforming to the subsidiarity principal because stabilising transfers are determined at the federal level but implemented locally (van der Ploeg, 1993: 144).[5] Moreover, if borrowing were permitted to promote counter-cyclical stabilisation, whilst ensuring that the budget is balanced over the economic cycle, the EFTS would avoid inter-temporal debt redistribution (van der Ploeg, 1993: 144). Careful design can generate an EFTS that is a more efficient stabiliser than existing tax and transfer systems that were developed to fulfil alternative objectives.

One proposal made by Italianer and Vanheukelen (1993) aims to achieve a similar degree of stabilisation as the fiscal federalism of the USA for an average annual cost of ECU 11.2 billion, which is the equivalent of only 0.23 per cent of EU GDP (Italianer and Vanheukelen, 1993: 500). A more recent EFTS proposal places the average annual cost at between 0.17 per cent and 0.86 per cent of EU GDP for securing an 18 per cent stabilisation of an initial shock within an EMU consisting of all current member states, whereas a more substantial 40 per cent stabilisation target would cost between 0.38 and 1.9 per cent of EU GDP per annum (Whyman, 1997).[6] Thus, both studies conclude that a similar degree of stabilisation may be achieved at a fraction of the central budget increases advocated by MacDougall, due to the greater efficiency of a stabilisation system designed solely to perform that function. The efficiency associated with conscious design, rather than a by-product of a fiscal system intended to pursue other priorities is not, however, restricted to automatic stabilisers. Indeed, Costello (1993: 274–7) noted that the EU structural

---

5   One criticism of a federal, rule-based system is that it may insufficiently reflect the heterogeneous preferences of voters regarding a unemployment/inflation trade-off. Many economists dispute the existence of a long-term trade-off between unemployment and inflation, nevertheless the existence of a potential conflict between policy goals is accepted by the author, at least in the short-term. It is at this point that democratically expressed preferences may diverge between individual member states in such a way as to disadvantage countries more actively pursuing full employment.

6   Precise estimates depend upon assumptions concerning the elasticity of output loss associated with higher unemployment.

funds achieved a slightly greater proportionate redistributive impact than the much larger German fiscal transfers.[7]

Distributional Effects of Federal Fiscal Policy Alternatives

Evaluation of discretionary and automatic federal fiscal policy measures depends upon their ability to stabilise EMU combined with their distributional impact upon the individual member states. The MacDougall Report recommended that the second element would require a federal budget equivalent to 5 per cent of EU GDP. For a twelve nation Euro-zone, this budget would be equivalent to €380 billion, whereas for a twenty-five nation union, a budget representing 5 per cent of total GDP would increase to €510 billion (EC Commission, 2004a).

In order to try and indicate the distributional consequences for EU member states arising from MacDougall's proposal, Table 9.2 highlights the considerable resource transfers involved were this recommendation to be achieved without the transfer of whole areas of national responsibility to the federal sphere. Bearing in mind that the latest available data concerning member state contributions to, and receipts from, the EU budget relate to 2003, the analysis is restricted to a fifteen member state union (EC Commission, 2004b). The estimates for EU contributions contained in the table are based upon the simplifying assumption that member state contributions are increased in line with present budget contributions. One immediate criticism that might be raised concerns the fact that contributions paid into the EU budget are complicated by the multiple sources of EU 'own resources' and therefore they do not relate as closely to the relative GDP levels of the individual nation states (EU Commission, 1998). A second alternative, therefore, might be to suggest that contributions made to the EU budget are exclusively based upon relative GDP levels, so that this form of 'taxation' is based upon the ability of a member state to pay. Nevertheless, this alternative is not adopted here in order to simplify the essence of the distributional consequences arising from the payments side of the increase in fiscal expenditure.

The estimated expenditure arising from the enlarged EU budget, and therefore benefiting individual member states, is based upon two simplifying options; firstly, that the additional resources are allocated in the same proportion as current EU expenditure or, secondly, structural funds are allocated the entire increase, which is subsequently transferred in the same proportion as existing structural fund payments to recipients. Clearly, neither option is defensible in and of itself, because a straightforward expansion of current EU spending priorities would expand CAP expenditure by the same factor as all other elements of payment; a consequence that would do little for stabilising EMU, would distort international trade (to the

---

7 Costello found that, in 1992, transfers equivalent to 6.24 per cent of German GDP achieved a 5.2 per cent change in the Gini coefficient, whilst EU structural funds equivalent to 2.51 per cent of EU GDP achieved a 2.53 per cent change in the Gini measurement. Thus, the EU structural funds were slightly relatively more efficient, although their absolute redistribution was only half of that Germany achieved due to the considerably smaller fiscal transfers involved.

detriment of poorer nations) and would encourage a decline in productivity through enticing people to move back into low productive agricultural employment across the EU. Similarly, allocating the entire increase in fiscal expenditure to structural funds, given their current priorities for expenditure, would vastly expand redistribution of resources across the eurozone from rich to poorer nations. However, whilst this is likely to be preferable in terms of stabilising the union against the consequences of asymmetric shocks, when poorer nations are likely to be economically weaker at any given point, the scale of the transfers may simply be too great and create perverse incentives towards dependence upon internal 'aid' and/or stimulate the potential for corruption of state officials. Therefore, it is probable that the precise method of calculating contributions and transfers would be based upon different criteria to those outlined in this section. Nevertheless, the assumptions made do at least enable a comparison to be made between those nations that would greatly benefit from this reform and those that would bear the brunt of the cost. It has the additional advantage of projecting the distributional impact based upon current policy choices, which may have the effect of stimulating a reassessment of how budget contributions and transfers are presently determined.

Table 9.2 illustrates the distributional impact upon the EU(15) nations had the expansion of the EU budget to 5 per cent of total EU GDP occurred in 2003. Under the assumption that EU expenditure increased in line with current priorities, it is not surprising that the existing differences between member states remain, although they are magnified by a little over four times due to the larger tax and revenue streams. Therefore, Germany, the UK and the Netherlands remain the largest contributors to the EU budget, providing 77.2 per cent of total tax payments, whereas Greece, Spain and Portugal benefit from 83.4 per cent of total EU expenditure. Germany, alone, would be expected to raise its net contribution from €8.6 billion to €34.5 billion, and increase of €25.9 billion, or 1.2 per cent of the German national GDP. This additional burden would add approximately 0.6 per cent to the German budget deficit, thereby worsening their breach of the SGP rules. In contrast, Ireland would receive net transfers equivalent to 8.1 per cent of its GDP, Spain 10.4 per cent and Portugal 13.6 per cent. This degree of redistribution is not warranted by the recent economic record of either Ireland or Portugal, with the former, in particular, having enjoyed a dramatic record in terms of economic growth in recent years, but which benefits from disproportionate agricultural expenditure and structural programmes initiated when Ireland remained a relatively impoverished nation.

This issue is magnified if the additional fiscal expenditure is entirely channelled through the existing structural funds, in proportion to existing spending priorities, as this skews the figures further to the benefit of the poorer nations. Thus, Ireland would receive a net benefit from the enlarged EU budget of €16.4 billion, equivalent to fully 10 per cent of Irish GDP, whereas the corresponding values for Spain and Portugal would be €77.1 billion (9.7 per cent Spanish GDP) and €30.1 billion (29.2 per cent Portuguese GDP), respectively. The consequences for other EU member states is not, however, so clear cut, as Germany would actually have a slightly lower burden under this alternative system, whilst French contributions would exceed the German value, whilst Belgium shifts from a moderate net recipient to a large contributor under the structural-based scheme. Nevertheless, its remains the case that Greece, Portugal and Spain would receive 93.6 per cent of total net expenditure under the stabilisation scheme, thereby further concentrating payments upon the relatively poorer nations, whilst Germany, the Netherlands and the UK would have a slightly less onerous burden of taxation under this alternative system, as they would be expected to contribute only around half of total EU taxation. The relative importance of the expansion of the structural funds is illustrated in terms of the proportion of national GDP that net payments and receipts represent for individual member states. Therefore, as a consequence, it is of little surprise that ten of the fifteen nations would prefer the distributional consequences derived from simply scaling taxation and expenditure up according to the current EU budget, than enhancing redistributive expenditure, however targeted.

This exercise raises a number of potential problems with a straightforward expansion of federal fiscal policy, of the magnitude recommended by MacDougall. Firstly, an expansion of discretionary expenditure of this magnitude would impact significantly upon national budget composition and spending limits. It would seem difficult to graft fiscal federalism upon the existing policy and institutional foundations developed to support EMU. Indeed, there would be a particular clash between the motivations and policy consequences of fiscal federalism and the SGP.

Secondly, increased payments to the poorer EU nations will only achieve greater stabilisation to the extent that the economically weaker countries are more likely to diverge as the result of asymmetric external shocks. As the recent experience of Ireland has amply indicated, the two elements are not always connected. It is possible that this problem would be at least partially solved by the introduction of ten new member states, which would dramatically alter the balance of structural fund expenditure, leading to the new member states absorbing most of this additional expenditure in place of the formerly poorest EU member states. It might be anticipated that the new member states may find greater difficulty maintaining their competitiveness within EMU, whenever they are permitted full membership.

Finally, accommodating such an increase in payments to the EU would require a substantial rise in taxation, real reductions in public provision and/or the transfer of significant areas of present national determination to the EU. It is unlikely that member states would welcome a substantial increase in the burden of taxation, and moreover the split between nations preferring the distributional consequences arising from the two methodologies relating to taxation and expenditure, as devised in this chapter, might prevent its enactment. It is unlikely that the German Chancellor would accept a substantial increase in budgetary expenditure to transfer to poorer EU member states at a time when it is committed to substantial annual transfers to former East Germany to reconstruct its economy and suffers from five million unemployed. Similarly, it is most unlikely that a request for a four or six-fold increase in net UK contributions to the EU budget would do anything more than harden the opposition to continued EU membership amongst a considerable proportion of the British population.

Another option might be to enact a transfer of responsibility for one or more areas, currently determined on a national basis, to the enlarged federal budget. One possibility could be defence, which is often portrayed as the next stage of political integration. Another could refer to the creation of EU-wide social security transfers such as unemployment benefits, although complicating factors here would include the level set for such benefits, and whether these would damage the competitive edge of poorer member states.

Table 9.2   **Estimated additional contributions to the EU budget to sustain EMU, 2003**

	TAX (existing payments into EU budget)	EXPEND (existing receipts from EU budget)	NET (balance of receipts minus tax)	NET (as per cent of national GDP)	NET (per cent of budget (TAX or EXPEND)
	(ecu bn)	(ecu bn)	Negative figure represents net TAX, positive net EXPEND (ecu bn)	Negative figure represents net TAX, positive net EXPEND	Negative per cent represents net TAX, positive net EXPEND
Austria	1.9	1.6	-0.3	-0.2 per cent	-1.8 per cent
Belgium	3.5	4.2	+0.7	+0.2 per cent	+4.0 per cent
Denmark	1.8	1.5	-0.3	-0.1 per cent	-1.4 per cent
Finland	1.3	1.3	+0.0	+0.0 per cent	+0.0 per cent
France	15.2	13.4	-1.7	-0.1 per cent	-8.7 per cent
Germany	19.2	10.6	-8.6	-0.4 per cent	-43.4 per cent
Greece	1.5	4.9	+3.3	+2.0 per cent	+18.0 per cent
Ireland	1.1	2.7	+1.6	+1.0 per cent	+8.5 per cent
Italy	11.8	10.7	-1.1	-0.1 per cent	-5.5 per cent
Luxembourg	0.2	1.1	+0.9	+3.4 per cent	+4.7 per cent
Netherlands	4.9	2.0	-2.9	-0.6 per cent	-14.8 per cent
Portugal	1.3	4.8	+3.5	+2.6 per cent	+18.9 per cent
Spain	7.4	15.9	+8.5	+1.0 per cent	+45.9 per cent
Sweden	2.5	1.5	-1.0	-0.4 per cent	-5.3 per cent
UK	10.0	6.2	-3.8	-0.2 per cent	-19.0 per cent

Table 9.2   Continued

	NET Position Expand EU budget to 5 per cent EU GDP	NET (as per cent of national GDP)	NET Position Expand EU budget to 5 per cent EU GDP	NET (as per cent of national GDP)	Preference for CURRENT contribution or the expansion of STRUCTURAL funds
	EXPEND and TAX both based upon current contribution proportion (ecu bn)	Negative figure represents net TAX, positive net EXPEND	All additional EXPEND financing structural funds TAX based on current contribution performance (ecu bn)	Negative figure represents net TAX, positive net EXPEND	
Austria	-1.4	-0.6 per cent	-4.2	-1.8 per cent	Current
Belgium	+3.0	+1.0 per cent	-12.6	-4.5 per cent	Current
Denmark	-1.1	-0.6 per cent	-5.9	-3.0 per cent	Current
Finland	+0.0	+0.0 per cent	-1.5	-1.0 per cent	Current
France	-7.0	-0.4 per cent	-37.7	-2.3 per cent	Current
Germany	-34.5	-1.6 per cent	-32.5	-1.5 per cent	Structural
Greece	+13.4	+8.1 per cent	+16.4	+10.0 per cent	Structural
Ireland	+6.3	+4.3 per cent	2.6	+1.8 per cent	Current
Italy	-4.4	-0.3 per cent	6.4	+0.5 per cent	Structural
Luxembourg	+3.5	+13.6 per cent	-0.8	-3.0 per cent	Current
Netherlands	-11.8	-2.5 per cent	-17.2	-3.7 per cent	Current
Portugal	+14.0	+10.4 per cent	+39.1	+29.2 per cent	Structural
Spain	+34.1	+4.3 per cent	+77.1	+9.7 per cent	Structural
Sweden	-4.2	-1.5 per cent	-5.4	-1.9 per cent	Current
UK	-15.1	-0.9 per cent	-23.7	-1.4 per cent	Current

Sources: EU Commission, 2004a, and 2004b

The alternative to a large increase in discretionary federal expenditure would be the establishment of a semi-automatic stabiliser which would target transfers at those economies which suffered relatively severely from external shocks, as reflected in changes of either unemployment or GDP relative to the EU average. Had such a scheme existed between 1982 and 1996, Whyman (1997a) calculated that average annual transfers would have ranged from only 0.17 per cent to 1.9 per cent of EU GDP, depending upon the selected stabilisation target and the estimate of the relationship between unemployment and lost output adopted. The surprisingly modest cost of the scheme results from the fact that it was explicitly designed to stabilise EMU participants in the aftermath of an external shock, rather than stabilisation being a by-product of a tax and transfer system primarily intended to achieve different goals. However, the degree of stabilisation achieved is significant, especially since the two main recipients, Spain and Italy, receive 72.4 per cent of total warranted transfers, accounting for between 1.3–7.1 per cent and 0.6–3.2 per cent of relevant national GDP accordingly. Average annual transfers on this scale would impact heavily upon the member states concerned. Moreover, transfers worth approximately 0.26 per cent of EU GDP were concentrated around the 1983–1984 and 1992–1994 trough periods of the business cycle, with only 0.004 per cent during the 1990–1991 high point, thereby reflecting the pronounced counter-cyclical nature of the scheme.

The distributional consequences of the stabilisation scheme are illustrated in Tables 9.3 and 9.4. Table 9.3 assumes that it is financed according to GDP-based contributions, whilst Table 9.4 calculates payments to the scheme according to those member states with unemployment below the national average. It is apparent that a GDP based system spreads the burden of financing the system more evenly than a 'stabilising' tax system, with the largest contributors having their payments proportionally reduced. However, Spain, Ireland and Italy benefit most from the 'stabilisation' method of payment since they contribute nothing, whilst French payments are reduced by 90 per cent.

One practical problem that a stabilisation scheme of this type might encounter, as illustrated by Whyman (1997a), is that more member states may be required to contribute than the number of recipients. This means that there will be a ready majority of votes in the Council of Ministers to prevent the expansion of the federal EU budget (Burkitt *et al.*, 1996: 17–20). This issue is particularly acute at a time when the SGP constrains national fiscal expenditure, and national governments will hardly wish to cede a larger proportion of the tax revenues they are committed to raising from their citizens to federal rather than national priorities. Moreover, the additional cost of such a scheme, established at a time when 18 million EU citizens are unemployed and draining public expenditure in the majority of member states, will prove politically problematic.

Table 9.3   **Average net warranted contributions made to, and payments received from the stabilisation scheme, assuming the 'neutral' (EU-based) form of taxation (1982–1996)**

	1996 EU budget contributions	Net payments received from (+) or contributions made (-) to stabilisation scheme, depending upon estimate of elasticity (ecu million)					
	(ecu million)a	elasticity = 1.5		elasticity = 2.25		elasticity = 5	
Stabilisation target (%)		18 %	30 %	18 %	30 %	18 %	30 %
Belgium	3107	-143	-239	-217	-361	-477	-795
Denmark	1564	-236	-394	-359	-592	-788	-1305
Germany	24421	-3646	-6077	-5318	-9182	-12153	-20255
Spain	5188	4237	7063	6435	10672	14125	23541
France	14338	-1084	-1808	-1647	-2731	-3615	-6025
Ireland	768	371	618	563	934	1236	2059
Italy	9869	2924	4874	4441	7365	9748	16247
Luxembourg	183	-25	-43	-38	-64	-84	-141
Netherlands	4729	-296	-494	-450	-746	-987	-1646
Austria	2349	-354	-591	-538	-893	-1181	-1969
Portugal	1212	-145	-241	-219	-364	-482	-803
Finland	1239	73	122	111	184	244	406
Sweden	2340	-465	-775	-706	-1171	-1550	-2584
UK	8816	-1034	-1722	-1569	-2603	-3445	-5741

Source: a = EU Commission 1996

A further complicating factor inherent in the attempted implementation of a budget-based fiscal federalism scheme concerns the on-going conflict within the EU around the British budgetary rebate, which was originally awarded due to the fact that a combination of high VAT and excise receipts, and relatively low levels of inward flows of resources from communal (particularly CAP) budget expenditure. This is particularly significant because Britain's GDP has risen relative to the EU average, whilst other member states – notably Germany, the Netherlands, Austria and Sweden – have begun to identify their own budgetary imbalances as a significant factor involved in their opposition to further expansion of the EU budget (EU Commission, 1998).

Table 9.4   Average net warranted contributions made to, and payments received from the stabilisation scheme, assuming the 'stabilisation' form of taxation (1982–1996)

	1996 EU budget contributions	Net payments received from (+) or contributions made (–) to stabilisation scheme, depending upon estimate of elasticity (ecu million)					
	(ecu million)	elasticity = 1.5		elasticity = 2.25		elasticity = 5	
stabilisation target (%)		18 %	30 %	18 %	30 %	18 %	30 %
Belgium	3107	115	192	175	290	384	640
Denmark	1564	-15	-24	-22	-33	-49	-73
Germany	24421	-8586	-14310	-13038	-21624	-28620	-47700
Spain	5188	5301	8836	8050	13351	17671	29451
France	14338	1231	2051	1869	3099	4102	6837
Ireland	768	486	810	738	1225	1621	2701
Italy	9869	5265	8775	7995	13260	17550	29250
Luxembourg	183	-202	-337	-307	-510	-675	-1125
Netherlands	4729	−60	-100	-91	-151	-200	-333
Austria	2349	-1803	-3005	-2738	-4541	-6011	-10018
Portugal	1212	-516	-860	-784	-1300	-1721	-2868
Finland	1239	-49	-81	-74	-122	-161	-269
Sweden	2340	-1728	-2880	-2624	-4352	-5760	-9600
UK	8816	561	935	852	1413	1870	3116

Conclusion

The sustainability of EMU in the medium- and long-term will partly depend upon the implementation of a fiscal policy initiative, located at the federal rather than national level, which is sufficiently well resourced and targeted to stabilise member state economies in the face of asymmetric external shocks. Failure to do so leaves monetary union fatally exposed to asymmetric external shocks and divergent economic forces. In the absence of exchange rate or monetary autonomy, and with insufficient labour mobility and wage flexibility, individual regions may become characterised by persistent unemployment, low per capita income and ensuing social tension, coexisting in the EMU zone with neighbours enjoying full employment, high growth and greater prosperity. The cost, in terms of lost output and avoidable human misery, is compounded by the probability of countries withdrawing from EMU should such inequalities continue over a long period. The reluctance of many economists and policy-makers to address this problem is therefore of particular concern.

This chapter suggests that the development of a discretionary or semi-automatic stabilisation mechanism is both feasible and essential for EMU to succeed. However, this will involve significant claims upon the productive resources of the majority of EU member states and generate difficult budgetary considerations for national governments. In this respect the greater targeting embraced by the EFTS may possess an advantage over the expansion of discretionary fiscal policy of the magnitude advocated by MacDougall. Nevertheless, average annual German contributions to a similar stabilisation scheme, had one been in operation between 1982 and 1996, may still have been as high as 2.8 per cent of GDP and 5.5 per cent of its national budget (Whyman, 1997b). A charge upon national finances close to this estimate would require consideration of compensating tax rises, public service reductions or the transfer of certain areas of public expenditure from national to federal level.

Conflicts of interest between member states likely to be net beneficiaries of a fiscal stabilisation mechanism, and those destined to be net contributors inevitably arise from any transfer scheme. However, such tensions must be overcome if member states are to create the social solidarity upon which a common currency and monetary policy ultimately depends. The maintenance of an economic union amongst diverse nations, which refuse to share its burdens as well as its benefits, is unlikely to succeed in the long-term. Consequently, the creation of a mechanism whereby those member states who are adversely affected by external shocks are compensated by their partners is likely to enhance feelings of solidarity as well as embodying efficient economic practice. Therefore, the architects of European integration need to analyse these arguments and turn their attention to the design of a stabilisation mechanism without delay.

Chapter 10

The European Social Model and EMU

Introduction

One of the more sophisticated arguments in support of participation in the process of Economic and Monetary Union (EMU), currently being established between the majority of European Union (EU) member states, concerns its facilitation of the development of a *Social Market* version of capitalism within the newly created Euroland. This position, typically held by those of a social democratic political viewpoint, suggests that the intensification of international competition associated with globalisation has undermined national government strategies aimed at decommodifying labour, regulating capital and ensuring a full employed economy consistent with egalitarian objectives. *Keynesianism in one country* is therefore increasingly viewed as obsolete and should be replaced by *supra-national Euro-Keynesianism*.

Pressures upon national social policy and industrial relations systems may additionally be resolved at European level due to the lower level of international penetration, whilst common levels of social support prevent strategies of social deconstruction to secure competitive advantage. Moreover, Euro-bargaining could provide one solution to the tensions created amongst national labour markets due to transnational corporations pursuing internally consistent labour strategies, whilst national competitiveness depends upon real wage moderation best secured through co-ordinated bargaining. The multiplicity of demands made upon labour market actors might be better resolved through their active participation in *social partnership*.

The social democratic vision of a social market Euroland, combining full employment though a variant of Euro-Keynesianism, an advanced common system of social protection and an inclusive form of industrial relations, certainly offers an alternative to neo-liberalism and minimal market regulation. Indeed, it has been memorably presented by the then President of the EU Commission, Jacques Delors, when thrilling the 1988 British TUC Congress with his vision of a 'social Europe', which embraced labour rights as core elements (Strange, 1997). However, whilst attractive in its own terms, this social democratic scenario is generally presented with little consideration of its plausibility and internal coherence. This chapter therefore seeks to provide an analysis of this position. In particular, it questions whether the creation and maintenance of a social market is consistent with the demands made upon individual economies by the form of EMU adopted by the EU member states in the TEU.

European Social Market

When most commentators refer to a *social market* type of capitalism, they almost inevitably refer to the post-war German system of interlocking relationships, which has combined a successful, competitive market economy with generous welfare provision and labour protection. Germany has attracted envious comparisons with other member states as the strongest European economy, but also because the rights available to German employees and citizens remain amongst the most extensive of any capitalist economy throughout history (Glasman, 1997). Consequently, it has been the achievements of the German approach, rather than the specific organisational blueprint itself that has appeared attractive to European social democrats. Nevertheless, it the main features of the social market model can be summarised under its specific contribution towards the macro-economy, social policy and industrial relations (see Figure 10.1).

Economy

The German social market approach has, at its essence, social institutions that mediate between state and market to safeguard the decommodification of labour and knowledge (Glasman, 1997: 136). Thus, the vocational training system produced skilled workers of sufficient quantity and quality, thereby rectifying the corporate tendency to under-invest in skill formation (Teague, 1997). Similarly, the relationship between banks and industry enables corporate managers to govern in the interests of stakeholders not simply shareholders. These social institutions are reinforced by the combination of co-ordinated wage bargaining, delivering labour market peace at an internationally competitive price, together with a suitable national macroeconomic policy.

   In the German system, the anti-inflation credibility of the Bundesbank is credited with maintaining the 'economic miracle' throughout the post-war period, by ensuring that social partners do not cause inflationary pressures that may undermine international competitiveness. However, it is quite possible that this particular institutional arrangement is over-emphasised, as it failed to prevent mass unemployment and recession in the 1980s and 1990s as effectively as it had succeeded against inflation. Indeed, the Bundesbank may have been partly responsible for an undue tightening of macroeconomic policy during this period, when a more balanced economic agency might have delivered a superior trade-off between inflation, unemployment and economic growth. Indeed, one of the attractions for social democrats in other countries is the possibility of re-introducing elements of Euro-Keynesianism as part of an economic strategy aimed at reducing the continent's stubbornly high levels of unemployment.

European Social Market

ECONOMY

- Competitive market economy, but where social institutions mediate between state and market

- Decommodification of labour and knowledge – facilitates investment in human capital

- Relationship between banking sector and industry produces long term relationship – encourages long term investment decision

- Co-ordination of wage formation – stable labour market at internationally competitive aggregate wage rates, prevents high quality producer being undercut by sweatshop employer

- Macroeconomic policy – Bundesbank – low inflationary credibility

- Euro-Keynesianism – full employment

- Social partnership between trade unions and employers – includes trade union recognition

SOCIAL WELFARE

- Individuals treated as citizens, with rights and responsibilities, not just factors of production

- Universal welfare state

- High transfer replacement ratio – enables participation of all citizens in society

- Socialisation of risk – increased efficiency of entire economy

- Redistribution of national income – narrows social and economic disadvantage

INDUSTRIAL RELATIONS

- Inclusion – 'voice' not 'exit' - Improved morale and lower employee turnover

- Social partnership – co-operation in adapting to change if through negotiation

- Dual-level industrial relations system enhances flexible adaptation at *micro* and *macro* levels - collective bargaining (distribution) and plant-level codetermination + works' councils (integrate employee interests into micro-level flexible adaptation)

- Stakeholder model – broader interests than shareholders - corporate decision making process

Figure 10.1   Features of a social market version of capitalism

One powerful argument supporting the development of a Euroland social market refers to the impact of globalisation of production and international freedom of movement of capital, which have combined to weaken the ability of national governments to pursue social democratic policies (Notermans, 2000). Indeed, Coates (1999) claimed, 'an increasingly integrated global economy will allow fewer and fewer spaces for social democratic models of capitalism'. According to this argument, full employment policies could only be re-created on a larger geographical basis, namely in the new Euroland. The fact that the 1997 Luxembourg summit committed the EU to place greater emphasis upon reducing the organisation's jobless figures is advanced as further evidence to support this position (Monks, 2000). Unfortunately, the persistence of mass unemployment across the continent indicates either the inadequacy of strategies proposed to reduce unemployment levels, or the lack of commitment demonstrated by governments, which prefer to enshrine price stability targets, but not equivalent levels of unemployment, in international treaties.

Social welfare

A distinctive feature of a social market, as opposed to a neo-liberal conception of a market economy, is the treatment of individuals as citizens rather than factors of production. This requires the development of a generous system of welfare provision, combining quality public services with high social transfer replacement ratio, to enable all citizens to participate fully within society. The socialisation of risk through the collective provision of social insurance frees employees to undertake greater risks if this increases efficiency and hence standards of living. Income redistribution narrows social and economic advantage based upon inheritance rather than merit. Decommodification empowers employees and enables the development of work relationships based upon trust and loyalty, rather than the market nexus; a difference increasingly important in the dynamic knowledge-based sectors of the economy.

Industrial relations

The emphasis upon the inclusion of workers and their unions in the working of the economy facilitates an expression of *voice* rather than *exit*. This, in turn, leads to co-operation in adapting to change, superior morale resulting in enhanced productivity and lower employee turnover, and finally the prevention of low-skill, low investment competitive alternatives stimulates productive investment and innovation (Streeck, 1992; Hutton, 1994; Coates, 1999: 654–5). Moreover, it provides the European social democratic labour movements with an alternative model to the neo-liberal prescription of market superiority to social institutions and the commodification of worker-citizens.

Co-ordinated sectoral wage bargaining, undertaken with national competitiveness in mind, facilitates industrial order and rational planning, taking the price of labour out of competition and providing favourable costs for all companies. Numerous studies have demonstrated that co-ordinated wage formation produces a superior macroeconomic flexibility in real wages and hence industrial adjustment to external shocks to the economy (McCallum, 1983; Bruno and Sachs, 1985; Calmfors and Driffill, 1988; Rowthorn and Glyn, 1990). However, the dual nature of German industrial relations provided for additional micro-flexibility as distributional issues were divorced from plant level codetermination, which enabled management to integrate employee interests and demands in corporate governance (Hassel, 1999). It is the combination of micro- and macro- forms of labour market flexibility that are necessitated by the external pressures provided by globalisation, introduction of lean production techniques, and EMU, requiring wages to rise no faster than in competitor nations.

Measures generating a type of Euro-corporatism are undoubtedly popular amongst those union officials frustrated with a decline in power and authority within many of the EU nation states (i.e. the UK), as it provides an alternative means of influence and rationale for continued membership of their organisations. Thus, recent moves to allow agreements between UNICE and ETUC to become law, in order to increase the flexibility of legislation, has created significant precedents in this direction. Furthermore, the EU Commission has provided generous material support to facilitate social partnership between trade unions and employer organisations, in order to promote their concept of European collective bargaining and develop this aspect of a European transnational civil society. This support has provided a significant proportion of the ETUC's budget, rising from 5–8 per cent of its total income in the early years of integration, to approximately 13 per cent as the single internal market programme was introduced (Knutsen, 1997). Moreover, this does not include indirect support through EU provision of free meeting venues and interpreters, the payment of travel expenses and provision of technical assistance for the ETUC as a means of facilitating consultative processes in which it has an interest (Abbott, 1997). The establishment of European Works Councils (EWCs) will have further increased this level of support (Knutsen, 1997: 300).

Is the Social Market Compatible with EMU?

The claim that a social market version of capitalism can be created on the foundations of an EMU established between EU member states depends upon two key assumptions. Firstly, that EMU is a net economic success, whose benefits in terms of lower prices and higher rates of economic growth outweigh the costs of transition. Secondly, it is assumed that the EU Commission will ultimately be prepared, or indeed able, to establish the fundamental principles of a social market within the newly created Euroland. Unfortunately for the proponents of this viewpoint, there is a considerable body of evidence to cast doubt upon both of these assumptions, thus necessitating the type of rigorous evaluation provided in this chapter to ascertain to what degree the assumptions may be reliable.

Economic impact of EMU

The net economic effect of EMU membership is understandably uncertain because it has no historical precedent (Goodhart, 1995). Supporters of the process claim that EMU will produce greater exchange rate stability, reduced transaction costs, enhanced competition deriving from price transparency, and low real interest rates, resulting from a successful anti-inflation strategy pursued by the independent ECB. If true, these factors would combine to provide a virtuous cycle of increased business confidence, trade, investment and growth. However, opponents of the process suggest that the loss of monetary and exchange rate autonomy will exacerbate economic instability amongst incompletely converged countries. The ECB will be incapable of moderating the resulting asymmetric shocks through the sole instrument of a common Euroland interest rate, whilst its attempts to gain anti-inflation credibility might lead to over-tightening monetary policy and resultant unemployment in a stagnant economy.

Deflation is an inevitable consequence of the implementation of the rigid targets established in the TEU to ascertain those member states capable of joining monetary union, and hence to provide a stable framework for the establishment of the single currency (EU Commission, 1992). The consequence of these rules has been to depress growth rates throughout the EU for a most of the last decade, thereby exacerbating already high levels of unemployment across the continent (Holland, 1995; UNCTAD, 1996).

The repercussions of budget restrictions included a series of strikes and demonstrations led by public sector workers across the continent, due, partly, to increasing pressure from governments to moderate pay and, secondly, as a result of recruitment crises. The EU's strongest economy, Germany, was forced to make public expenditure cuts of £30 billion (DM70 billion), representing its single largest fiscal entrenchment in post-war economic history (Strange, 1997: 13–14). Weaker economies, for example Italy and Portugal, negotiated corporatist social pacts with their union movements to legitimise reductions in pensions and restructure labour regulation (Teague, 1998). Unlike previous forms of corporatism, these agreements offered labour few benefits and indeed promised to *reduce* the social wage in order to meet the TEU convergence criteria. Nevertheless, many trade unions defended their agreements on the grounds that they are the best strategy to ensure that trade unions remain important economic and political institutions in a single currency Europe (Teague, 1998: 120).

The Stability and Growth Pact (SGP) ensures that fiscal restrictions are tightened for members of the monetary union, requiring maximum budget deficits of 3 per cent to be immediately reduced or the member state may face fines of 0.5 per cent of GDP per annum. Exceptions require national income to have declined by 0.75 per cent in a given year. Thus, in all but truly exceptional periods, budget balance variance of up to 10 per cent over a trade cycle implies that member states need surpluses approximating 7 per cent of GDP in boom periods to prevent violation of the 3 per cent limit when in recession. This would require even larger public sector cuts or tax increases to be implemented by virtually all EMU participants. Even if it is true that structural budgetary reforms are in any case necessary to reduce cyclical deficits, this does not imply that the convergence criteria has no real cost, because this process could have been pursued according to a more flexible timetable, with reductions occurring only when economies were growing steadily.

The argument that globalisation and the integration of world financial markets has made monetary *sovereignty* illusory, and therefore the forfeit of these instruments when joining EMU has no negative consequences, may be widely held but is quite simply inaccurate. It is certainly the case that a greater proportion of industrial production flows from trans-national corporations which resist devaluation to maintain common international prices to prevent price competition between identical subsidiaries. Moreover, if complete international integration of world financial markets were ever to occur, it would result in a single global interest rate, with the addition of a variable risk premium associated with the probability of default or devaluation. However, neither of these factors alters the fact that since sterling was ejected from the ERM, the British economy has operated a significantly different monetary strategy to its neighbours, with a reasonable degree of success. Thus, nation states retain a large degree of autonomy in monetary and exchange rate policy.

Trans-national production remains a minority element within the output of most industrialised nations, whilst world financial markets are certainly not yet completely integrated, thereby leaving room for differential inflation rates as seen within the EU at present. International capital flows might have circumscribed national economic sovereignty, but the *image* of globalisation as an overwhelming force is overblown. Indeed, it is this image that has 'mesmerised analysts' and paralysed 'radical reforming national strategies', producing 'over-diminished expectations' (Hirst and Thompson, 1996). In reality, nation states have considerably more autonomy than they probably realise, as demonstrated by Norway, which shrugged off rejection of EU member ship by popular referendum and, rather than entering a period of disinvestment and economic decline, has restored full employment and resumed a period of strong economic growth.

The minimum benefit accruing to EMU must be sufficient to exceed to costs of transition for the project to prove an economic, rather than political success. Estimates of the transition costs vary from €30 billion (£18.75 billion), cited by Arestis and Sawyer, to £107.4 billion for the largest 3,000 UK firms alone, calculated by Whyman, with additional costs for smaller firms and public organisations (Arestis and Sawyer, 2000; Whyman, 2001).

Employee relations

Industrial relations under EMU faces a number of distinct challenges. Firstly, the maintenance of international competitiveness, in the absence of exchange rate variation, requires a greater degree of flexibility in wages and prices. Thus, wage formation can fulfil the macroeconomic goal of ensuring that aggregate wages grow in line with productivity. However, corporations are simultaneously demanding greater internal flexibility in the setting of wage and working conditions to implement elements of lean production and human resource management, which require employees to be tied closely to the goals of their employers to maximise productivity. The difficulty arises from the conflict between *macroeconomic* and *microeconomic* objectives (Marsden, 1992). The former can be best achieved through co-ordinated bargaining, as indeed is the strategy pursued by the Netherlands, Germany and Ireland to ease their respective transitions to EMU (Rhodes, 1992; Teague, 1998). The latter, however, may encourage employers to demand wage bargaining decentralisation, flexible contracts to ensure factor mobility and wage flexibility to match the fluctuations in market forces.

It is further suggested that wage discipline will increase within EMU, thereby exacerbating the difficulties for the trade union movement (Melitz, 1997; Pissarides, 1997). Wage transparency resulting from a single currency facilitates wage comparisons within the EMU area, stimulating demands for wage equalisation (Peters, 1995; Berthold and Fehn, 1998). This strategy may be supported by union confederations in high wage areas, as this will reduce the threat of wage competition undermining their preferential labour market position. However, if attempted in the absence of an equalisation of productivity, this will lead to job losses in the less productive region.

The combination of an over-valued currency being irrevocably fixed in value against its closest competitors and wage equalisation stimulating inflationary pressure, have predictably negative macroeconomic consequences. Hence, the German unification case represents a stark warning of the dangers of mishandling a rapid transition towards EMU (Doyle, 1989; Horn and Zwiener, 1992; Goodhart 1995). Wage equalisation must not be allowed to proceed the narrowing of productivity differentials, unless the less efficient economy is to suffer unemployment and recession.

Industrial relations systems are additionally under pressure throughout Europe due to the tendency for TNCs to focus upon internal labour markets, establishing multiple cost centres and implementing initiatives to tailor working conditions to their specific business requirements in order to react flexibly to changing patterns of demand. Innovation in information technology has enabled the devolution of responsibility for production to lower levels of organisations, which in turn encourage central management to attempt to assert influence through designing the terms and conditions to suit their individual organisational challenges (Sisson and Marginson, 1995). Multi-employer bargaining is ill suited to this process and therefore trade unions face being marginalised due to employer preference for company-level 'productivity coalitions' rather than centralised concentration or sectoral bargaining (Lash and Urry, 1989).

The harmonisation of pay and conditions for employees, irrespective of the location of production, together with the European Works Council (EWC) directive, which is intended to expand pan-European corporate consultation, are both influences towards the establishment of a form of 'arms length' Euro-pattern bargaining (Teague, 1991; Rhodes, 1992: 45). Nevertheless, it is possible that this pan-European labour market may be limited to certain key groups of workers, possessing specific technical and managerial skills, and for particular categories of highly mobile labour, notably managers, construction workers, labourers and young people (Walsh *et al.*, 1995). In this scenario, the higher incomes, which are commanded by key employees, may disrupt national labour markets by increasing income inequality or through low-wage countries losing skilled labour to higher-wage member states (Marsden, 1992: 593). Furthermore, while the advent of Euro-bargaining could provide new opportunities for trade unions and their members, it could equally fragment unions along supranational company lines, and thereby undermine class solidarity.

The divergent tensions, threatening to further complicate European industrial relations, are likely to effect EMU because current arrangements show no clear evidence of converging to a uniform pattern across Euroland. Demands for greater firm-centred flexibility fit very poorly with the macroeconomic imperative of maintaining wage moderation and thereby international competitiveness. Hence, the most likely prediction is for an uneven and spasmodic development of industrial relations, with the eventual emergence of an ad hoc, partly institutionalised system of pan-European labour relations (Rhodes, 1992: 43–44).

Social policy and labour regulation

A third element associated with a social market concerns the degree of social protection afforded to citizens, especially the development of a comprehensive welfare state and labour regulation. Social protection is a necessary element of an efficient social market as it frees individuals from fear of potential future crises and therefore facilitates full participation in an efficient economy and society. Concern over future health problems may inhibit risk-taking in production and curtail consumption patterns, thereby reducing the long-run growth rate. Social insurance therefore provides an efficient means of ensuring comprehensive coverage at low administration costs.

Furthermore, the socialisation of risk may be extended to provide educational grants, thereby socialising the risk associated with investment in an individual's skill enhancement. Similarly, high replacement ratios associated with social transfers, together with state subsidised re-training and re-location programmes, minimise the cost to those individuals who lose their jobs due to technological change and, thereby, reduce the degree of opposition to industrial rationalisation, thereby raising long-run growth rates.

To many of a social democratic persuasion, the comparison of a social market approach with an alternative of unfettered capitalism is one of the most persuasive arguments in favour of full participation in further economic and political integration in Europe. Accordingly, EMU is perceived as *part of the EU package* rather than a beneficial reform in its own right. However, the case for joining EMU would certainly appear more compelling had a social market actually been established in advance. Yet it remains largely an unrealised aspiration. The high fragmentation of social policy within, and between, EU member states implies that European regulation may only be possible for non-contentious issues, where nations share common interests and goals, such as health and safety matters. Otherwise, social protection may be restricted to the lowest common denominator (Konstanty and Zwingmann, 1996; Keller and Sorries, 1997). Consequently, Barnard and Deakin claim that the existing body of EU social legislation is nothing more than an 'eclectic body of employment law', whilst others claim the approach has a 'hollow core' (Barnard and Deakin, 1997; Leibfried, 1994; Leibfried and Pierson, 1995). Moreover, Streeck claims that the 'retarded advancement of European-level political rights' and the 'almost complete absence of a European system of industrial citizenship' demonstrates that there is little reason to anticipate further social initiatives to prove more successful (Streeck, 1992: 218–9).

This negative conclusion can be challenged by the argument that existing gaps in the EU social dimension will be progressively filled, even if this relies upon a degree of wishful thinking. A more robust defence can be made that, although sporadic in coverage, EU Directives have had a measurable impact upon the lives of EU citizens. In particular, social legislation has provided a degree of protection for workers involved in company take-overs and faced with redundancies, has placed restrictions on long working hours, established European Works Councils, enshrined minimum maternity rights, enhanced health and safety protection and introduced equal treatment for workers on irregular contracts. Although the main effect has been experienced in member states with minimum existing social regulation, such as the UK, EU legislation has nevertheless achieved a degree of progress towards the type of social policy anticipated in a social market.

The realisation that a social market remains a distant aspiration, despite the advances that have been secured through the EU sponsored social partnership, have inspired a number of previously sceptical trade union leaders to support EMU, but to make this conditional upon the EU's continued commitment to enact proposals designed to create a fully functioning social market model in the new Euroland. For example, John Edmonds (2000), leader of the GMB trade union and member of the TUC General Council of the UK, argues that:

> Trade union support for the single currency should be fully conditional on the EU commitment to the European Social Model. If the politicians of Europe have nothing to offer working people but an unregulated labour market with rising insecurity and even more powerful employers, trade union support for the single currency must be forfeit because there will be no benefit to justify the risk.

This clear statement of conditional support for EMU therefore rests upon the assumption that the social model is the most likely model the EU Commission and governments will select to use in the development of the new Euroland. This is, however, by no means certain. Indeed, it ignores the increasingly vocal neo-liberal critique of welfare states, labour regulation and centralised wage bargaining, as causes of *Eurosclerosis* (Lawrence and Schultz, 1987; Minford, 1996).

Highly developed welfare states have been criticised by a number of economists as being responsible for a decline in economic performance (Feldstein, 1974, 1976; Lindbeck *et al.*, 1994; Dowrick, 1996; Henrekson, 1996; Atkinson, 1999). Increases in taxation to fund higher levels of government transfers are suggested to reduce work incentives, increase the rate of natural unemployment and depress economic dynamism, whilst social security reduces personal savings rates, thereby reducing the stock of capital and hence national income. Job security legislation is claimed to produce hysteresis, where an individual's duration of unemployment is negatively related to their probability of getting a job (Lawrence and Schultz, 1987). However, the evidence is rather mixed, with welfare expenditure acting as an automatic stabiliser to prevent a drift into recession, whilst social insurance may enable workers to take greater risks in their working lives, which may produce greater returns for society as a whole (Korpi, 1985, 1996; Barr, 1992). Moreover, when utilising the appropriate mix of active labour market policies and co-ordinated wage formulation, corporatism tends to present an improved unemployment-inflation trade-off (Jackman *et al.*, 1990; Rhodes, 1992: 29).

Nevertheless, the neo-liberal viewpoint has influenced leading members of the European political and financial elite. For example, British Prime Minister, Tony Blair (2000), has repeatedly emphasised the need for all EU member economies to restructure their traditional approaches to social welfare and labour regulation. In a recent speech, Blair pointedly rejected the 'old social model' in Europe, and stating that 'our welfare systems and labour markets will require fundamental reform'. Moreover, despite the adoption of the social chapter and introduction of the minimum wage, Blair prefers to concentrate upon the fact that the UK still has 'the most lightly regulated labour market of an leading economy in the world'.[1] In addition, there is a similar debate raging in Germany, home of the social market approach, concerning *Standortfrage*, the question of whether the costs of welfare provision has rendered the country uncompetitive as a production location (Flockton, 1998: 79). Furthermore, the European Central Bank's (ECB) senior economist, Otmar Issing, recently argued that the poor performance of the Euro was due to 'the adverse impact of minimum wage and employment protection legislation', which can only be overcome by a 'comprehensive programme of structural reform'.[2]

The natural conclusion to be reached from this neo-liberal criticism of the fundamental features of the social market is that influential figures within the European project desire a shift from welfare state to *competition state*, in which policies are determined by the perceived demands of maintaining international competitiveness within the global economy (Cerny, 1990). The adaptation of economic and social policy to demands made by global markets is in direct conflict with a social market approach, as individuals are recommodified and social protection replaced by state-provided means for individuals to better compete in a global labour market. Social partnership becomes nothing more than a hollow shell of its potential development in a social market. Trade unionists are encouraged to increase productivity and adopt management objectives, with little consideration of the merits of greater codetermination in the workplace and a more equal redistribution of income and economic power throughout society. Consequently, it appears paradoxical that many social democrats are justifying their continued support for EMU upon the basis that the future Euroland will be a worker-friendly social market, at the very time when EU governments and other influential figures are increasingly questioning the future of this very model. Indeed, the social model is presently looking to be a less viable future model for Euroland than at any time in the previous few decades (Whyman, 2000).

Conclusion

The social market version of capitalism, enacted by Germany in the aftermath of the Second World War, has proved attractive to social democrats throughout the world, due to its ability to combine an efficient market economy with citizens and employees enjoying amongst the most extensive social and economic rights amongst industrialised nations. Thus, it is not surprising that, with Germany committed to the process of the EMU and with other initiatives based upon German precedents (i.e. the ECB and EWCs), social democrats should eagerly anticipate the possibility of their benefiting from an extension of the social model throughout the newly created Euroland. However, there is little evidence to substantiate this position.

This chapter has demonstrated that the balance of the economic forecasts indicates a relatively neutral impact upon the Euroland economy at best, and at

---

1   Introduction to the DTI White Chapter Fairness at Work (cited in Coates, 1999: 653).
2   Cited in *The Guardian*, 13 May 2000, p. 24.

worst the combination of convergence criteria and inflation-obsessed ECB will result in decades of slow growth and persistently high levels of unemployment. The stringent conditions applied to fiscal policy under EMU by the convergence criteria and SGP will effectively prevent the construction of Euro-Keynesianism and its use to drastically reduce EU unemployment. Furthermore, despite recent commitments to reduce unemployment, little effective action has been taken. The absence of economic consensus on how best to reduce unemployment is an additional factor undermining successful macroeconomic co-ordination at supranational level.

In terms of industrial relations, the expectation that a social market will facilitate the emergence of a form of Euro-bargaining and/or Euro-corporatism can be encouraged by a number of identifiable trends in this direction. For example, the ability for the ETUC and UNICE to reach agreements which are translated into Directives, is a potentially powerful corporatist tool. Nevertheless, employer resistance to supranational negotiations, except where these avoid more prescriptive alternative legislation, fatally weakens the development of this process into a formalised corporatist structure. Similarly, whilst EWC's undoubtedly provide the opportunity for unions to collaborate within TNCs, and may even provide a channel for an attempt at pattern bargaining across national boundaries, employers are more concerned with the development of internal labour markets according to their own agenda. Indeed, whilst TNCs may provide an impetus for Euro-bargaining through a uniformity of terms and conditions across countries in which they operate, their increasing disinterest with national labour market outcomes (as opposed to internal developments) may instead fracture existing industrial relations systems.

Finally, the desired expansion of social protection and labour regulation, as fundamental elements of a new Euroland social market approach, appear contrary to the available evidence. The EU's Social Chapter measures that have been implemented are minimalist in nature, and cautious in design. Indeed, few workers in the majority of EU member states will benefit from these measures, except those with the weakest forms of social protection. Thus, it would appear the intent is to prevent *social dumping* from being used as a competitive tool by fellow member states, rather than the establishment of a social market. Indeed, influential elements within the EU political and economic elite are committed to the deregulation of European labour markets, and a reduction in the nature and coverage of welfare programmes. Thus, in certainly two out of the three fundamental elements examined in this chapter, the evidence undermines the stance taken by those social democrats whose support for EMU participation is conditional upon the commitment to, and development of, a fully functioning Euroland social market.

In view of the implausibility of Euroland developing as a social market, social democrats have only three alternative positions to take. Firstly, they can ignore all of the evidence and blindly cling to the hope and belief that their loyalty might be rewarded eventually. This is, of course, possible, but adopts an unnecessarily high risk. Secondly, they can oppose the TEU version of EMU. This might have the impact of re-opening discussion concerning how the monetary union should operate, enabling the reform of the convergence criteria, SGP and providing the ECB with additional objectives of full employment and high growth, onto its solitary existing goal of price stability. However, it is by no means certain that this ill occur, particularly in light of the political capital invested in agreeing the existing formula. Thus, this option might involve a degree of isolation from the deepening of European integration and there might be a political price to pay in lack of leadership. Against this, however, their governments would be less constrained to develop their own versions of a social market in their individual nation states.

The final alternative would be to adopt John Edmonds' suggested strategy, namely to make support for EMU *conditional* on the delivery of a social market. This would necessitate a spirited opposition to the TEU version of monetary union in the absence of a compromise agreement concerning the establishment of a social market system, complete with detailed timetable of contributory reforms. Otherwise, this strategy would simply be a deceptive restatement of the first alternative. However, it is clear that none of these choices is easy, nor will this choice be particularly palatable to those who have hitherto championed EU integration in the anticipation of future benefits. The absence of evidence that this is likely to occur should, however, provoke a reconsideration of the basic strategy.

Chapter 11

EMU and Trade Unions

Introduction

The EU's economic integration project has substantially transformed a large segment of the continent, creating a single internal market, the abolition of border controls, agricultural subsidies and support for areas of industrial degeneration, together with the provision of a degree of fiscal redistribution to maintain internal 'cohesion' and assist development in the poorer member economies. The momentum of the European 'project' is, moreover, accelerating. Initiatives range from a common police force, rapid response EU army, common foreign policy and other moves towards ultimate political union, alongside possibly the most extensive project attempted to date, namely the creation of EMU between selected member states. The monetary union element involves the irrevocable fixing of exchange rates between the twelve initial participating EU member states, through the mechanism of the replacement of previous national currencies with a common currency, the euro. Economic unification involves the transfer of monetary policy to the control of the ECB, together with acceptance of a set of rules intended to limit the scope of national fiscal policy.

The UK has to date remained uncommitted in relation to the EMU initiative. The previous Conservative government, led by John Major, negotiated an opt-out from having to join the single currency, once convergence criteria were met. This has enabled the current Labour government to maintain a 'wait and see' policy, ostensibly until economic cycles coincide and five economic tests are met to ensure that participation is in the national interest. However, the Labour Party is officially committed to joining the single currency, albeit at an optimal moment as expressed by five economic tests adopted by the UK Treasury. Nevertheless, it is interesting to note that, although support for the European 'project' has remained a fundamental New Labour constant, nevertheless where this appears to conflict with the maintenance of successful macroeconomic management of the national economy, participation in the euro has shifted to a secondary, not primary, target for the government (Carter, 2003: 5–6).

The stance adopted by British trade union leaders is slightly more complex, with the TUC and certain leading affiliates (i.e. AEEU) maintaining strong support for further economic and political integration, whilst others have remained largely detached from the issue, despite occasional critical comments made by individual general secretaries.[1] Sporadic criticism has not, however, prevented the British trade union movement from adopting a policy ostensibly similar to that of the Labour

---

1 For example, Derek Simpson (General Secretary of AMICUS) and Tony Woodley (General Secretary of TGWU), writing in *The Guardian*, 30 June 2004, p. 19.

Party, although typically trade union support for EMU relies upon the simultaneous achievement of a social dimension to European integration. However, such subtleties are often lost in the cut and thrust of political debate, and this gives rise to the interesting phenomenon that the British labour movement is associated with support for further European integration, whilst the majority of the Conservative Party firmly opposes the deepening of economic integration. This is a reversal of the balance of opinion two decades ago.

This chapter will therefore seek to answer two main questions. Firstly, why the labour movement altered their previous critical stance towards European economic integration and became amongst its staunchest supporters. Secondly, whether this new enthusiasm towards further integration, and particularly membership of EMU, is in the national interest, or at least the interest of those working people and their families organised labour seeks to represent.

Evolution of Labour Movement Opinion

The British labour movement was initially opposed to EU membership on the grounds that it was designed to benefit multinational capital at the expense of workers. A larger market facilitated economies of scale, which enhanced industrial profitability but also provided trans-national capital with the opportunity to threaten national workforces with disinvestment and the relocation of production abroad if wage concessions were not made or strikes abandoned. The location of trade unions within nation states implies that any weakening of democratic government autonomy potentially reduces the strength of national labour. Corporatist pacts in which organised labour exchanges wage moderation for increases in employment and an improved social wage are less feasible if governments have ceded control of their economic instruments. The free movement of capital undermines the maintenance of full employment as high rates of fiscal expenditure and the pursuit of a 'cheap money' strategy may cause capital to flow out of the economy in search of better returns and to avoid the risk of currency depreciation, thereby causing a currency crisis and decline in investment. Moreover, internationally minded labour activists disliked the fact that EU membership meant establishing higher external tariffs against the developing world, particularly commonwealth countries (Nairn, 1972: 7, 66–73, 147).

The leadership of the Labour Party abandoned this policy in 1974, and successive leaders have become increasingly favourable to further integration, pledging the intention to keep Britain at 'the heart of Europe'. This policy stance, on behalf of the labour leadership, may partly reflect a genuine desire to create a social democratic Europe, but it simultaneously distinguishes 'New Labour' from 'old Labour' whilst magnifying current differences between an increasingly Eurosceptic Conservative Party. Furthermore, support for this reversal of policy appears widespread amongst Members of Parliament (MPs), according to an influential 1996 survey (Baker *et al.*, 1996). This found that only 16 per cent of Labour MPs opposed EMU entry whilst 12 per cent rejected rejoining the ERM, despite 29 per cent believing EMU would institutionalise neo-liberal economic policy in Britain and therefore severely constrain the ability of a Labour government successfully governing the country. However, the overwhelming majority of Labour MPs (88 per cent) identified globalisation as making membership of EMU a necessity. This analysis therefore suggests that euroscepticism would appear to be concentrated amongst a small group of the 'old' Left, thereby forming a 'declining legacy of Labour's past' with the party's 'centre of gravity ... shifted decisively in favour of Europe and EMU' (Strange, 1997: 15). The contributions contained within this book, however, tend to indicate that this conclusion is an over-simplification of the truth.

The UK trade union confederation, the Trades Union Congress (TUC), was more reluctant in altering its opposition to EU membership, and only did so after the 1975 referendum produced two-thirds support for continued membership (Strange, 1997: 16). The position of the TUC and leading British trade unions is superficially similar, particularly as loyalty to the Labour Party platform is a dominant trait amongst the more moderate unions. However, close analysis reveals trade union backing for closer integration, and EMU in particular, to be conditional upon the successful achievement of wider objectives (Edmonds 2000). Indeed, union support only swung enthusiastically behind the federalist vision of closer economic and political integration after the 1988 TUC Congress, when the then head of the EU Commission, Jacques Delors, outlined his vision of a 'social Europe' which embraced labour rights as core elements (Strange, 1997).

This vision of a social democratic Europe was extremely tempting to a trade union movement marginalised from political influence by successive Conservative governments, and having haemorrhaged membership due to mass unemployment and laws restricting major aspects of trade unionism. Moreover, although John Monks (currently ETUC General Secretary – previously TUC General Secretary) noted an initial scepticism amongst many trade unionists, due to a monetarist bias ingrained within the TEU, establishing the operating framework for EMU, this opposition became increasingly muted over time (Monks, 2000).

One factor in the marginalisation of the sceptics within organised labour, derived from a change in the economic strategy supported by the leading figures in the union movement, namely an acceptance of the benefits of fixed, rather than floating, exchange rates. This involved advocating membership of the European Exchange Rate Mechanism (ERM) and accepting the loss of monetary policy sovereignty, together with the readjustment of the remainder of macroeconomic policy to secure a similar inflation rate to that of the strongest EU economy, Germany. Devaluation was dismissed as 'anti-worker', since it reduced real incomes, and the neo-liberal case was partially accepted in so far as changes in nominal exchange rates are not necessarily reflected in changes to real values. Thus, the further step towards EMU membership was perceived as less threatening than it would be had the previous policy of competitive exchange rates been maintained.

The European Trades Union Congress (ETUC) had, furthermore, secured a commitment from the EU Commission to place greater emphasis upon employment matters, cumulating in the Luxembourg jobs summit in November 1997, thereby diffusing concerns that EMU might accentuate Europe's existing unemployment problem (Monks, 2000: 186–7). This required each member state to prepare an annual 'jobs plan' as part of a European co-ordinated strategy to reduce the persistently high rates of unemployment across most of the continent. Unfortunately, this procedure has, thus far at least, had little appreciable success in reducing unemployment figures, and in practice, employment policy remains subservient to the monetary discipline enshrined in the SGP and the price stability objective pursued by the ECB.

A second, and altogether more important factor encouraging British organised labour to support further European integration was the belief that EMU was 'part of the EU package' which included the establishment of a 'European Social Model' (ESM). This vision of a new, worker-friendly European society was outlined in the previous chapter. This facilitated the TUC's strategy to recover lost ground in terms of membership, industrial and political influence, through offering a positive-sum 'partnership' with 'good' employers (Monks, 2000).

European Social Model (ESM)

The ESM in question would perform a number of functions:

1. Implemented through an international treaty, it would provide a bulwark against the renewal of radical Conservatism, intent upon weakening trade unions through restrictive industrial relations legislation and thereby unravelling labour protection.
2. It incorporates trade unions as a legitimate social partner and counterpoint to organised business organisations, thereby promoting employee involvement in relevant aspects of working life at both local and super-national level. This provided a new legitimate role for unions to fulfil and thereby justified continued membership.
3. A fully developed ESM would involve the establishment of a generous system of welfare provision, including high quality public services together with social transfers combining a high replacement ratio with income redistribution. The combination of a more comprehensive system of social policy with increased labour regulation produces partial labour de-commodification and thereby enhances trade union power resources (Korpi, 1985; Esping-Andersen, 1990).
4. The EU Commission have provided significant material support to facilitate social partnership between trade unions and employer organisations, thus promoting an European version of collective bargaining. This has totalled 13 per cent of ETUC income in the years following the introduction of the SIM, together with the provision of free meeting venues and interpreters, together with providing travel subsidies and technical assistance (Abbott, 1997: 472; Knutsen, 1997). Further payments to facilitate European Works Councils may have totalled approximately €57 million, over a three year period between 1992 and 1994 (Knutsen, 1997: 300). Thus, the ETUC has a direct financial interest in supporting further European integration.

Contradictions within the Trade Union Case

The stance taken by leading figures in the trade union movement appears to be consistent with their traditional aims and values only as long as certain key assumptions hold. These are, first, that EMU proves to be an economic success, which outweighs the costs of transition and it's potentially less favourable effects upon national economies. Second, the unions are correct to believe that the EU Commission will ultimately create an ESM for Euroland which will prove consistent with the requirements of EMU. Unfortunately, as demonstrated in Chapter 10, there is a considerable body of evidence to cast doubt upon both of these assumptions. Consequently, the trade union case for supporting EMU must be subjected to rigorous evaluation to ascertain which elements are likely to prove unreliable and, therefore, whether the strategy followed by most leading trade union figures is fundamentally flawed. This analysis may be made in terms of the economic impact of EMU, the importance of wage formation for the ultimate success of this initiative, the potential 'Europeanisation' of industrial relations, together with developments in the fields of labour regulation and social policy.

Economic impact of EMU

Although the net economic effect is uncertain, there is sufficient evidence to indicate that the monetarist 'Maastricht' model is inherently deflationary, due to the combination of MCC, SGP and the operation of the ECB. The repercussion of restrictions placed upon public expenditure will generate industrial conflict, particularly in a public sector starved of resources, and hence exacerbate recruitment difficulties for high quality staff. For greater detail, see the material discussing the ESM in the previous chapter.

Wage formation – crucial for successful EMU

Labour market outcomes will become increasingly important within EMU as alternative instruments, previously used to adjust the competitiveness of an industry (or economy), are no longer available. Pay bargaining systems will be faced with two problems during the transition to EMU. The first is to ensure that aggregate wages grow in line with productivity, whilst the second is to facilitate the anticipated industrial restructuring resulting from the completion of the single market and increased competition resulting from price transparency across Euroland. The difficulty for government, employers and unions, is that there may be a conflict between a *macroeconomic* definition of flexibility of real wages, and a *microeconomic* objective of rapid adaptation to diverse patterns of industrial change (Marsden, 1992: 594–5).

The former may be best achieved through co-ordinated wage bargaining, occurring at central or industrial level, where all parties can internalise the inflationary implications of their decisions, whilst a solidaristic wage structure should minimise social conflict and encourage self-restraint in exchange for increased employment opportunities.[2] Indeed, the Netherlands, Germany and Ireland have sought to promote wage bargaining moderation through national or sector-level pay bargaining structures to facilitate the transition to EMU (Teague, 1998: 119–120). However, the microeconomic objective may be best advanced via a decentralised wage bargaining structure, flexible contracts to ensure factor mobility and wage flexibility to match the fluctuations in market forces. It is clear that trade unions would not wish to accept such an extreme form of decentralised, deregulated market without at least having the opportunity to negotiate certain limitations upon microeconomic flexibility. However, rivalries between unions, whether due to organisational competition, religious or ideological reasons, might equally impair co-ordinated bargaining across the entire Euroland (Turner, 1996: 330). Furthermore, it is suggested that wage discipline will increase within EMU, thereby exacerbating the difficulties for the trade union movement (Melitz, 1997; Pissarides, 1997).

A third consideration, arising out of concern that wages do not expand faster than productivity, derives from Keynes' observation that *relative* wages were at least as significant as real wages when formulating negotiating objectives. Thus, the transparency resulting from a single currency facilitates wage comparisons within the EMU area, stimulating demands for wage equalisation (Peters, 1995: 321; Berthold and Fehn, 1998: 530). This strategy may be supported by union confederations in high wage areas, as this will reduce the threat of wage competition undermining their preferential labour market position. However, if attempted in the absence of an equalisation of productivity, this will lead to job losses in the less productive region.

This is precisely the pattern observed in former East Germany, whereby the 1989 economic and political unification process ignored productivity differentials whilst political expressions of equal citizenship prompted currency fixing at parity.[3] Furthermore, trade unions were not dissuaded from demanding wage equalisation; partly to discourage large-scale labour movement out of the former East Germany in search for improved living conditions. This was despite the East German economy being only about half as productive as their Western neighbours, although this efficiency gap was reduced by 20 per cent longer working hours and wages no higher than one-third the equivalent West German rates (Lumley, 1996: 26). Wage equalisation reduced East German competitiveness, however, because wage rises in the East were not matched by increasing productivity. In 1991, gross wages in manufacturing in the East averaged 138 per cent of net value-added. Predictably, manufacturing collapsed under the twin cost pressure of wage rises and exchange rate appreciation, with output falling by 67 per cent in the first year after unification and leading to 25 per cent of the entire labour market losing their jobs. A year after

---

2   Studies supporting this position include: McCallum (1983); Cameron (1984); Bruno and Sachs (1985); Crouch (1985); Calmfors and Driffill (1988); Calmfors and Nyomen (1990); Rowthorn and Glyn (1990); Amoroso and Jespersen (1992: 79–80); Henley and Tsakalotos (1995: 186–9); Marshall (1995: 209); Sawyer (1995: 28).

3   The decision to adopt parity conversion of Ostmark to DM occurred despite official debts being valued at an exchange rate of 24:1 and the unofficial exchange rate was between 6:1 and 10:1 (Incomes Data Services European Report, 1990c).

monetary union, only 44 per cent of the previous 9 million workforce of the DDR remained in the same employment relationship (Buechtemann and Schupp, 1992: 95–7, 102–4). At the same time, between 1991 and 1997, transfers from West to East Germany averaged a staggering DM 140bn (4–5 per cent of GDP) per annum, with an equivalent sum provided by local government, pension funds, the Federal Labour Office, German Unity Fund and Inherited Debt Amortization Fund (Flockton, 1998).

The combination of an over-valued currency being irrevocably fixed in value against its closest competitors and wage equalisation stimulating inflationary pressure, have predictably negative macroeconomic consequences. Hence, the German unification case represents a stark warning of the dangers of mishandling a rapid transition towards EMU (Doyle, 1989; Horn and Zwiener, 1992; Goodhart, 1995). Wage equalisation must not be allowed to proceed the narrowing of productivity differentials, unless the less efficient economy is to suffer unemployment and recession.

Europeanisation of industrial relations?

The third element of an ESM relates to its contribution towards the legitimisation of trade union activity and establishment of a European system of industrial relations. The importance attached to real wage flexibility for member states within EMU may provide one opportunity for the creation of new forms of national labour market co-ordination between social partners, perhaps on corporatist lines (Rhodes, 1992: 45). Furthermore, there may be a tendency for TNCs operating throughout Europe to facilitate an embryo European system of industrial relations through the harmonisation of pay and conditions for employees irrespective of the location of production. The EWC initiative is considered to further strengthen co-operation and the pooling of information between EU trade unions, potentially leading to euro-bargaining to establish universal minimum standards of training, anti-discrimination practice, promotion procedures and so forth. A form of 'arms length' bargaining may evolve whereby management and unions do not negotiate directly with one another, but unions are able to have an additional form of input into the decision-making process. The result could be a type of European pattern bargaining, although TNCs are unlikely to concede such an arrangement whilst productivity differentials persist (Teague, 1991; Rhodes, 1992: 45).

It is equally possible, however, that the creation of an European labour market may be limited to certain key groups of workers, possessing specific technical and managerial skills, and for particular categories of highly mobile labour, notably managers, construction workers, labourers and young people (Walsh *et al.*, 1995: 85). In this scenario, the higher incomes, which are commanded by key employees, may disrupt national labour markets by increasing income inequality or through low-wage countries losing skilled labour to higher-wage member states (Marsden, 1992: 593). Furthermore, while the advent of euro-bargaining could provide new opportunities for trade unions and their members, it could equally fragment unions along supranational company lines, thereby undermining class solidarity. Accordingly, unions risk becoming 'partners ... of regional capital trying to survive in inter-regional free market competition' rather than 'agents of inter-regional redistribution' (Streeck and Schmitter, 1991: 55).

There are, additionally, a second group of factors, which may cause a general decentralisation of industrial relations systems. The intensification of international competition has led many companies, particularly TNCs, to focus upon internal labour markets to establish multiple cost centres and implement initiatives to tailor working conditions to their specific business requirements in order to react flexibly to changing patterns of demand. Advances in information technology have facilitated a shift from administrative to performance-based control, with responsibility and accountability devolved to business units at lower levels of large organisations (Sisson and Marginson, 1995). These systems of 'managed autonomy', in which central management maintains control through an extensive web of formal and informal performance measures, place a premium on the bottom-line responsibility of individual business unit managers for labour as well as other costs. Multi-employer bargaining is ill suited to this process (Marginson and Sisson, 1996: 177–8). Furthermore, there is a claim that deregulatory pressures are the consequence of a 'paradigm shift' from Fordist to post-Fordist industrial organisation, implying a duality of labour markets split between core and periphery workers (Atkinson, 1984). Thus, trade unions face being marginalised due to an employers' preference for company-level 'productivity coalitions' rather than centralised concentration or sectoral bargaining (Lash and Urry, 1987; Windolf, 1989). According to this viewpoint, euro-bargaining is irrelevant to the needs of post-Fordist flexible production (Rhodes, 1992: 28).

The divergent tensions, threatening to further complicate European industrial relations, are likely to persist into EMU because current arrangements show no clear evidence of converging to a uniform pattern across Euroland. Demands for greater firm-centred flexibility fit very poorly with the macroeconomic imperative of maintaining wage moderation and thereby international competitiveness. Hence, the most likely prediction is for an uneven and spasmodic development of industrial relations, with the eventual emergence of an ad hoc, partly institutionalised system of pan-European labour relations (Rhodes, 1992: 43–44). Irrespective of the eventual evolution of industrial relations throughout Europe, trade unions face increasing challenges. One problem concerns the changing composition of the European labour market and lower unionisation amongst groups being increasingly represented in the labour force and in the expanding sectors of the manufacturing and particularly service sectors. Another relates to the tension between union objectives of social solidarity and maintaining membership through delivery of real material benefits. The former may be better served by national or sectoral wage formation, where employers and government may participate to secure aggregate wage moderation, whilst the latter may be best achieved by decentralised bargaining for workers in the most profitable companies.

Social policy and labour regulation

The final element of the ESM concerns the combination of European social policy and labour regulation, which the EU Commission promotes as being sufficient to counterbalance excessive pressures on employees emanating from a combination of the single market and EMU. Directives already implemented have ensured a degree of protection for employees in cases of collective redundancies, restrictions on working hours, the establishment of European Works Councils, minimum maternity rights, enhanced health and safety protection, and equal treatment for workers on irregular contracts. However, whilst it would be unfair to dismiss such achievements as meaningless, nor treat the social dimension as though it were a complete and coherent approach, it is nevertheless grossly insufficient for the EU Commission to portray this as a distinct ESM (see Table 11.1).

Table 11.1   Comparison between fully developed ESM and current EU 'social dimension'

	EU Social Dimension	**European Social Model**
Welfare State		
– Type	Minimalist	Comprehensive
– Coverage	Safety net	Universal
– Replacement Ratio	Low	High
– Association with labour market	Re-commodification	De-commodification
– Response to globalisation	Competitive – improve labour market skills	Protective – social citizenship requires non-market income source to make effective choices
Industrial Relations		
– Recognition of collective bargaining	Patchy	High/Comprehensive
– Corporatist	Diverse – some member states deregulated wage formation, whilst others rely upon social contracts to secure budget cuts	Established – facilitates superior inflation: employment trade-off
– Euro-level IR	Minimum – EWC, consultation only	Developed – framework bargaining between federal-level social partners
– Labour regulation	Minimum – complements single market; over-regulation impedes competitiveness	Fundamental – basis of social accord, combining industrial adjustment with employee protection

The high fragmentation of social policy within, and between, EU member states suggests that social and labour regulation at European level may only be possible for non-contentious issues, where nations share common interests and goals, such as health and safety matters. Otherwise, social protection may only occur at the lowest common denominator. Hence, discussion of the ESM, or even presentation of the contemporary social dimension as a logical response to European economic integration, is premature (Streeck, 1992: 218–9). Furthermore, as specified in the previous chapter, neo-liberal and 'third way' theorists have criticised the 'traditional' version of ESM and the generosity of their welfare states, on the basis that their tax take stymies economic growth whilst social provision undermines individual incentives (Feldstein, 1974 and 1976). Despite an absence of decisive empirical proof to support this position, it has influenced key players in the ECB, together with 'modernisers' like Tony Blair, who is determined to reform the 'old social model' and replace it with a more market-orientated social policy (Blair, 2000).

Conclusion

Trade union support for continued European integration has been one of the most consistent features of the debate surrounding membership of EMU, particularly in Britain since at least Delors' address to the TUC in 1988. However, distinct from business supporters of the process, union members and activists support EMU because their fundamental objective, the establishment of an ESM, depends upon continued support for the entire package of measures. Analysing the rationality of this support must therefore question whether the construction of an ESM throughout Euroland is realistic, and more fundamentally whether this would be consistent with the demands made upon member states by EMU itself.

The result of the analysis contained within this chapter is that the British trade union leadership is mistaken in their assumptions and naive in believing that membership of EMU is likely to lead to the creation of an ESM type society. There are simply too many contrary indications. For example, the economic evidence is relatively balanced over whether membership will deliver any significant dynamic gain. One problem feature is that the deflationary impact of the convergence criteria and SGP, combined with the tight monetary policy operated by the ECB, is likely to reduce growth rates across Euroland as budget balances are further consolidated. A continual squeeze upon public expenditure is a particular problem for the public sector unions, potentially threatening the future of national pay bargaining, whilst further wage restraint will exacerbate an already large income gap compared to the private sector, thus fuelling recruitment problems and possible industrial unrest.

Predicted developments in industrial relations and wage formation hold as many problems as solutions for unions and their members. Trends towards euro-corporatism seem weak and where they do exist, the value to government's lies in the possibility of securing lower real wage growth – hardly a long-term strategy to appeal to union members. The tendency for TNCs to concentrate more closely upon internal labour market arrangements than national wage formation implies that any form of euro-bargaining emerging from the EWCs will be company-orientated and therefore undermine class solidarity. Furthermore, there is a clear tension between the deregulated, decentralised labour market desired by TNCs in order to maximise microeconomic adaptation to change, and macroeconomic flexibility as measured by variations in real wages.

Finally, after two decades of construction, the EU's social dimension is a poor reflection of the type of generous, universal welfare state assumed by an ESM. Indeed, the minimalist and work-related nature of the EU's social charter does not encourage the belief that an ESM, of the type favoured by trade unionists, is even on the long-term agenda of Euroland. Instead, certain EU leaders have accepted elements of the neo-liberal critique of welfare states as too passive and in need of reform to ensure they enhance international competition. Such reforms are hardly consistent with an ESM dedicated to decommodify labour, as they instead recommodify individuals, having first sought to improve their relative market position.

In short, the trade union case for supporting EMU is fatally flawed and those leading figures in the movement who advocate support for EMU do so based upon a number of questionable assumptions. A deflationary, neo-liberal Euroland, whose economy is managed by an ECB charged with the sole objective of producing stable prices, is inconsistent with the development of an ESM capable of guaranteeing social citizenship based on generous welfare provision, protection at work and employee input into their working lives. Trade unionists therefore must reconsider their position on this important issue.

Chapter 12

The Impact of EMU upon Business

Introduction

A British Government survey, conducted in 1998, revealed that 95 per cent of small and medium-sized enterprises, defined as those employing less than 250 employees, had at that time made no preparations for the impact of the euro and that 65 per cent considered that none were necessary (Simon, 2000). Whilst perhaps rational in a climate of considerable uncertainty concerning the UK's possible future membership, there was a working assumption that a second general election victory by the Labour Party would result in an attempt to take Britain into membership.

This chapter seeks to evaluate how EMU will transform the current and future performance of UK enterprises, in terms of its micro, macro and dynamic impact.

The Micro-Impact of EMU

Four main direct theoretical benefits are assumed to arise from the introduction of a single currency. They are:

1. A reduction in transaction costs;
2. The elimination of exchange rate uncertainty;
3. Price transparency reducing information costs;
4. Enhancement of the SIM, thereby stimulating increased competition and industrial reorganisation.

The most obvious advantage concerns the elimination of the transaction costs involved in changing EU currencies, both for the travelling public but more significantly for trading purposes. The European Commission estimated that savings could amount to 0.4 per cent of total EU GDP per year, which could provide a significant stimulus to competition and saving for European consumers over a long period of time (European Commission, 1990). It may also lead to a certain degree of trade-diversion as companies might switch transactions from suppliers outside to inside the eurozone due to the lower costs involved. These gains will not be equally distributed across all member states. The UK, with a higher proportion of trade outside the eurozone, will gain less than most other potential participants. Moreover, whilst transaction costs may be a relatively onerous burden for small exporting companies, their larger competitors typically face costs as low as 0.05 per cent for transactions exceeding $5 million (Burkitt et al., 1997).

The second direct benefit generated by monetary union concerns the elimination of exchange rate uncertainty between participating member states, which is assumed to lead to more efficient business decisions. Firms no longer have to set foreign prices to include a buffer in case of adverse shifts in exchange rates. Nor do they have to incur the cost and management time involved in hedging international transactions, through forward and swap markets. The manufacturing sector, with its long-lived factories and other assets, is predicted to derive most benefit. Reduction in exchange rate risk is expected to lead to lower real interest rates, and hence higher economic growth. The European Commission estimated that the combination of these factors could boost the EU economy by between 0.7 and 1 per cent of EU GDP per annum (European Commission, 1990). Such optimism appears at odds with a number of academic studies, which have failed to discern a significant relationship between exchange rate volatility and trade (De Grauwe, 1992; Frankel and Wei, 1993; Sapir *et al.*, 1994).

The introduction of a single currency creates price transparency, thereby reducing information costs and enabling traders to make cheaper purchases and increase competition across the eurozone SIM. This, in turn, should exert downward pressure upon prices, to the benefit of European consumers. The EU's SIM is currently incompletely integrated, with price segmentation persisting between markets as, for example, new car prices in the UK and the Netherlands.

The eurozone will form a market comprising eleven countries, 300 million customers and accounting for approximately one-fifth of the world economy. British enterprises, which currently export to only one EU country, will find it easier to expand into others without the need to redesign new packaging, brochures and promotional literature, each with different pricing structures and accounting systems. Moreover, the reduction in these costs lowers the barriers to smaller companies exporting their products or services. The European Commission estimates these savings may boost EU GDP by 0.3 per cent of EU GDP per annum. However, a Price-Waterhouse study estimated that the *entire* benefit, including transaction, information and exchange rate stability elements, may be no higher than 0.3 per cent of EU GDP per annum across the entire EU (Hallet and Vines, 1993; Burkitt *et al.*, 1997). Nevertheless, the 'menu cost' approach indicates how even small reductions in costs can theoretically exert a much greater impact upon output and employment.

The combination of lower information costs, price transparency and the elimination of exchange rate uncertainty, within a more competitive SIM, provides British firms with new opportunities to realign their products both geographically and in terms of product positioning.

A further consideration, arising from the introduction of the single currency, derives from the outcome of transferring from bilateral exchange rates to the euro, which can result in less psychologically inviting figures, requiring the company to decide whether to set a more attractive price. If raised, it might incur consumer suspicions that retailers are profiting from conversion. If lowered, it will reduce revenue and profits unless suppliers are squeezed or the quantity (or quality) of the product is adjusted, thereby incurring costs associated with the re-tasking the production line. The impact of currency conversion will be restricted to UK exports were the UK to remain independent of EMU. However, membership would require the transformation of all prices currently represented in sterling into euros, and therefore imply similar changes to many domestic products in terms of marketing, size or quality of the product.

Negative features arising from the introduction of the single currency include transition costs. This includes consumer psychological adjustment to a new monetary value system. However, the adjustment costs for business are likely to be considerably larger. These include the changeover in record and accounting systems, requiring the adaptation of computerised systems and the need to open euro bank accounts, coupled to a temporary need for dual pricing. The European Banking Federation calculated that the EU banking sector is required to spend between £6.3 and £7.9 billion over a three to four year period (Taylor, 1995). This amounts to 2 per cent of operating costs for each changeover year, a sum exceeding £900 million per annum for the UK banking sector. The British Retail Consortium has estimated the cost of currency changeover to be approximately £3.5 billion, 17 per cent of which resulting from six months of dual labelling of all products after the introduction of the single currency (Henderick, 1998).

Extending industry analysis to produce an economy-wide estimate of transition costs is difficult to achieve due the large number of autonomous variables. One study suggested a $30 billion (£18.75 billion) total adjustment cost (Arestis and Sawyer, 2000). However, extrapolation from a more recent study, based upon a survey drawn from the largest UK companies, generates a far higher value. The KPMG report estimated that each of the 3,000 firms employing over 5,000 workers faced a total cost of adaptation to the single currency of €56.5 million (£35.8 million), comprising half short-term IT project costs and the remainder the result of dynamic costs associated with consolidation and price transparency (KPMG, 2000). Simply applying this predicted cost to the largest 0.1 per cent of UK firms produces a total cost of £107.4 billion. However, even this substantial amount is a gross under-estimate, because all employers, whether public sector organisations or micro-businesses, will have to change accounting packages, price lists/catalogue, PAYE systems and so forth. Consequently, the KPMG results imply that the UK will incur transition costs of *at least* £200 billion, at a conservative estimate. This requires the dynamic gains produced by EMU to be substantial for UK participation to make economic sense.

The transition cost experienced by small and medium-sized enterprises is likely to be *disproportionately* higher than for large corporations. For a small, privately owned company, the cost of re-calculating and printing price sheets and catalogues, purchasing an updated accounting package together with adjusting employment-related costs for the business, may be extremely significant. It could occupy a large proportion of scarce management time, which could be spent improving the efficiency of the company in view of the increased competition it is likely to face from the completed SIM. These challenges may be sufficient to force marginal firms out of business. Firms operating out of non-EMU countries may therefore possess a degree of competitive advantage over competitors within the EMU-zone, which may result in enhanced market share through lower costs and prices.

A second negative feature for business follows from the prediction that prices are likely to be forced downwards by the combination of improved information and price transparency, particularly for those goods most accessible to cross-border trade. The development of Internet shopping will reinforce this trend. The consequence will be that inefficient firms will be exposed and be driven out of business. However, intensified competition will also reduce profits for all enterprises, unless falling prices stimulates demand sufficiently to offset this process. The reduction in exchange rate risk exacerbates this tendency, as competition causes a reduction in the risk premium added to price and which, in the absence of negative exchange rate movements, enhances profitability. Lower prices may further reduce firms' expected future profits (Burkitt, 1996). One response might be to intensify merger activity to secure greater economies of scale and scope, typically leading to rationalisation of production and job losses.

Financial sector

Although monetary union is likely to have a significant impact upon all elements of business, its impact will be particularly profound for the financial sector, due to the integration of Europe's capital markets. This will reduce home country bias in the consumption of investment products, and thereby complete the SIM in financial services. Barriers to entry into the eurozone will be reduced, thereby intensifying competition and promoting the rationalisation of the industry. This should result in cheaper, improved service, which enhances customer choice. The unified financial market will be on a similar scale to the US and thereby reduce the cost of finance for European business. The negative side of this process will be the reduction in employment in the financial sector across Europe. However, British financial institutions have largely anticipated this process and are far leaner and innovative than a decade ago, placing them in a prime position to take advantage of the opportunities to expand into other national sub-markets.

Competition is assumed to stimulate the development of new products and encourage the rapid growth in the electronic transfer of funds for retail transactions. Foreign exchange transactions will be eliminated for trade occurring *between* participant countries, although this loss of business for the banking sector may be partially replaced by dealing between the euro and other currencies, particularly dollar and yen trading against the euro. This will be influenced by the degree to which the euro becomes attractive as a 'vehicle currency' in world trade, absorbing a proportion of the trade currently occurring in dollars. Monetary union will also possess implications for transactions in securities, creating a large market in government debt denominated in *euros* together with a substantial stock of euro-equity.

The implications for the City of London are of great importance for the whole UK economy, since international financial services employ approximately 150,000 people and generate between £10 and £15 billion in annual invisible exports (Taylor, 1995). With the utilisation of information technology, the new business will gravitate towards the most efficient financial centre, measured by cost, speed and integrity of transaction. The fact that the City of London is one of the three principal world financial centres, and that international business tends to gravitate towards a single location within each time zone, creates a virtuous circle reinforcing its pre-eminence within Europe. This centralisation is reinforced by a preference for deep, liquid markets, accommodating legal, regulatory and tax frameworks, skilled labour, and a cluster of supporting services including accountancy, law, software and telecommunications. High volumes of trade ensure that economies of scale generate competitive terms, whilst existing pre-eminence in financial services makes it easier to attract leading institutions and highly skilled experts. Providing complacency is avoided, the existence of such advantages should ensure the City's continued dominance whether or not Britain joins EMU.

The Macro-Impact of EMU

The micro- or firm-centred consequences of the introduction of monetary union will be experienced directly by most enterprises; requiring many to reassess their pricing and marketing policy to avoid losing market share in the increasingly competitive SIM. However, EMU has an equally substantial bearing upon the prosperity of enterprises via its impact upon the European economic environment. Monetary union will fundamentally change the behaviour of many economic agents, complicating the assessments made by economists as to whether the single currency will enhance future prosperity or will retard the economic development of the continent.

Favourable consequences

One gain resulting from EMU derives from enhanced nominal exchange rate stability, which should reduce real interest rates, whilst lower transaction and informational costs facilitate lower prices. This, in turn, should encourage an increase in market demand, causing firms to expand investment and production to satisfy expected market conditions. A low inflation rate can further enhance the business climate. Price stability is the sole objective established for the European Central Bank (ECB) by Article 107 of the TEU (European Commission, 1992). As one of the most independent central banks in the world, it is generally assumed that the ECB will secure lower inflation for those countries participating in the single currency, securing reductions in real interest rates, which provide a further stimulus for investment and economic growth.

The favourable climate for business activity, created by EMU and the ECB, is reinforced by the requirement for participants to have first met the convergence conditions established in the TEU. It established targets that all EU member states are *compelled* to meet in order to provide a stable framework for the single currency. These conditions apply equally to the UK because its 'opt-out' only provides Britain the right to decide whether or not to join the single currency, the third stage of monetary union. It does not present an opportunity to avoid the entire process.

The TEU convergence criteria institutionalise the desire for sound finance in order to prevent the participation of member states with unsustainable fiscal debt burdens or current budget deficits. High government borrowing could increase interest rates, thereby undermining some of the benefits created by EMU. Thus fiscal restraint is further encouraged amongst all members of the monetary union by the Stability and Growth Pact (SGP), which will affect governments whose deficits exceeded a target rate of between 1 and 3 per cent. In the absence of compliance with the target, the EU will impose significant fines upon the member state. The only exception occurs if a member state suffered a fall in GDP exceeding 2 per cent in the given year, whilst a decline between 0.75 and 2 per cent would be subject to the discretion of the European Council.

An additional benefit derived from EMU is the avoidance of protectionist retaliation from other participants. Failure to join could leave the UK vulnerable and incapable of influencing the monetary policy of the EMU-zone from outside. Potential threats include the risk of losing markets due to 'unofficial' protectionism (i.e. standardisation regulations) preventing the free passage of UK goods and services across the rest of the EU, declining political influence within the EU and jeopardising the position of the City of London as the ECB strengthens the prestige of the Frankfurt financial market. Inward investment could also be placed at risk, as investors 'gravitate' towards a potentially more stable common currency area. These fears are groundless because they violate the Treaty of Rome, the Single European Act, the Treaty on European Union and the rules of the World Trade Organisation.

In summary, the proponents of monetary union suggest that its introduction has the *potential* to stimulate investment, employment and growth. However, these benefits accrue *only* if firms take advantage of the new opportunities available to them and individual economies are sufficiently converged with one another and flexible enough to adapt to changed circumstances. Hence, Healey (2000: 19–20) concludes that 'while the benefits are significant, cumulative over time and reasonably uncontroversial, the costs are much more uncertain, widely exaggerated and almost certain to diminish with the passage of time'.

Detrimental consequences

The positive account of EMU does, however, omit a number of important points. The first relates to the deflationary impact upon the economies of certain EU member states, caused by the reductions in public spending and/or increases in taxation required by the TEU criteria. Estimates range from a deflation of between 4.5 and 5 per cent of GDP during the 1990s for 'EMU aspirants', resulting in between seven and ten million people losing their jobs (Holland, 1995; Baimbridge *et al.*, 1998; Minford, 2000). Compliance with the convergence criteria requires Britain to rejoin the ERM, despite its two-year membership costing an estimated £68.2 billion in 1992 prices (equivalent to 11.5 per cent of UK GDP) in terms of lost output and one-and-a-quarter million more unemployed. Moreover, the TEU requirement to maintain budget deficits below 3 per cent of GDP over the full business cycle means that budget surpluses in the region of 6–7.5 per cent must be secured at the peak of the boom given recent trends in Britain's fiscal path. This necessitates further reductions in public expenditure and hence sub-trend growth rates (Burkitt *et al.*, 1996; Burkitt *et al.*, 1997).

The rigidity of the TEU conditions and SGP is exposed by the fact that all five criteria were fulfilled on only thirteen from a possible 120 occasions over the 1990–1997 period, an achievement rate of only 10 per cent. Indeed, the SGP would have been met by EU member states on only thirteen of 450 occasions over the past three decades (Baimbridge *et al.*, 1998; Eichengreen, 2000). Accordingly, EMU is likely to result in Europe remaining locked into high levels of unemployment, entrenching *laissez-faire* orthodoxy when active macroeconomic policy is required to reduce unemployment. Economic policy restrictions imposed by international treaty constitute a fundamental loss of democracy in terms of the limited choice available to European citizens. Furthermore, the 'generous' interpretation of the convergence criteria made by the European Commission, allowing as many countries as possible to participate in EMU, ensured that deflation will be prolonged into the period when monetary union is established, thereby lowering growth and increasing unemployment within the eurozone.

The loss of control over monetary and exchange rate policy may weaken national economic management which, when additionally constrained by restrictions upon fiscal expenditure, reduces a country's capacity to respond to internal or external shocks, thereby exacerbating the danger of national destabilisation. External shocks have an asymmetric impact upon individual member states to the extent that they are insufficiently converged prior to entering monetary union.

The UK has a notably different industrial structure from most other EU member states. Specifically, it has a more highly developed energy sector, together with competitive advantages in financial and media services, together with high technology exports in the fields of aerospace and pharmaceuticals where its principal competitors are US or Japanese firms and the products are typically priced in dollars. The sterling-dollar exchange rate will remain far more important to this key element of British manufacturing than sterling-euro, so that participation in the single currency might increase exchange rate volatility for this crucial sector of the UK economy. Inter-EU trade is a much smaller proportion of the UK's total international trade than for most member states, whilst the UK depends upon the continuation of overseas earnings from foreign investment (Burkitt *et al.*, 1996). The UK has a higher concentration of owner-occupation, principally financed by variable-rate interest borrowing. Hence, the UK economy is approximately four times more sensitive to changes in short-term interest rates than the EU average (Taylor, 1995; Bank for International Settlements, 1996; Burkitt *et al.*, 1996; Eltis, 1996).

Differences in industrial structure largely explain the findings by Bayoumi and Eichengreen (1993) that the UK economy is out of step with other EU member states 87 per cent of the time. This implies that the UK's economic interests cannot be properly served by a common interest rate determined by a central ECB operating by majority decision. Integration might, in itself, reduce the asymmetry of shocks, but this will take time and monetary union could be irreconcilably damaged in the medium- and short-term, though the absence of alternative means of stabilising the eurozone.

Wage and price flexibility is unlikely to alleviate more than minor external shocks or regional disequilibria due to the persistence of well-documented European labour market rigidities. Similarly, labour mobility within EU member states is three times lower than between US states, despite the existence of greater regional inequality and unemployment (OECD, 1986; Eichengreen, 1992). Moreover, as these figures relate to labour mobility *within* countries, mobility *between* countries is likely to be much lower due to language barriers, differences in culture and non-recognition of qualifications. As a result, many theorists have advocated a form of fiscal federalism to offset recessionary external shocks.

At 1.24 per cent of total community GDP, the current EU budget is *far* too small to sustain EMU over the long-term. It needs to increase to a minimum of 5 per cent of Community GDP and ultimately to between 20 and 25 per cent of GDP (MacDougall, 1977; European Commission, 1996). This would involve UK annual payments rising from £6.3 billion to a minimum of £28.7 billion, or the transfer of large areas of national public sector competence to Brussels. A substantial rise in taxation would either directly affect enterprise through changes in Corporation Tax, or indirectly as income or consumption taxation reduces market demand. A more cost-effective alternative may involve the creation of a European Federal Transfer Scheme (EFTS) charged with the sole objective of the stabilisation of the eurozone. Smaller implementation time lags, and a cost perhaps as low as 0.23 per cent of EU GDP are more attractive than either enlarging the central EU budget or widening its competence to incorporate additional areas of expenditure.

Critics express doubt that the ECB can deliver lower real interest rates, which depends upon a prior reputation for sound finance. Indeed the presence of formerly high-inflation nations upon its board of governors may cause the financial markets to conclude that the euro may be a weak currency, requiring higher real interest rates to sustain its value. As a result, the ECB might try too hard to develop credibility and over-deflate the EMU economy, resulting in political pressure for the relaxation of monetary policy. Therefore a potential conflict of policy aims and objectives, caused by the separation of monetary and fiscal authority may therefore have negative consequences.

Minford (2000) predicts that the operations of the ECB will double the size of national recessions due to its inability to respond to differential shocks on a national basis. Its task becomes more difficult if the introduction of the single currency affects the demand for money, thereby destabilising monetary indicators whose large, unpredictable shifts may generate either a Community-wide inflationary or deflationary shock. Moreover, the ECB lacks democratic accountability due to its insulation from political influence, so electors can no longer influence macroeconomic policy. Finally, no conclusive evidence exists of a casual relationship between low inflation and central bank independence; the weight of the evidence suggests that countries with more independent central banks have suffered deeper recessions than other nations, thereby implying that central bankers share a deflationary bias (Barro, 1997).

Opponents of EMU entry conclude that, in terms of the standard economic objectives of high and sustainable growth, full employment, balance of payments equilibrium and stable prices, national economic management is more effective than EMU. Minford's computer simulation indicates that floating exchange rates provide the policy framework most conducive to economic stability, given appropriate budgetary and monetary measures.

Dynamic Effects

Having evaluated the principal consequences that the introduction of EMU is likely to exert upon corporate marketing and pricing policies, this final section outlines four further ways in which monetary union may impinge upon business activity over the longer term. The first relates to the possible acceleration of industrial restructuring across Europe. The removal of non-tariff barriers resulting from the completion of the SIM was predicted to stimulate cross-country mergers and a relocation of production in order to create larger plants, which could better secure economies of scale. The enhanced competition facilitated by the single currency may accelerate the trend, with the implication that medium-sized British companies are more likely to be subject to take-over than would otherwise be the case, whilst large British multinationals have the opportunity to increase their output by absorbing smaller European competitors. However, economies of scale require industrial relocation into fewer, larger production plants, which will increase the competition between European regions in terms of hidden 'sweeteners', offered to attract or hold large employers in their area. Employees may also be in closer competition with workers in other European plants to lower unit costs and increase product quality to secure the future of their national plant.

A second consequence of EMU may involve an increase in labour market rigidity, resulting from the greater transparency of pay differentials, between workers doing similar jobs in different countries. The danger is that this may generate demands for pay equalisation, irrespective of productivity variance. The result could be devastating in terms of jobs and output. A recent example of this process concerned the introduction of a single currency between East and West Germany (at 1:1 parity) whilst, at the same time government and unions pressed for wage equalisation across the new unified labour market. Government support for this process involved the wish to avoid mass emigration of Eastern workers to Western cities in search of higher living standards, together with electoral considerations. Equalisation occurred despite East German productivity levels being between half and one-third of equivalent West German rates, albeit compensated by 20 per cent longer working hours and wages one-third of West German rates. The combination of currency appreciation and wage equalisation undermined this competitive position, leading to the collapse of manufacturing output by 67 per cent in the first year after unification. A year after monetary union, only 44 per cent of the previous 9 million workforce of the DDR remained in the same employment relationship (Buechtemann and Schupp, 1992; Peters, 1995; Lumley, 1996; Berthold and Fehn, 1998).

The requirement for multinationals, operating in a number of member states, to establish European Works Councils to act as a forum for information dissemination and consultation between management and the workforce, created a potential focus for demands for equalisation. However, a determined management can resist such claims, because few workers will move to other countries in search of higher wages, due to language, social and cultural differences. Moreover, the greater transparency of productivity differences between production plants in separate countries could act as a spur to rationalisation and greater efficiency, with the prospect of higher wages as the incentive for worker co-operation.

A third dynamic result of EMU membership is the exposure of the UK to Eurosclerosis, under which a combination of high taxes, regulation of labour and product markets, and state subsidies, reduces the flexibility of European economies. Eltis (2000) cites the 14 per cent higher European tax wedge compared to the USA, together with labour market inflexibility, as the reasons why Europe failed to generate sufficient private sector employment growth over the past two decades. To the extent that such criticisms are valid, structural reform of European fiscal, welfare and labour market arrangements is necessary to stabilise EMU in the medium and long term, whilst reducing structural unemployment. However, many supporters of European integration wish to preserve the European 'Social Model' and believe that the creation of a larger economy, less exposed to outside forces, will facilitate their objective. It is significant that leading figures in the British trade union movement express qualified support for EMU membership 'in order to bind Britain more tightly into the European Social Model', to protect workers from the results of increased competition arising from the SIM and the single currency (Edmonds, 2000: 196).

A fourth factor focuses upon the possibility that EMU acts as precursor to political union. Historical experience supports this argument because no monetary union has ever existed separately from political union, whilst no independent country has unilaterally abandoned its own notes for another's currency. The nearest previous arrangement was the Latin Monetary Union of the 1870s (between Belgium, France, Italy and Switzerland) which standardised coinage between the four countries, but without a common central bank to control exchange rate and monetary policy. Additionally, Luxembourg fixed its exchange rate at the same value as Belgium, thereby allowing intercirculation of currency between the two countries, without control over monetary policy. Consequently, although political union does not necessarily follow the introduction of a single currency and a uniform interest rate, it would be unique if it did not eventually occur. Political integration necessarily affects the business environment, in ways that cannot be predicted.

These four long-run consequences of EMU will not necessarily occur, and would only become significant issues for employers over a considerable period of time. Monetary union does not generate a single, one-off shift in market conditions, but represents a *dynamic* process, which will continue to have a distinctive impact over many decades. A virtuous cycle will generate greater prosperity and employment opportunities over the medium-term and long-term, whilst a vicious cycle will imprison the Continent in a pattern of low-growth and mass unemployment for decades. The consequences for business are enormous, so it is vital for enterprises to react immediately to the opportunities available to them, for a British opt-in or opt-out, in order to secure maximum gains and minimal costs from the process.

Conclusion

The task of forecasting precisely how the current establishment of EMU in Europe will affect British business is bedevilled by contradictory evidence. This chapter has explored the principal forms in which monetary union will impinge upon existing market conditions, causing firms to reassess their pricing and marketing strategies.

The balance of the available evidence indicates that monetary union will have a significant impact upon British business whether or not the UK decides to participate in the project. All firms that export to participating countries would have to replace their existing catalogues, packaging and pricing policies, due to the change in currency and translation of current prices necessitating a re-evaluation of product volume and marketing strategy. Intensified competition across Europe would tend to force prices downwards in the UK, which provides opportunities for companies to break into foreign markets but similarly threatens their market share in the domestic market. This process would be more intensive if the UK adopted the single currency. The lower inflation and real interest rates promised by the ECB would be secured for UK business only if the UK joined EMU. However, there is an equally powerful case that the euro will be a weaker currency than Sterling, so that British business would enjoy lower real interest rates by remaining outside of the single currency.

The balance of the macroeconomic impact of EMU is hard to predict. It is certainly the case that compliance with TEU convergence targets both prior to and during EMU has reduced European growth rates. However, it is arguable that this reorientation of fiscal policy would have occurred anyway, particularly for those countries whose debt burden exceeds the value of their annual output. Asymmetric shocks are likely to prove problematic for participating member states, particularly for the UK, due to its cyclical and structural divergence from the EMU-zone. Nevertheless, the combination of fiscal federalism, supply-side reforms and the convergence produced by further integration, may reduce the impact of external shocks over a period of time. Consequently, a tentative prediction may be that EMU will prove problematic for the UK economy in the short-term and medium-term, but as long as such problems were properly compensated by other member states, structural divergence may reduce over time. Significant differences will remain, however, as many are due to relative competitive advantage and therefore should not be sacrificed on the basis of arguments claiming closer integration. The efficiency of the world economic system, together with the future prosperity of the UK economy, requires the allocation of resources towards areas of competitive advantage to facilitate production at low cost via specialisation.

The crucial test, which will determine the ultimate success of the EMU experiment, is whether it can achieve stable prices and low real interest rates, whilst simultaneously maintaining high or full employment. Unfortunately, the answer to this question is almost impossible to discern without observing how monetary union operates in practice over a longer time period than is currently available, leaving theorists divided on the advisability of membership.

PART IV
Alternative Futures for Britain

Chapter 13

Alternative Relationships Between Britain and the EU

Introduction

The relationship between the UK and the EU has always proved to be difficult, juxtaposed between periodic elite-level enthusiasm for closer European economic (if not political) integration and a general lack of enthusiasm for such measures on behalf of a majority of the electorate, as indicated by successive opinion polls. Thus, Aspinwall (2003: 146) is correct in his assertion that 'the question of whether to sacrifice domestic autonomy in favour of European integration is one of the most volatile and passionately discussed issues in British politics'.

There are many inter-related reasons that may explain this phenomenon. Political and business elites are likely to benefit the most from economic and political integration, with the creation of a host of new career opportunities created due to the formation of new supra-national regulatory and representational structures, whilst trans-national corporations benefit from economies of scale available from larger markets, and their activities less subject to overview and control.

The evidence presented in this study demonstrates that, on balance, EU membership, and the momentum towards further political and economic integration, has tended to weaken UK national interests. The costs of EU membership have been found to exceed those benefits that have accrued to the UK, and the impact of participation in EMU would likely further exacerbate this economic deficit. Additionally, a number of complementary estimates have emerged on the viability of EU membership. For example, Black (2000) argues that unilateral withdrawal from the Common Agricultural Policy (CAP) alone would result in significant budgetary savings, where the loss in revenues to farmers would be more than compensated by significant welfare gains to consumers from cheaper food prices arising from trade diversion and creation effects. Similarly, Pain and Young (2004) suggest that UK food prices could be reduced by as much as 20 per cent on leaving the EU. This assertion is also supported by Hindley and Howe (1996) and Leach (2000), who predict a UK net cost of approximately 1 per cent of GDP from EU membership largely due to the CAP, whilst Minford (1996) suggests that the figure could be as high as 1.5 per cent. However, Pain and Young (2004) remain sceptical, arguing that UK 'special relations' with transatlantic partners are heavily dependent on our continued membership and influence within the EU.

The most obvious areas where EU membership has imposed as significant net costs upon the UK economy relate, firstly, to the net UK contribution to the EU budget of over £50 billion. Secondly, agricultural protectionism through the CAP has caused food prices to remain 7 per cent above world prices, costing an average British family £36 per week (Burkitt *et al.*, 1996). Black (2000) argues that unilateral withdrawal from the CAP alone would result in significant budgetary savings, where the loss in revenues to farmers would be more than compensated by significant welfare gains to consumers from cheaper food prices arising from trade diversion and creation effects. Similarly, Pain and Young (2004) suggest that UK food prices could be reduced by as much as 20 per cent on leaving the EU. This assertion is also supported by Hindley and Howe (1996), Leach (2000), Milne (2004) and Minford *et al.* (2005: 6) who predict a UK net cost of ranging from 1–1.5 per cent of GDP, some £10–15 billion, from EU membership largely due to the CAP. Thirdly, Deva (2002) calculates that approximately 40 per cent of all legislation that affects Britain arises from the EU, whereby the costs of regulation and harmonisation of goods and services will have a significant net cost for companies and organisations operating within the UK. Thus, in terms of UK GDP, regulation is estimated to cost between 2 per cent (Milne, 2004) and 6 per cent (Minford *et al.*, 2005: 14). Finally, EU experimentation with fixed exchange rates has proven to be disastrous for the UK economy, with its 1990–92 ERM membership resulting in GDP shrinking by 3.8 per cent, unemployment rising by 1.2 million thereby cumulatively costing the UK economy over £67 billion or 11.3 per cent of 1992 UK GDP in terms of lost potential output (Burkitt *et al.*, 1996). There is little reason to assume that membership of EMU would prove any more fruitful in terms of the operation of the European Central Bank, together with the tight fiscal rules established in the Stability and Growth Pact, which have contributed to the eurozone economy suffering a decade or more of slow growth (Baimbridge, 2006; Michie, 2006; Ormerod, 2006; Sawyer and Arestis, 2006; Whyman *et al.*, 2006).

In relation to trade, the one area where many authors tend to find strong benefits for continued UK membership of the EU, the data is more complex. For example, whilst the EU does represent approximately 48 per cent of UK trade (and the eurozone 43 per cent), more exports are priced in terms of dollars (i.e. oil and gas, aerospace, pharmaceuticals) than in euro's. Furthermore, it is the net balance of trade that is important for the prosperity and future development potential of the UK economy, not the absolute amount of trade taking place. Thus commentators frequently include erroneous measures such as emigration and the number of holidays that UK citizens take abroad in warmer countries as evidence of a 'profound europeanisation' of the UK economy (Aspinwall, 2003). Far more significantly, the UK has suffered a total accumulated trading deficit of over £90 billion with the EU, whereas during the same period it has enjoyed a trading surplus of over £70 billion with the rest of the world. Such a substantial volume of resources, drained from the British economy, will have contributed to lower economic growth, leading to fewer jobs in the UK (particularly in manufacturing industry) than would otherwise have been the case (Baimbridge and Whyman, 2006). Moreover, the substantial expansion in European growth rates that the EU's *Cecchini Report* (Cecchini, 1988) predicted would result from the creation of the Single Internal Market (SIM) have not materialised as predicted (Burkitt and Baimbridge, 1990, 1991). Consequently, Milne (2004) and Minford *et al.* (2005) estimate a net cost for the UK economy, arising from trade-related matters, varying between 0.1 per cent and 2.5 per cent of UK GDP.

All mainstream British politicians assert, regardless of the weight of evidence, which demonstrates that the UK bears a heavy financial burden from its EU membership (Milne, 2004; Minford *et al.*, 2005; Baimbridge *et al.*, 2005), that no viable alternatives exist to the strategy of remaining 'at the heart of Europe'. However, it makes little sense to allow a nation's democratic self-determination to be undermined through participation in further initiatives leading towards deeper economic and political integration without first considering a range of alternatives that exist for the UK, and that may facilitate more economic prosperity coupled with enhanced democratic accountability via the national parliament. This chapter outlines a number of these policy options and seeks to briefly evaluate their potential.

The Status Quo Position

This is the most obvious alternative short-term position, whereby the UK retains EU membership but relies upon its opt-outs from EMU and refuses to participate in further economic and political integration. The maintenance of a national veto over economic proposals (i.e. taxation) remains a consistent feature of UK government policy towards the development of the EU, irrespective of the composition of government. Moreover, there are a number of precedents where individual member states have continued to pursue their individual national interests even if this threatened to hamper the effectiveness of the EU institutions. For example, Italy delayed the successful conclusion of the 1994 Edinburgh summit over a dispute concerning their milk quota, whilst the French refused to permit the creation of additional European Parliament seats until the new European Parliament building was located in Strasbourg. Indeed, de Gaulle at one point utilised the negotiating tactic of the 'empty chair' to prevent the unanimity needed for decisions to be taken until other EU member states accepted key French demands.

The extension of qualified majority voting (QMV) has weakened the potency of this tactic somewhat, in recent years. Nevertheless, a determined effort may produce compromises. The key question to be resolved, if adopting this approach, is to determine whether the ultimate goal involves the non-compliance with future integrationist initiatives, which other nation states are free to pursue if they so wish, or an attempt to roll-back the momentum leading the EU towards deepening economic and political integration. In other words, consideration must be given to whether the strategy is to create a multi-dimensional, Europe 'á-la-carte', or to press for the re-empowerment of the European nation states.

A second question, to be resolved if adopting the status quo strategy, relates to Britain's ability to establish a bilateral trade agreement with a third party, even if this related to an alternative trade association. This may involve closer ties with the North American Free Trade Association (NAFTA) and/or commonwealth countries. These options are explored in more detail later in this chapter, on the basis that Britain forms these alliances subsequent to withdrawal from the EU. However, the point at issue in this section is to explore whether these potential trade advantages can be secured without the need to reject EU membership, and indeed, it would appear that such actions are indeed compatible with current EU rules. For example,

Denmark negotiated an agreement with fellow Nordic states, which permitted the free movement of people, goods and services despite the fact that Norway, Sweden and Finland were not at the time members of the EU single market. This precedent does not, however, apply to the establishment of *new* unilateral trade agreements post-EU membership, but rather applies to the acceptance of *existing* trade agreements at the time of a nation's accession. Consequently, the benefits arising from closer co-operation with other trade blocs might cause difficulties within the constraints of EU membership.

These problems would, however, be in the most part political and not economic in nature. The practicalities of the UK being a member of two trade organisations are relatively easy to reconcile, requiring that all imported goods and services bear the mark of the country of origin, to prevent differential tariff rates creating a market for arbitrage in order to avoid paying higher rates of import taxation. Objections that such labelling is contrary to a single EU market can be dismissed due to precedents created by the solution to the BSE beef health crisis, whereby beef exported from Britain will have been labelled according to the country of origin to facilitate consumer choice. Once labelled according to the country of origin, if re-exported from the EU to US (or vice versa), the correct tariff charge could be applied when it enters the final market.

This strategy rests upon the premise that maintaining EU membership at its current status is both desirable and tenable. It maintains UK access to the SIM and provides the forum for participation in the determination of harmonised trade rules which define the marketplace. Yet, it avoids probable additional costs implied by EMU and moves to further limit national sovereignty through extending QMV. Moreover, it is perhaps the easiest position for politicians to defend, since it means doing nothing new and therefore avoids offending any section of their own parties.

The strategy is, however, at best a compromise solution. While further integration measures can be vetoed, and the UK can avoid participating in future experiments that may damage its economic potential, it remains committed to those that already exist. Apart from the obvious direct costs associated with the CFP and CAP, being a net contributor to the EU budget, together with the long-term trade deficit with other EU member states, disadvantages include the net budget contributions, continuing trade deficits and the fact that, technically, the UK has an opt-out only from the final stage of EMU (i.e. having to accept the single currency) but not from earlier stages including the requirement to meet the convergence criteria established in the TEU. These require the UK to maintain inflation rates no higher than 1.5 per cent above the lowest three participating member states and interest rates no higher than 2 per cent above the average interest rates set by the same group of countries, budget deficits no higher than 3 per cent, and government debt no higher than 60 per cent of GDP, respectively, and finally a requirement for stable exchange rates pegged to other member states through participation in the Exchange Rate Mechanism (ERM). Thus, the UK would be economically tied to a slow growth area, and be required to implement deflationary policies perhaps unsuitable to the particular requirements of a recession or wider national interest. Moreover, recent demands made by the EU Commission that Britain reduces public spending, at a time when the international economy was particularly sluggish and government spending provided one means of stimuli to the domestic economy, was contrary to the preference specified by the British electorate in the 2001 General Election in addition to being economically illiterate.

Furthermore, the Treaty of Rome obliges member states to allow the free movement of goods, services, capital and labour. Whilst in many circumstances the inhibited movement of goods and services is preferable, prevention of imposing even temporary restrictions upon the free movement of capital and labour may have greater consequences. The current controversy over a potential influx of individuals of working age from new EU member states highlights one possible problem area. Control over a national labour market is made more difficult, with the consequence that migrant labourers could place additional stress upon national health and social security systems. Moreover, they might provide a pool of exploitable labour and thereby undermine the competitiveness of 'good' employers who comply with minimum wage legislation and provide satisfactory levels of health and safety, and in the process cause episodes like the recent Morecambe Bay Chinese cockle-picker tragedy. Similarly, although the unimpeded movement of capital is conventionally assumed to be desirable, it can be destabilising for an economy that is damaged by a flow of 'hot' capital searching for a temporary profitable haven. Recent examples of Mexico, Brazil, Russia, and the 'Tiger economies' of South East Asia, all demonstrate the tremendous chaos that financial speculation can cause. Yet, the fundamental rules governing the EU would prevent a nation state from imposing restrictions, even if this was purely temporary, in order to prevent the disruption caused by speculative attack.

One further example involves EU rules prohibiting industrial subsidies because, whilst this is generally considered to enhance competition 'on a level playing field', there are circumstances in which the national interest may be served by such policies. One example might relate to facilitating the development of emergent technology, where future income streams are uncertain and therefore private financial markets either do not provide sufficient finance, or else reduce investment in the sector through demanding large risk premiums. A second example might relate to the emergence of an infant industry, which has the potential to grow into an internationally competitive venture, thereby enhancing the future prosperity of the UK economy, but which might be swallowed up by more established competitors in its early stages of development. A third case might relate to a nationally significant sector of technology, such as aerospace or the maintenance of a national car industry. It might involve support for space exploration, on the basis that the scientific and technological advances this might produce will enhance the competitive position of the national economy. Or it might be for reasons of national prestige, by keeping Concorde flying, for example, and thereby reminding consumers in other nations that British industry can produce products simply years ahead of their time – hence, raising the prestige of the 'Made in Britain' brand identity.

The status quo strategy may facilitate an 'a-la-carte' or 'variable-geometry' form of EU membership so that individual member states only need proceed with measures they favour and thus nations move at different speeds or even in different directions. Thus, a small number of EU member states could establish ever-closer political and economic integration between themselves, perhaps even resulting in the formation of a single, federal state, whilst other EU member states do not need to follow this initiative, and might alternatively wish to reallocate certain functions back to the control of local, regional or national governments through the principle of subsidiarity. However, whilst this scenario is popular in the UK, it is unlikely that supporters of federalism will easily acquiesce to the implied repatriation of powers to nation states.

Renegotiation of EU Membership Obligations

A second option available to the UK is to press for renegotiation of the obligations posed by membership of the EU. This would have the potential for resolving many of the issues that have generated the greatest costs for the British economy. It would involve withdrawal from some or all of the EU's drawbacks, for the British economy, whilst remaining within the organisation. Thus, targets for renegotiation could include the reconstitution of the CAP and CFP, renegotiation of the UK's budgetary contribution, together with opt-out's from specific policy initiatives (i.e. EMU, European foreign and defence policy, etc).

This option has a number of precedents, including John Major's negotiation of an opt-out from the final stage of EMU (i.e. Britain remains bound by the TEU rules but is not compelled to take the final step and replace sterling by the euro-currency), together with the budget rebate that Margaret Thatcher forced from reluctant partners in Fontainebleau in 1984. Moreover, the current preoccupation with the establishment of a EU Constitution and institutional reform, in advance of the further enlargement of the EU, demonstrates a degree of flexibility in redesigning the organisation to limit its generosity to new entrants. This process will, if completed, significantly change the character of the organisation and modify existing arrangements established by international treaty. Thus, it is possible to secure renegotiation when the incentives are sufficient to encourage widespread compliance. Nevertheless, the requirement to achieve unanimity makes a general renegotiation difficult. For every advance secured by the UK, in reducing one of the various burdens on the British taxpayer, this financial cost will be redistributed amongst the remaining EU member states, and not surprisingly they are likely to be reluctant to accede to domestic unpopularity without some sort of trade-off.

One obvious source of negotiating strength for a British renegotiation derives from the fact that the UK is a net budget contributor and would probably remain so even after further contribution rebates and/or opt-outs from specific programmes had been achieved. In addition, the remaining member states enjoy the benefit of a large trade surplus with the UK, and therefore leverage might be forthcoming if renegotiation was pursued as the least disruptive alternative to full withdrawal from the EU. For this strategy to work, the threat of withdrawal would have to be credible. Indeed, the more Britain debated withdrawal, and the greater the public popularity of this option, the greater the concessions a government might be able to secure from other EU member states.

The renegotiation strategy need not necessarily isolate Britain from all other member states. Proponents of the strategy argue that a loosening of the ceaseless pursuit of increasing integration will be popular in other nations, particularly in Denmark and possibly Sweden, where small populations proud of democratic achievements are unwilling to have this diluted into mass electorates too large to canvass personally and therefore increasing reliance upon a media-based campaign largely isolated from the electorate. Thus, the renegotiation strategy could be pursued in isolation or as part of an attempt to redesign the format of the EU at a more fundamental level.

Weaknesses with this strategy include its reliance upon the maintenance of negotiating strength and/or the ability to secure concessions written into international treaty. Otherwise, pressures might cause periodic challenges to any successful renegotiation – i.e. in the way that the French government has periodically challenged the British budget rebate. It is also based upon the premise that concessions can be secured through negotiation. However, the enlargement of the EU, and increased pressures on the EU budget that this might bring, would increase the difficulty of this proposition. Indeed, the conception of a significant number of member states casting off current obligations would be more difficult to achieve than appeasing a single recalcitrant nation. Furthermore, all of this presupposes the achievement of some sort of compromise that, inevitably, implies that Britain will not secure all of its preferred objectives, and that some costs are removed from the British citizens at the detriment of enshrining others more deeply in the new arrangements.

Creation of an Associated European Area (AEA)

One interesting proposal that Britain could pursue as part of a larger renegotiation of obligations to the EU, made by Conservative Member of Parliament, Bill Cash, involves changing the rules to facilitate the creation of an Associated European Area (AEA). This would provide a distinctive choice in the type of European integration and pan-national, regional collaboration – pursuit of ever-deeper integration via an inner core group of EU member states, and a looser, co-operative arrangement between members of the AEA. The former could pursue their goal of creating a united states of Europe, complete with single currency, single central bank and convergence of economic policy, together with other trappings of a nation state, such as a federal president, foreign policy, police force, army, flag, parliament, passport and national anthem. At the same time, members of the AEA could continue their co-operation with the 'fast track' countries in trade and environmental areas, but retain national control over other areas of policy – i.e. macroeconomics, currency, social policy, labour market, foreign and security policy. It would remove the requirement that each member of the EU has to accept the *acquis communitarie* (i.e. the existing rules and regulations agreed by existing member states) in full upon membership. This innovation would require modification of Article 43 of the Amsterdam Treaty. It would, additionally, restore authority to national parliaments, by removing the requirement of qualified majority voting from those areas of EU business where this currently applies. Nevertheless, it might prove possible because it would simultaneously release the impediments to a small group of countries accelerating their integrationist agendas, whilst providing nations with their preference of a looser arrangement through association.

In the Cash proposal, the AEA initiative is perceived as a means of securing more than simple renegotiation of EU membership commitments, however, because it is viewed as a means of forging a bilateral free trade agreement with NAFTA and used to challenge the customs union lying at the heart of EU economic arrangements, and its replacement with a free trade area. Therefore, this more far-reaching interpretation of the AEA has more than a degree of similarity with other options highlighted in this and the following chapter. However, in so far as the intention is to release Britain from most of its obligations imposed by EU membership, but retaining membership of a trade-bloc through the single internal European market, this might be more easily achieved through membership of the already-existing European Free Trade Agreement (EFTA) and European Economic Area (EEA). Rather than having to create a new institutional arrangement, Britain could make use of existing structures, agreed by the EU, to fulfil its goals.

Membership of the Single Market Through EFTA and the EEA

This strategy would involve the UK formally withdrawing from the EU and re-joining the European Free Trade Association (EFTA) that it helped found four decades ago. In the process, the UK would be eligible for membership of the European Economic Area (EEA). Article 41 of the convention establishing EFTA states that any state may accede provided it receives the approval of the EFTA Council, or alternatively the Council may negotiate bilateral agreements with individual states subject to its unanimous approval by all member states. Article 42 establishes the right to withdraw from the convention after 12 months advance notice. Similarly, Article 128 of the EEA Agreement states that any European state becoming a member of EFTA can apply to the EEA Council to be party to the agreement, with the terms and conditions subject to negotiation. All future EU members are required to apply to become party to the agreement.

The EEA is an agreement made between EFTA (less Switzerland) to extend the internal market of the EU and that of the EFTA participants to create a trading area of 28 countries and some 462 million people. This is the world's largest and most comprehensive multinational trading area that came into force on 1 January 1994. Under the agreement, there is free movement of goods, services and capital across the entire area, whilst Article 28 provides for the free movement of persons and a single labour market across all 18 countries. Participants are encouraged to co-operate in the fields of environmental protection, social policy, education and research and development programmes. Exceptions to coverage include agriculture and fisheries, whilst the EEA has no common external tariff and therefore requires the identification of country of origin for all goods and services.

As a member of the EEA, the UK would possess full access to the SIM and retain some influence over the rules that affect trade with EU nations. The EEA ensures free trade without the discrimination against external nations created by a customs union. The terms of the EEA stipulate that the UK business sector would operate under the same general conditions as its EU competitors, whilst ensuring that EEA member states develop relevant legislation *jointly* without the EU imposing standards arbitrarily. The EEA provides member states with the right to oppose and veto EU law if they feel that it operates against their national interest. It also offers the possibility to participate in EU research projects and co-operation on the environment and the social dimension of EU legislation should any EEA participants find these beneficial.

A net transfer of income to the EU budget is part of the requirement for EEA membership, but it would be significantly lower than the high budgetary burden imposed by full EU membership upon UK taxpayers. Membership of the EEA also releases the UK from pressure to participate in the ERM, stipulated by the TEU and in eventual EMU. Given the UK's previous unfortunate experience of ERM membership, and the still larger disadvantages it would suffer through EMU, this constitutes a significant advantage. Thus, the EEA provides many of the advantages of EU membership without some of the costs.

Norway can be used as a precedent since their electorate rejected EU membership in a national referendum and yet was able to participate in the EU single market by means of the EEA. The EU have not sought to 'punish' Norway for failing to persuade its people to become full members, and on the contrary appear eager to take advantage of their addition to the single market to export goods and services, whilst having Norway pay a contribution towards the EU bureaucracy that manages the market.

One disadvantage of the EEA over full EU membership is that a power imbalance may arise between EU states and EFTA/EEA members, which could undermine many of the benefits that the agreement currently provides. However, if the UK reduced its membership to that of EEA status, this problem would be partially reduced in magnitude since the UK and Norway would jointly provide a far more credible counter-balance to the EU in future negotiations.

An advantage is that EFTA is a similar type of trade agreement to NAFTA in that it does not impose undue costs and restrictions upon member governments, barring those minimum rules necessary to maintain the effectiveness of the free trade area. The only significant differences are that the EEA is not as explicit on the issues of intellectual property and foreign investment, whilst it progressively adopts updated rules on trade harmonisation once these are agreed between the EU and EFTA members. Thus, UK membership of the EEA and NAFTA could establish closer co-operation between the two trade blocks around a two very similar free trade agreements.

Bilateral Free Trade Agreement between EU and UK

One further option that the British government could consider relates to formal withdrawal from full EU membership and its replacement with a bilateral trade agreement between the EU and UK. This is sometimes referred to as the 'Swiss position'. Equally, it could refer to the 'Israel position', because it has successfully negotiated a bilateral trade agreement with the EU.

Since the UK is ill served by participating in the CAP and the CFP, a restriction of free trade with EU nations to industrial and financial goods and services would prove more beneficial than the present status quo. The remaining EFTA countries negotiated such a free trade agreement with the EU in 1972, after the UK, Denmark and Ireland had joined the EU, thus escaping from the financial burdens and policy constraints imposed by EU membership. As with membership of the EEA, this approach would allow the UK to reorientate its economic policy to serve its own perceived national interest rather than those of competitor EU countries. The money saved by non-contribution to the EU budget could be used to increase incentives for productive investment within the UK, and for state expenditure on infrastructural and research-based projects that increase long-term competitiveness. This option provides greater freedom than EEA membership, which implies the agreement of common rules and equal conditions for competition, so that greater pressure would be placed upon EEA participants to accept EU regulations to ensure continued co-operation. Restricting EU relations to a free trade agreement would remove the possibility of such behind-the-scenes pressure.

The third option closely resembles Switzerland's current position, after a majority of its citizens and cantons voted against EEA membership in December 1992. This decision was motivated partly by a desire to preserve its 700 year independence from the rest of Europe, and partly by a disillusionment with an EU model which would undermine the country's tradition of direct democracy for a federation operated by an elite largely unaffected by its member states' citizens (*The Economist*, 28 November 1992). Although Switzerland's political and business elite favoured EEA membership, the Swiss voters did not agree. Indeed, in March 1995, a referendum voted to ban transit lorry traffic through the Alps by 2004 to force traffic onto the railways. Such democratically inspired national action to safeguard the environment was not welcomed by the EU.

These decisions did not haemorrhage economic vitality; instead they strengthened the Swiss economy. For instance, a sharp influx of foreign funds occurred after the 'No' vote, raising the stock market by 30 per cent and strengthening the value of the Swiss Franc. Moreover, Switzerland has managed to maintain relatively low levels of inflation, interest rates and unemployment, together with a significant balance of payments surplus, particularly when compared to the larger continental EU member states. Thus Switzerland is benefiting from its arm's-length relations, despite a continued eagerness amongst its political elite for future EU membership. These relations are based upon over 100 bilateral treaties, including a 1972 Free Trade Agreement, which covers industrial goods (Church 1993). Amongst OECD countries, agriculture apart, there is no economy more open to the outside world than Switzerland. Exposure to such competitive pressures encouraged the development of some of the world's most international-orientated companies. Switzerland is the fourteenth trading nation in the world and the second trade partner with the EU (after the USA) and the third supplier after the USA and Japan. Consequently non-membership of the EU has failed to hamper its economic development or its trading potential.

Despite economic success outside the EU, the Swiss authorities express two fears, which are familiar to UK citizens when confronted with the possibility of a change in relations with the EU. First, since the majority of trade is done with EU nations, membership may prove essential to protect it. Second, absence from the EEA may result in EU discrimination against Swiss-made goods through technical barriers. These concerns may be over-exaggerated. For example, in the Swiss case only 58 per cent of exports and 71.5 per cent of imports relate to the EU, so that its economy is less orientated towards the EU than most commentators claim. Additionally, like the UK, an increasing proportion of its international trade is being conducted with the fast growth areas in Asia and the USA rather than with the slow-growing EU. Thus Switzerland's dependence upon the EU market is likely to diminish in the future. The trend would be accelerated if the UK, Switzerland's fifth most important trading partner, left the EU.

In answer to the second point, the EU nations benefit far more than Switzerland from their trade so that they are unlikely to engage in discriminatory practices that could endanger their own more sizeable exports. Moreover, the Uruguay GATT (latterly WTO) agreement prevents arbitrary treatment of a nation's exports in any market, thus preventing active discrimination against Swiss, or any other countries', exports by the EU. Of course unofficial barriers to trade do exist, but EU membership is no guarantee that these will be dismantled.

Conclusion

The evidence reviewed in this book indicates that Britain's current relationship with the EU may have imposed net costs, not benefits, upon the domestic economy. Consumers pay higher prices due to the interaction of agricultural subsidies and budgetary mismanagement. Businesses pay the cost of over-complicated regulation and harmonisation growing out of the specific conception of single market introduced amongst EU member states. Moreover, future costs relating to a low growth environment, deflationary economic policy infrastructure surrounding EMU and the introduction of the single currency, the euro, together with uncertain initiatives relating to the development of a social market, regulated labour market and aspects facilitating political unification (i.e. defence, foreign policy, immigration controls, etc). As a result, this chapter has outlined a number of potential alternative approaches to the relationship between Britain and the EU. Each possess advantages and disadvantages, and therefore government should make its selection at least partly on the basis of a cost-benefit analysis.

These alternatives strategies possess a common characteristic, namely that they are designed with the UK retaining some degree of attachment with the EU. However, they would in all probability only mitigate against the pernicious effects of the EU. Moreover, they do not completely reflect the fundamental differences between the UK and its current EU partners in terms of economic structure, political and legal systems, let alone social and cultural identity. Therefore it is vital that the UK's future options for economic prosperity and democratic self-governance are not limited to these five alternatives or variations therein. Thus, the next chapter focus upon the alternative of withdrawal from the EU, and specifically how this could provide a number of new options for the British economy. Rather than withdrawal

Chapter 14

An Independent Britain

Introduction

Successive British governments have sought to place the UK at 'the heart of Europe', and in the process have accepted the idea of the inevitability of a drift towards broader and deeper economic and political integration across a large swathe of the European continent. This is not to say that leading British political figures have not made personal stances against this process, together with a larger number who have argued for a loosening of the constraints imposed upon nation states by the integration process (Abbott, 2000; Redwood, 2000; Benn, 2006; Gould, 2006; Mitchell, 2006; Owen, 2006; Shore, 2006). Moreover, both Conservative and Labour governments have drawn their 'red lines' or vetoed specific new initiatives usually seeking to limit national self-determination. However, notwithstanding these efforts, the process of ever-closer unification has progressed from the trade-related common market, through the creation of a SIM, to the recent establishment of EMU.

Withdrawal from the EU provides one means of escaping these increasing constraints imposed by the EU upon the UK's economic behaviour, and which are not fully eliminated by those options involving retained EU membership. The status quo option implies similar costs to EMU unless the UK breaks the TEU convergence rules, for example, concerning ERM re-entry, whilst the EEA involves a budgetary cost and a general acceptance of the EU's regulations for the long-term survival of the agreement, which implies a de facto submission to the EU on many matters. Renegotiation could reduce many of these direct costs, but would be exceptionally difficult because a gain for the UK would involve a net cost for other member states. The Swiss option is the most palatable but if this is achieved with the UK remaining bound by the Treaty of Rome, economic policy remains fundamentally constrained and speculators could therefore 'punish' Sterling for non-compliance with EMU rules. Therefore, in view of the varying but substantial costs implied by any form of EU membership, a fourth option for the UK is complete withdrawal, so that it can repatriate the ability to employ those economic policy tools it sees fit to better manage the economy in its natural interest.

Withdrawal would take the form of Parliament repealing the European Communities Act of 1972 under which EU directives take precedence over UK law, as well as the 1986 and 1993 European Communities (Amendments) Acts which added the SIM and the TEU. Following the example of Greenland, which left the EU after 12 years of membership in 1985, the UK could negotiate a Treaty of Separation to annul the Treaty of Accession and establish formal future trade co-operation on a mutually beneficial basis under the auspices of GATT/WTO rules.

Once attained, the UK is free to operate any economic policy it wishes. It could take the form of a determined effort to rebuild large sections of the UK's industrial base, decimated by EU, and accelerated by ERM, membership. Burkitt *et al.* (1992) outlined the essential elements of one such strategy. It could pursue a low-tax, market-orientated strategy, or else seek to stimulate growth rates through a combination of national Keynesianism, an active labour market and industrial policy. However, the crucial point is that UK citizens would possess the power to decide how they are governed and how the economy is run, rather than exercising merely a token vote at election time because important decisions concerning fiscal, monetary, exchange rate and trade policy are taken in Brussels. The economy would be free to react to external shocks in a way that suited its particular circumstances, not what suited Germany as the strongest EU state, or the 'average' member state, whether or not such a creation of statistical indexes actually exists! Indeed, as the German and Japanese economic 'miracles' were partially based upon a competitive currency and long-term low interest rates for industrial finance, the UK could adopt a similar approach to compete more successfully with EU members rather than be restricted by EU economic policies that are not in its interest.

Supporters of EU economic integration not surprisingly, dismiss the potential arising from renewed economic independence as illusory. They argue that sterling would be susceptible to speculative destabilisation once outside the ERM or EMU, requiring higher interest rates to be maintained than would otherwise be necessary, and thereby deterring productive investment. It has been further suggested that the only way in which the UK can exercise any power in world affairs is as part of the EU, because it is too small to do so on its own. Finally, withdrawal may endanger foreign investment in the UK and cause negative reactions from remaining EU members. Concern over these issues has effectively prevented detailed consideration of withdrawal as a viable policy option, even though this would prove popular with a large minority (and perhaps a majority) of the British population.

Far from the Euro-sceptics having won the battle of ideas, the reverse is actually true. Whilst opinion polls consistently show that UK voters do not like the EU, and would be free of it if they had a choice, the supporters of European integration control the agenda so firmly that whenever an opportunity arises to debate Britain's future, concern over the costs of withdrawal have obscured the best available evidence concerning the likely implications.

Many of the issues raised, however, enjoy little factual basis. For instance, after the ERM experience, it is disingenuous of the supporters of European integration to suggest that disengagement from the EU, and consequent floating of the currency, would damage sterling. During the two years of being fixed to the other EU currencies, the UK lost over a million jobs, and between £5–20 billion expended in defending sterling's value which could have been devoted to productive ends. At total economic value of some £85.4–99.2 billion, equivalent to 8.2–9.5 per cent of 2004 GDP. Moreover, it is unlikely to suggest that the world's financial markets will be fooled into believing that a permanently fixed exchange rate system will operate significantly better than the ERM, without inflicting permanent damage upon weaker EU countries and/or regions. International speculation does not occur against currencies set at the equilibrium level or against rational exchange rate systems but, as with the ERM in the Autumn of 1992, it will undermine any moves towards EMU that are not viable, whatever EU politicians suggest. Destabilising speculation is best prevented by *international*, not EU, action, perhaps with a Tobin tax on currency transactions which are reversed within a short period of time, as suggested by President Clinton at the time of the ERM crisis (Tobin, 1994). The history of free floating currencies is not as successful as its advocates often claim, but managed floating is certainly preferable to the damage inflicted by an inflexible single currency.

The argument that the UK can only exercise any influence on world events within the EU is perverse, appearing to be simultaneously defeatist yet hankering for a world leadership role. The UK lost its former dominant world position because of economic problems. Decades of slow economic growth reduced the UK from being the leading world economy before the turn of the century to a medium sized economy in the 1990s, with political power declining accordingly. Japan and Germany obtained increased international influence not because of foreign policy or military might, but because their economic strength compels attention. If the UK is to regain influence, it must be based upon economic success, which is less likely to be secured within the monetarist-inspired EU-EMU policy straitjacket. Furthermore, the UK could secure international influence far in excess of its size through less conventional means. The Scandinavian countries, for example, achieved significant prestige for their environmental and human rights campaigns. The UK, when it established the National Health Service, was likewise a model that countless other countries used when constructing their own welfare systems. Likewise, the British democratic system is still admired by many sections of the globe as the 'mother of parliaments'. International influence does not, therefore, have to be of the traditional type. Even the latter can be more effectively attained through UK participation in the G7 summits than by being one voice amongst 27 (or more) within the EU.

The belief that withdrawal would reduce the flow of foreign investment into the UK is widely held, but a UK economy growing faster outside the EU with a permanently competitive exchange rate is more attractive to foreign markets than a EU member state. Foreign-based companies locate productive facilities in the UK to enhance their profits through producing output it can sell in the British and European markets, utilising the skills and abilities of a well-educated and flexible labour force. If firms remain profitable irrespective of British membership of the EU, they will continue to invest in the British economy in large numbers, as they currently do with few indications that the UK will participate in the most visible extension of European economic integration, namely the single currency.

Nor is the idea that withdrawal from the EU would provoke retaliation from current EU 'partners' any more probable. Apart from EU political pressure attempting to persuade the UK to change its mind, the other EU countries will not engage in a trade war because their surplus with the UK means that it would hurt them most. The UK habitually runs a large trade deficit with the EU, which means that they sell to us more then we sell to them. Consequently it would be self-damaging for the EU to engage in any measures that reduced trade with the UK. Indeed, if the UK could reorientate its economic policy outside the EU to promote greater economic growth, the UK would be able to buy more EU goods than if it stayed a member and remained a low growth economy within a low growth bloc. Thus the UK is in a strong position to bargain with other EU member states. Any impression of the UK as a weak nation, having to accept EU dictates, is a misconception propagated by the enthusiasts for further integration.

Withdrawal from the EU is only a first, necessary step. Once achieved, the UK can develop whatever trading relations with other nations it desires. It could remain non-aligned, taking advantage of the lower tariffs predominating in the world economy today, due to the success of successive GATT/WTO trade agreements. Or it can make alternative trade alliances. For instance, one possibility is to rejoin EFTA, so taking advantage of a free trade area without the pretensions of economic and political union. EFTA could be expanded to include those East European nations currently desperate to join the EU as a 'badge' of their market economy credentials, but which the EU is hesitant to admit because of the agricultural costs. An EFTA free trade area in manufactures, without agricultural protection, would assist all nations.

A second alternative could be to reinvigorate the Commonwealth trading bloc (West, 1995). Australia, New Zealand and Canada were severely damaged by the UK's decision to join the EU (Burkitt and Baimbridge, 1990) and subsequently reorientated much of their trade towards the emerging economies of East Asia. However, ties of language, culture and mutual advantage may ease a resumption of trade between them, other Commonwealth nations and the UK. The Commonwealth is an asset that the UK often underestimates, particularly since it now includes some of the fastest growing economies in the world, which often possess closer links with other fast growth areas than the UK. Consequently, reorientation of British trade policy will prove profitable.

A third alternative is to form an association with the North American Free Trade Agreement (NAFTA), which comprises the USA, Canada and Mexico. Since approximately one quarter of UK trade is already done with the USA, this bloc, together with the Commonwealth link to Canada, would be beneficial for the UK. Furthermore, talks between the USA, China, Japan and fifteen other Pacific nations concluded with their determination to form a Pacific Free Trade Area by the year 2010 for the industrialised countries, which would encompass most of the fastest growing economies in the world. It may arguably be in the UK's economic self-interest to negotiate a trade agreement with such countries rather than to remain within the EU, since the potential for export sales is significantly higher. Consequently, whilst withdrawal from the EU provides the UK with an opportunity to operate an independent trading policy relying upon bilateral agreements with major trading nations, a combination of free trading areas between EFTA, the Commonwealth, NAFTA and in future the Pacific nations would create superior trading opportunities for the UK than remaining trapped within the EU could do.

Alternative Trade Blocs

(i) Membership of NAFTA

If the UK were to join NAFTA, it would be required to leave the EU since the latter compels its member states to adopt a common external tariff and to subscribe to an EU-wide uniform external trade policy. There are, however, a number of compelling reasons why both the US and the UK should actively promote such a development.

As demonstrated, the UK and US economies are closely intertwined; further trade liberalisation would result in immediate benefits, in terms of trade creation, for both. Over the last decade, for instance, UK net direct investment in North America was more than double its investment in the EU. In 1997 British direct investment in the US was $18.3 billion greater than any others country's, which represented 30 per cent of all FDI in the US. Similarly, America invested more in the UK than anywhere else, $22.4 billion amounting to 20 per cent of the total of all US foreign direct investment.

From the past, the US and UK share a common culture and language, which make a contemporary trade relationship between them more likely to prove successful. A free trade area centred around an Anglo-American nexus is a more efficient fit than any conceivable alternative economic arrangement; it would also be building upon success, because over the past 15 years the US and Canada have created 2 million more jobs than EU countries.

For the future, the telecommunications revolution has led to the 'death of distance'; sharing borders no longer necessarily translates into increased trade and financial transactions, compared to a geographically distant country, as it has tended to do throughout history. A US-UK focal trading relationship would not work well in the era of the sailing ship or even when the Treaty of Rome was signed in 1957. Today information technology makes it eminently practical.

If Britain joins NAFTA, the larger group will help to protect both the US and the UK from whatever outcome emerges from the EU experiment in supranationalism. A more broadly based NAFTA can counter the impact of either an imploding or a successful integrating, but by necessity largely inward looking, EU.

NAFTA countries have already expressed interest in establishing closer trading relations with EFTA and Chile. If Britain participated in such a grouping, a revamped NAFTA could ultimately be transformed into a global free trade association, which could potentially incorporate such countries as Australia, New Zealand, South Africa, the Caribbean countries, Denmark, Sweden, Norway, Ireland and Switzerland. It would be a grouping, based solely upon a commitment to free trade between them. It would seek no control of member states' trade relation with non-members nor would it possess the motivation to pursue 'ever closer union' that renders the EU unpalatable to many people within the UK. By contrast, NAFTA would prove more consistent with the democratically accountable sovereignty of each individual participating nation state.

Impact of a 'North Atlantic' FTA

One important factor for potential partners in a free trade area to consider relates to the degree of comparability of the economies in question. In particular, what possibilities for economies of scale exist for firms taking advantage of the larger free trade area, and whether trade creation will exceed trade diversion resulting from the creation of the larger trade bloc. The former benefit will result from companies currently stymied from expanding to their optimum size due to the limited size of the domestic market, and therefore are unable to offer consumers products as cheaply as would be the case in a larger market. This potential for lower prices will also be more likely to be realised in a larger market, where competition will prevent former national monopolies or oligopolies from exploiting their market power and maintaining high prices.

A second type of potential benefit accruing from the enlargement of NAFTA would refer to the degree of trade creation less diversion. This relates to the fact that, in a global market characterised by free trade, the most efficient producer(s) in a given commodity should specialise in its production, thereby optimising consumer benefits from low prices and efficient production. However, the existence of trade restrictions (i.e. tariffs) means that less efficient internal producers might be able to produce goods and services more cheaply, thereby transferring production from more to less efficient companies, and consequently wasting precious resources through this unwarranted diversion of trade. The benefit of a free trade area is where former tariffs levied on foreign firms now inside the tariff barriers might result in more efficient producers taking market share from less efficient domestic firms, thereby consuming less scarce resources and thus potentially increasing world production.

US and UK – partner economies?

The UK and US enjoy close links in terms of trade and investment. British exports to the US are now larger than those to France and Germany combined. Table 14.1 provides the relevant details for 1998.

Not only is British trade with NAFTA growing, whilst that with the EU is stagnant. Inward and outward direct investment is overwhelmingly with North America. Table 14.2 provides the evidence over the decade from 1987 to 1996.

Table 14.1   The UK's largest ten markets (total exports, 1998)

Country	£ billion	%
USA	61.39	17
Germany	34.2	10
France	26.89	8
Netherlands	25.7	7
Italy	17.25	5
Ireland	14.85	4
Belgium and Luxembourg	14.23	4
Japan	13.08	4
Spain	11.44	3
Sweden	7.01	2
UK's top ten	226.04	64
Other countries	125.12	36

Source: Global Britain (1999).

Table 14.2   UK inward and outward direct investment (1987–1996)

Outwards A	Inwards B	By region	Balances
63.64	58.64	North America	4.96
31.83	15.04	EU	16.79
7.63	6.09	Other Western European countries	1.54
21.21	5.82	Other developed countries	15.39
47.87	1.87	Rest of the world	46.00
172.18	87.5	World	84.68
		By country	
59.02	55.55	US	3.47
4.62	3.13	Canada	1.49
13.11	2.83	Australia	10.28
7.05	4.09	Germany	2.96
6.09	5.32	France	0.77
1.69	2.83	Japan	-1.14
1.41	1.61	Netherlands	-0.2
4.84	0.27	South Africa	4.57

Notes: A – earnings flowing into the UK   B – earnings flowing out from the UK.
Source: Milne (1998).

Since its withdrawal from the ERM, the British economy has been convergent, both structurally and cyclically, with North America. Consequently sterling tracks the US dollar not the euro, whilst its divergence from continental euro has widened. Thus sterling has fluctuated in a range of 13 per cent against the dollar since September 1992, but over a range of 37 per cent against the (former) deutschemark. Such oscillations determine the efficiency of interest rate harmonisation, leading to the conclusion that the American and British economies are more convergent with each other than either is with the euro zone. Such a conclusion is supported by analysis of the growth rates of the UK, the US, France and Germany.

The correlation coefficients shown in Table 14.3 indicate that the timing of the UK economic cycle has been closer to that in the USA. For all period, the US and UK record high correlation coefficients consistently with relatively synchronised economic cycles, whilst in both the latest UK and international cycles there was little or no correlation between British and German growth. Similarly, higher correlation coefficients are normally recorded for the UK and the USA than for Britain and France although the difference is less marked. Therefore the economies of the UK and NAFTA are already deeply enmeshed commercially, whilst they tend to experience the different phases of the economic cycle simultaneously.

Table 14.3   Correlation coefficients of comparative growth rates

	UK/US	UK/Germany	UK/France
1970–1996	0.66	0.31	0.46
1979–1996	0.56	0.01	0.38
Economic cycles			
1975–1981 (UK)	0.86	0.82	0.82
1981–1992 (UK)	0.47	-0.14	0.48
1982–1993 (International)	0.52	-0.30	0.35

Source: Jamieson and Minford (1999).

The UK economy is the sixth largest in the world, after USA, China, Japan, India and Germany, when measured in GDP (PPP) terms and the thirteenth when measured in GDP per capita terms (excluding small island nations/financial havens) (CIA, 2005). When the 60 million people living in the UK are added to the NAFTA figures, this trade bloc would be far larger than the EU, with a population of 495 million, compared to the EU, which would be reduced in size to 397 million citizens (and 24 nation states) by Britain's departure (CIA, 2005). According to the OECD, in purchasing-power-parity terms Britain was ranked 17th of the organisation's 29 members in 1999, whilst among G7 economies, Britain was fifth, behind US (52 per cent wealthier), Canada (16 per cent), Japan (10 per cent) and Germany (6 per cent), although ahead of both France and Italy (both 2 per cent poorer). Although these figures are susceptible to significant variations due to changes in exchange rates, for example, the recent devaluation by the US dollar will reduce GDP figures when compared with the EU, although whether the figures were previously artificially inflated, or are not artificially deflated, only history can judge.

In terms of business cycle, the UK has traditionally had a closer statistical relationship with USA than with Germany and other leading EU member states (Bayoumi and Eichengreen, 1993). Indeed, whilst the US and UK economies have enjoyed years of relatively rapid economic expansion, many continental EU economies have been trapped in conditions of slow economic growth and high unemployment. The US has created 22 million new jobs over the last decade, whilst UK unemployment stands at a twenty year low. Comparable unemployment figures for leading EU member states are 9.1 per cent in Germany, 11.7 per cent in France and 12 per cent in Italy, whilst standing at approximately 5 per cent for the UK and US. Consumer confidence is high in both economies, and whilst America's output of goods and services has grown by an astonishing 58 per cent in 9 years, Britain's economic growth rate has recovered to rank in the middle of the Group of seven rich countries. Indeed, UK growth rates have outpaced those of Germany over the past two decades.

One noticeable change in both US and UK economies during the past decade has been the remarkable transition in their respective labour markets. The shift towards non-standard contracts, whether part-time, temporary or fixed-term working, together with the deregulation of the labour market, has increased the flexible adaptation of both economies to deal more effectively with industrial restructuring. One notable feature of this change is a decline in the non-accelerating inflation rate of unemployment (NAIRU), which denotes that level of unemployment, which is associated with a stable rate of inflation. If unemployment is forced lower, inflation accelerates; if unemployment exceeds this rate, inflation tends to fall. In a remarkable change from a decade previously, both economies have little tendency towards inflationary wage pressure despite low unemployment levels. Moreover, productivity has been rising quickly in both nations, with US productivity growth outstripping average wage growth. This, together with the high value of both currencies, has dampened remaining inflation pressure from increasing oil prices and property market booms.

One factor stimulating productivity increases, running at double the average of the previous 25 years in USA, is due to the impact of information technology. One estimate calculates that computers account for about a quarter of the overall increase in productivity, with increases in the use of information technology accounting for approximately half of this rise. The UK accounted for 44 per cent of all EU venture investment in high technology, with Germany a poor second with 17 per cent of the investment total. The diffusion of information technology and especially the internet throughout the economy is incomplete, thereby allowing for continued high rates of future economic expansion (*The Economist*, 2000). Stock market asset expansion has further stimulated consumer expenditure, with high technology shares securing the greatest value accumulation, before more recent market adjustment.

Macroeconomic strategy is similar for the UK and US, with restrained fiscal policy enabling a greater role for monetary policy loosening to facilitate economic growth and increased levels of investment though lower real interest rates. Supply-side policy seeks to reduce taxation to encourage entrepreneurship, together with stimulation of investment in human capital. Consequently, both nations are ranked in the top ten most competitive nations in the world; the USA maintaining its premier position. Moreover, of the most competitive EU nations, are the smaller, Scandinavian economies that tend to score well in the World Economic Forum international competitiveness index, with the larger, continental EU member states such as France, Germany and Italy receiving significantly poorer rankings.

(ii) Commonwealth

The greatest visible sign of economic weakness is the persistence of mass unemployment within EU nations, which is not matched by the North American, Asian 'Tiger' and Latin American areas. Indeed, it is interesting to note that many Commonwealth countries offer potentially faster growing markets than do other EU member states.

Historic links with Commonwealth nations could give the UK a potential advantage in establishing trading links with these dynamic economies. These include Singapore, India, Pakistan, Malaysia, New Zealand, Australia, Canada and the 'new' South Africa. The East Asian link is potentially also important as a bridgehead to closer trading links with China. A survey by Price Waterhouse suggested that out of the UK's top 250 quoted companies, 31 per cent have already invested in China and a further 37 per cent expressed their intention to follow suit (cited in *Sunday Telegraph*, 13 November 1994). In 1993, Commonwealth countries accounted for 12.8 per cent of all UK exports and 13.1 per cent of UK imports. Between 1991 and 1993 exports to the Tiger economies, North America, Latin America and Eastern Europe rose by 53 per cent, providing two-thirds of the total export gain in this period.

Over the 10 years from 1983 to 1992, £24.8 billion was invested in Commonwealth nations by UK companies, only £5.8 billion less than in the EU and half as much as in the USA, but nevertheless a significant volume for a trading bloc which receives little strategic attention compared with the supposed advantages emanating from the EU. This trade potential is likely to have become even more favourable as those regions with close Commonwealth connections out perform the IMF's estimated world growth rate of 3.7 per cent, whilst the USA, Eastern Europe and non-EU industrial countries were all anticipated to grow faster than the EU.

The World Bank (1993) estimated that the areas of the world which grew most during the past two decades, namely South and East Asia, will continue to expand more rapidly in the next decade (Table 14.4). Additionally, growth potential is expected to result in significantly higher rates amongst most developing, than amongst the developed, economies. Latin America, Africa and the Middle East join Asia in offering UK companies superior potential for increased export sales than does the EU single market. OECD nations are expected to grow slower than developing countries, with EU members more sluggish than the rest of the OECD, so that the focus for UK companies wishing to expand sales overseas must be where demand is rising the fastest. Because of developments in the world economy, the danger of the single market is that it might distract UK firms from pursuing their widest options for sales and encourage a parochial European mentality at a time when a more international focus is indicated, for both short- and long-term trade prospects.

Table 14.4   Real GDP growth, annual average (per cent)

Countries	Actual 1974–1993	Forecast 1994–2003
Rich Industrial Countries	2.9	2.7
Developing Countries	3.0	4.8
East Asia	7.5	7.6
South Asia	4.8	5.3
Latin America	2.6	3.4
East Europe and former USSR	1.0	2.7
Sub-Saharan Africa	2.0	3.9
Middle East and North Africa	1.2	3.8

Source: World Bank (1994); *The Economist* (1994).

Since Asia and Latin America are the world's fastest growing economies, their purchase of world exports is also likely to increase. In 1993, one-fifth of UK exports, amounting to 4 per cent of GDP, went to developing countries. Because of the rapid growth of these economies, their share of exports will rise and become more important for UK economic development than the EU single market within a relatively short period of time. However, the UK is distracted from taking advantage of such export opportunities by the publicity given to the SIM and by the EU's common external tariff. The latter is an impediment to free trade which encourages other nations to place tariffs upon EU nations' exports, thereby putting UK exporters at a competitive disadvantage with the rest of the world.

Naturally enough, predictions relating to future market shares must always be taken with more than a degree of scepticism due to the tendency to fail to predict external, or even internal shocks, which may alter national growth and competitiveness figures substantially. Suitable examples concern currency and financial crises involving EU member states in 1992, Asian economies in 1997 and Russia in 1998. Nevertheless, even including these effects, East Asia appears likely to expand more rapidly than continental EU economies over the next few years, and therefore trade relations are more likely to grow in importance over this medium-term time period.

(iii) A revitalised EFTA?

The possibility of using EFTA membership in order to access the SIM was discussed in the previous chapter. However, the potential offered by EFTA is worth exploring in the context of establishing supplementary trade relationships supplementary to those with the EU member states.

In this regard, a revitalised EFTA could provide an alternative to the EU as a looser form of co-operation between European nations. This might prove interesting for those political parties and segments of the electorate in nations currently waiting their opportunity to secure full EU membership. There is significant electoral opposition to European integration amongst a number of EU accession candidates, in addition to sizeable majorities within Norway, Sweden, Denmark, Iceland and Switzerland who are broadly sceptical towards further European political and economic integration. Many of these voters would certainly prefer the type of co-operative arrangements that could be forged through the auspices of EFTA than via the 'full-blooded' version pursued by the EU.

Conclusion

Concentration upon Britain's relationship with the EU is not, however, a sufficient response to the analysis contained within this book. Indeed, in part, it replicates one of the most fundamental problems that EU membership has imposed upon British businesses and government; namely, that it has forced an over-concentration upon the European region to the detriment of relationships with other potentially even more significant areas of the world. Indeed, it may have caused Britain to narrow its focus, and in the process to neglect previous significant partners in trade and commerce. It has caused too much of Britain's energies to be dedicated towards facilitating convergence with European neighbour economies, rather than concentrating upon developing markets for British goods and services amongst the fastest growing areas of the world.

This chapter examined a number of the main options available to the British economy following a decision to withdraw from EU membership, and its consequent freedom to craft an independent economic policy based upon national priorities and interests. This would allow a British government to design and implement an economic strategy irrespective of the rules and regulations arising from Brussels. It would additionally enable Britain to form new trade alliances with trade groupings or blocs that better represent the dynamic elements of the world economy. Rather than being tied into regional economic integration, as distinctive areas of British competitive advantage are sacrificed in pursuit of harmonisation across the European continent, British workers and companies could benefit from a change in focus – from a narrow, Euro-centred vision of the future, to a global, more enriching alternative.

Withdrawal would free Britain from many of the regulations and standardisations imposed by the EU in the cause of creating a fully-functioning single market. It would release a significant sum of money that the UK annually transfers to the EU budget (net of receipts), it would free the UK to adopt different trade policies with other nations and/or trade bloc's throughout the world. Moreover, it would prevent unwelcome constraints being placed upon national macroeconomic management, from the rules governing EMU to those adopted in the very early years of the Treaty of Rome. However, it also has the potential to provide Britain with the *freedom to* develop alternative economic and trade policies that are distinctly different from those pursued by EU member states. It could promote reindustrialisation, using all of the instruments of industrial policy to select, support and nurture strategic industries through the early and unknowable stages of their development, until they too achieve their own international competitive advantage. Governments may prefer to make use of fiscal, monetary and exchange rate policy instruments, unhindered by EMU dictates, to prioritise economic growth, low unemployment and low inflation above external exchange rate stability and compliance with the dream of a 'united states of Europe'. This issue is considered in the next chapter.

Chapter 15

Alternative Economic Policies

Introduction

Participation in further EU integration will place an additional straightjacket upon UK macroeconomic policy and increase the difficulty of pursuing its national interest. For example, the model for EMU seeks to impose a particular institutional framework that restricts the flexibility of action of individual countries in order to enable economic policy to be determined, or at least co-ordinated, from the centre. Many economists (Jamieson, 1998; Michie, 1999; Minford, 1999; Ormerod, 1999a) argue that greater autonomy for individual nation states, under the principle of subsidiarity, might provide a more stable economic environment in which to pursue further co-operation between countries. However, largely due to the political desire to tie members more closely together, the EU is seeking to progressively replace economic autonomy for a nation state by the requirement to co-ordinate its economic strategy with the EU norm, or else be subject to sanctions levied by the EU Commission (Pennant-Rea *et al.*, 1997).

A decision to reject such developments would restore to national government those economic instruments essential to the management of its economy. Governments will be able to devise different economic programmes and, once endorsed by the electorate, will possess the means by which to pursue their chosen objectives. Democracy will, therefore, be restored, so that citizens can once again enjoy the opportunity to choose the economic strategy pursued by the government of the day. Moreover, governments will be able to pursue a more balanced economic programme, pursuing the multiple objectives of full employment, high economic growth and a sustainable balance of payments as well as low inflation. The opportunities are substantial.

To illustrate the broad range of different policies that could be enacted, this chapter outlines a number of broad alternative economic strategies that could be pursued, once a nation is freed from the restrictive grip of the ECB and the requirements of the TEU, let alone any future developments. Additionally, it discusses the development of complementary industrial strategy and exchange rate policy. The former can only prove effective if supplemented by fiscal and monetary policies that target growth and reject deflation. Inflation is not the British disease but the symptom of an economy that cannot produce enough to satisfy domestic demand. Britain's basic economic problem is insufficient production. The solution is to boost demand but channel it to UK industry, improving profits, stimulating production and hence productivity, and providing the incentive to invest. Thereby cutting unit costs and inflation through a considered policy of economic expansion. It can be achieved, free from EU constraints, through control of the exchange rate and the accompanying interest rate changes. Such a policy makes it profitable to produce in the UK, by utilising the price mechanism to boost exports, encourage import substitution and lure British industry back into sectors it has abandoned. A tax on imports would provide crucial support. An effective exchange rate policy is critical to the successful implementation of the outlined options for macroeconomic policy. The intention is to demonstrate, not only that national economic management is still feasible, but also that it is preferable to transferring the main levers of macroeconomic policy into the hands of the EU which is incapable of using them consistently in the best interests of all member states simultaneously.

Tight Monetary Policy – Low Interest Rate Strategy

The first potential economic strategy seeks to follow the framework established by Alan Greenspan and the US Federal Reserve Bank, whereby national monetary authorities (whether in the hands of an independent or democratically controlled central bank) seek a higher long-term growth rate by providing a favourable climate for industrial expansion through low inflation and hence reduced long term interest rates. Fiscal policy is used to support the more dominant monetary policy by restraining inflationary pressures, thereby reinforcing the low interest rate objective. The globalisation of financial markets prevents governments from 'persuading' financial institutions to finance public sector borrowing at less than the market rate. Consequently, the higher the level of public sector borrowing on the international money markets, the higher the price for that borrowing in terms of long-term interest rates. This approach assumes crowding-out in the financial markets due to limited resources for lending to prospective borrowers because, were banks to create money simply to meet the additional demand for funds so that the supply of loanable funds was relatively elastic, interest rates would be unaffected. However, the strategy seeks to reduce government expenditure in order to reduce borrowing and hence interest rates.

In 'hard' versions of this strategy, the government endeavours to maintain a high value for the currency in order to squeeze inflation further. The objective is comparatively easy to accomplish if the country enjoys a trade surplus, because the pressure on its exchange rate is upwards due to the country's competitive position, assuming the absence of speculative motives to counter this fundamental relationship. However, since the UK typically suffers from a current account trade deficit, a rise in short-term interest rates is needed to attract sufficient short-term capital investment into UK securities to counterbalance trade-related downward pressures on the currency, thus maintaining a high value for sterling. However, these developments will impact long-term interest rates and thus conflict with the fundamental goal of the strategy. Nevertheless, there is no reason why sterling should not prove to be a stronger currency than the euro, particularly due to the participation of high-inflation southern European member states and an ECB forced to balance economic policy between conflicting needs (Baimbridge *et al.*, 1999b; Weber, 1991b). The ECB will require time to establish its anti-inflation credibility and to demonstrate that it can ensure the long-term stability of EMU.[1] Moreover, unemployment remains the greatest economic problem for Europe to solve; thus it is probable that, sooner rather later, the ECB will come under pressure to loosen monetary policy. The departure of German Finance Minister Lafontaine may have indicated an early victory for supporters of the independent ECB and the restrictive Maastricht rules, but it does not indicate which viewpoint will ultimately prove the stronger.

A Fiscal-based Strategy

A second distinctive economic strategy involves the more active use of fiscal as well as monetary policy in order to pursue both internal and external balance for the economy. Internal balance refers to more than just low inflation, but also to low unemployment and to high rates of economic growth. Accordingly, a mixture of demand-side reflation and supply-side labour market policies, particularly measures encouraging re-training and labour mobility, could reduce unemployment. Thus, the net stimulative effect is targeted upon specific sectors of the economy that most require assistance, rather than raising aggregate demand *per se* and creating inflationary bottlenecks. Economic growth could be facilitated by the maintenance of a competitive exchange rate through managed floating, perhaps based upon a trade-weighted basket of currencies, together with tax incentives for firms that increase productive investment. A mixture of fiscal and monetary policy could restrain inflation; if this proved difficult to achieve, rather than abandon the other internal objectives, governments could enact additional measures to restrain inflationary pressures. These might include the temporary re-introduction of credit controls, an incomes policy (tax-based or otherwise) or co-ordinated national bargaining. Although currently unpopular amongst economists who prefer the allocative efficiency of free markets, the reality of sticky wages and prices, due to oligopolistic markets as much as the existence of trade unions, gives rise to the possibility of market failure resulting in persistently high unemployment and slower-than-trend output growth. In this case, government intervention is justified to achieve a superior outcome. It is a fact that the majority of the world's nations still retain exchange controls to assist them to manage their economies, whilst Ireland's remarkable recent growth rates have been facilitated by 'social contracts' with trade unions to prevent wage pressures undermining its competitive position. Finally, external balance can be achieved through the provision of a competitive exchange rate, although structural problems in export sectors may require supplementary supply-side measures to improve product quality, reliability and to encourage a shift of resources to provide goods and services in growing rather than stagnant markets.

The 'Keynesian' strategy is notably different from the first approach due to its positive role for government action in wider areas of economic activity. Accordingly, an approach of this nature would be facilitated by an industrial policy designed to enhance the long run competitiveness of UK industry. An analysis of

---

1 Kydland and Prescott (1977) argue that rules or pre-commitment are more relevant when the monetary and fiscal authorities enjoy a reputation for discipline and consistency over time, whereas discretionary policy is more appropriate when such credibility is lacking.

trade flows indicates that Britain enjoys a comparative advantage in financial and media services, and those areas of manufacturing which rely upon a high degree of scientific innovation, such as telecommunications, pharmaceuticals, aerospace, energy exploration and generation, biochemicals and computer-related activity.[2] In contrast, Britain is less competitive in lower value-added manufactures, most notably in engineering and metalworking sectors. Outside the EU, Britain could strive to strengthen its competitive position by enhancing the productive potential of already strong sectors through *targeted* reductions in corporation tax, research and development tax credits, and greater spending upon education. Innovative research undertaken by universities and publicly funded research centres requires prioritisation in terms of the allocation of government resources, if higher growth is to be forthcoming. Labour market programmes designed to re-equip workers for the requirements of industries with a competitive advantage ensure that their maximum growth potential is not undermined by the lack of a skilled workforce, whilst facilitating the shift of resources to more productive uses. The promotion of firms based in the UK has the further advantage that it will substantially improve the balance of payments position in the long-run, whilst ensuring that the majority of the improvements in living standards and profitability remain in the UK economy and are not repatriated abroad by transnational corporations. Moreover, the trend towards foreign-owned plants demanding ever-increasing 'sweeteners' to retain production in existing plants raises the possibility that providing inexpensive finance or development grants to UK-based firms might prove a cheaper alternative that generates an improved long-term growth reward.

An Industrial Strategy

An active industrial strategy must be based upon understanding of what promotes industrial competitiveness. Porter's (1990) exhaustive research demonstrated that economic success is achieved through the development of 'clusters' of mutually reinforcing internationally competitive industries. Britain once enjoyed the benefits of clustering, as one sophisticated industry spawned and reinforced others; British goods pulled British services into overseas markets and vice versa, its multinationals served as loyal customers abroad, and the cluster of financial services and trade-related industries was highly self-reinforced. However, a gradual unwinding of industrial clusters occurred, with only pockets of competitive advantage remaining. British firms rely heavily on foreign inputs and machinery. As some UK industries became uncompetitive, they were increasingly poor buyers for other domestic products. The spiral continues downward, cushioned only by long tradition and the remnants of technological innovation. Thus many British manufacturing companies lag behind those of other industrial countries such as Germany, Japan and Sweden in process technology and in their willingness and ability to invest in new plant, undermining

---

2   It is worth noting that the international price structures of many of these key products are denominated in US dollars. Moreover, the Euro is likely to have a more volatile medium-term relationship with the US dollar than Sterling has experienced since the UK's withdrawal from the ERM in September 1992.

competitive advantage in industries producing manufacturing equipment such as machine tools, process controls and lift trucks. In the car industry, for instance, the UK lost competitive advantage in end products outside a small luxury sector and positions in a variety of automotive components eroded with it. The same process applied to an even greater extent in durable goods, such as appliances and consumer electronics.

The sectors where British firms sustain competitive advantage partly owe it to a cluster of related, supporting industries. In consumer goods and services, a vibrant retail industry creates pressures to innovate. Britain was among the first countries to permit television advertising, which created a fertile environment for companies to build skills in modern marketing. The City of London provides another sector where British strength relies upon the advantages of clustering. Britain's international position in financial services such as trading, investment management, insurance and merchant banking is concentrated in the City, along with supporting activities like information and telecommunications facilities, financial journalism, printing and publishing, legal services, financial advertising and public relations. The dynamism of this cluster attracts firms worldwide to locate in London.

However, British industry overall lacks dynamism and the ability to upgrade its competitive position unaided, due to cumulative disadvantages which reinforce each other negatively in the spiral of relative decline. Problems in one industry hurt others. Falling competitiveness reduces relative living standards, making consumer demand less sophisticated. Downward pressure on government revenue leads to cutbacks in resource creation and social services, weakening still more industries. Britain's remaining competitive advantages are insufficient to generate sufficient well-paid jobs for all its citizens. Therefore it is caught in the downward spiral of clustering and its relative living standards suffer accordingly. Loss of competitiveness creates its own momentum, which, once established, is hard to reverse without a major policy initiative. Indeed lingering market positions and customer loyalties allay any sense of urgency about the need for change.

A significant proportion of growth in skilled and value-added UK employment has occurred from investment by foreign firms. Much of this, however, is attracted by relatively low production costs. Foreign investments are largely in assembly facilities, taking advantage of poorly paid, mostly unskilled labour, or in service industries such as hotels, golf courses and retail outlets. While overseas capital benefits British industry, an economy whose growth depends on assembly outposts of foreign companies will be constrained in terms of productivity increases. Certainly such investment alone cannot break the vicious circle between a weak balance of payments, slow growth and declining manufacturing, which has developed in the three decades since UK accession to the EU.

Britain demonstrates the problems facing an economy needing to restart the upgrading process. A number of fundamental problems must be tackled by a coordinated industrial strategy if recovery is to occur:

1. The UK cannot regain innovation-driven competitiveness without a world-class educational and training system encompassing all socioeconomic and ability levels. The rate of investment in human skills must rise substantially,

standards must be improved and technical expertise must be stressed. This is perhaps the most pressing issue facing Britain over the next decade, for the need to improve the quality and quantity of its labour force is great. Research conducted in France and Germany by the National Institute for Economic and Social Research (Prais and Jarvis, 1989; Prais and Wagner, 1988; Steedman, 1988) demonstrated that the level of technical qualifications of craft workers is far superior in those countries to that achieved in the UK. A further report (Prais and Jarvis, 1989) on training in the retail industry concluded that the UK was creating a certificated semi-literate underclass'. Moreover, training trends are deteriorating in the UK; in 1964 240,000 young people were in apprenticeships and 148,000 in industrial or mercantile training, but some 20 years later these figures had dropped to 55,700 and 36,700 respectively.

2. British companies, as well as the government, face a busy skills agenda. They need to realise that without a broader pool of trained human resources, their competitive advantage will be limited. This need embraces managerial staff, where British firms have traditionally employed far fewer university graduates than other industrial economies. Unless companies accept greater responsibility for internal training of all workers, they will make little progress relative to their competitors. The multi-skilling of the industrial workforce provides the route to productive flexibility, quality and innovation, while enhancing individuals' occupational status. The inability of individuals to contribute to their full potential is reflected in the stunted economic performance of many sectors. Narrow vocational training is a contradiction in an economy that seeks to place workers at the forefront of innovation. Consequently the emphasis must be on quality training to reflect new economic requirements.

3. UK investment levels need to increase to match the improved labour force, primarily in manufacturing but also in the infrastructure of essential services. Machinery and plant in many sectors are currently antiquated, so that the development of advanced technologies as a basis for expanding into modern high value-added production is held back. The future competitive advantage of British firms can only be based on innovation in new products and new processes of production. Government aid to industry enabling the maintenance of high investment can play a crucial role in this process.

4. The UK lags behind other industrial nations in the share of GDP allocated to research and development (R&D). Government investment in R&D is among the highest as a percentage of GDP across OECD countries, but half is focused on defence that possesses limited spin-offs for civilian industry. Even more troubling is the low rate of overall R&D spending in firms. A reallocation of both government and company resources towards commercial R&D is necessary for successfully reversing the spiral of relative decline, by stimulating both the generation and the diffusion of innovation. Supporting reform of the accounting treatment of R&D expenditure would also prove beneficial.

5. Without sophisticated buyers, innovation and dynamism will be stunted. Britain already enjoys demand-side advantages in luxury and leisure-related commodities. The challenge is to upgrade industrial demand to broaden the

sphere over which British companies benefit from well-informed buyers. Improvement of managers' and workers' education contributes to this objective. The prosperous London and South East markets can be the cutting edge of new consumer demand conditions.

6. Some of the operations of London financial markets have become a barrier to British competitive advantage. Institutional investors often possess little commitment to companies nor do they play an active role in corporate governance. A group of large British conglomerates has emerged, which buy and sell unrelated companies, but whose financial orientation does little in the long-run to upgrade competitive advantage in domestic industry. The result of such trends is that US-style earnings pressures threaten to dominate UK management thinking. However, a long-run bias in industrial decision-making is in the interests of national prosperity.

7. British economic prosperity will never be complete without a faster rate of new business formation to make headway in reducing unemployment, because revitalisation of established industries sometimes reduces the size of the workforce. However, new business formation depends on skills and ideas, on appropriate motivation and goals, on active competition, and access to capital. One of the urgent reasons for upgrading British education, especially in universities, is to seed new ventures. The UK cannot rely on foreign investment for job creation and prosperity (*The Economist*, 1991).

These measures should reduce the level of joblessness, leading to the long-term restoration of full employment. By reducing, and eventually eliminating, the long-run growth of imports and by stimulating an expansion in exports, the strategy aims to reconcile full employment with the simultaneous achievement of payments equilibrium.

However, such an industrial strategy can be reconciled with current EU regulations, let alone its future federal aspirations, thus Britain's essential interests' conflict directly with EU moves towards greater integration. However, with determination and imagination, there is no reason why Britain cannot acquire again the significant comparative advantages in the production of goods that once made it the workshop of the world. Services are a crucial complement to this process, but do not alone provide the growth momentum of manufacturing industry nor can they be relied upon to substitute for the deficits in overseas visible trade. The construction of such a competitive economy in the UK involves the complete unravelling and reconstruction of its relationship with the EU. It is to this relationship that we now return.

The policies required to revitalise British industry run counter to current EU rules and would be frustrated by movement towards economic and political union. Major historical trends cannot be reversed quickly; a permanent increase in the British rate of productivity growth, for instance, requires sustained economic expansion, a difficult endeavour given the deflationary tendencies of EMU.

UK membership of the EU tends to frustrate the achievement of these objectives through three fundamental mechanisms. Firstly, Britain's relatively weak competitive trade position with other EU nations prevents market forces from generating unaided the profits required for industrial regeneration. Experience demonstrates that market operations tend to accentuate strengths and deficiencies rather than eliminate them. Secondly, The Treaty of Rome severely limits aid to industry, whilst the public expenditure needed to complement the price mechanism in promoting industrial regeneration is circumscribed by the TEU convergence criteria and SGP. Thirdly, the current functioning of EMU limits the scope for discretionary national economic policies. Therefore, both markets and governments are prevented from addressing the UK's basic problems by the very essence of EU operations and developments.

The scale of deindustrialisation is uniquely intense in Britain requiring the implementation of a solution geared specifically to British problems rather than a more blunt, less sensitive EU-wide programme. However, any strategy designed to confront the UK's deep-seated trading crisis within the EU will take many years to come to fruition. Therefore a danger arises that such a strategy could be jettisoned before it has had sufficient time to be effective, in the face of short-term pressures. This consideration suggests that government funds for industrial restructuring should be exempt from any immediate requirement for reducing public expenditure. Consequently a programme to stimulate industrial investment, boost jobs creation, and improve the quality of education and training must be rigorously maintained in the face of potential short-run problems. The benefits from such a programme would be reaped over a five to ten year period, if the constraints imposed by EU integration are prevented from undermining its potential. Survival in the interim requires the creation of a breathing space for the British economy until the programme becomes effective. The preservation of this essential space depends upon the UK government possessing an active exchange rate and trade policy, with discretionary control over movements in the external value of sterling and freedom to pursue independent fiscal and monetary policies.

Exchange Rate Policy

Export-led growth occurs because the firms that are competitive in world markets commence with the advantage of costs at least as low as their competitors given that an economy is usually required to sell its output to the rest of the world at a competitive price. If it does so, it will embark on export-led growth, otherwise import-led stagnation is likely to follow. Moreover, once export-led growth is established a number of forces operate to keep fast growing economies moving ahead. Particularly significant is the impact of successive waves of investment, which tend to reduce the cost of goods in the internationally-traded goods sector so rendering export prices increasingly competitive. However, a key determinant of competitiveness is to establish and maintain a competitive exchange rate, i.e. one that achieves balance of payments equilibrium at full employment.

If a policy of expanding the British economy through the export-led growth engendered by a competitive exchange rate is adopted, it is unlikely on the available evidence, to cause substantial inflation during its early stages. Indeed, it could lead to inflation falling. However, a further potential generator of price increases may be an overexpansion of domestic demand, so that the economy becomes overheated. Once demand exceeds the capacity to supply, prices begin to rise. Such a scenario must be avoided. However, these problems are not insurmountable; they can be contained through a variety of channels. First, the more resources that are deployed into sectors facing falling cost curves and engaged in foreign trade, the easier it is for self-sustaining growth to be achieved. Large returns on investment that can be obtained in these sectors can provide sufficient new profitability to finance additional new capital requirements. Second, for at least some shortages there is considerable scope for importing what cannot be obtained from domestic production. For many commodities there exists an elastic supply of foreign output to meet domestic shortages. Third, any attempt to reflate the British economy in order to achieve full employment has got to include an undertaking of training, retraining and education, particularly covering engineering and technical work. A competitive exchange rate cannot in itself be a panacea for all the UK's economic problems. It will take some years to recreate full employment. When the pound's external value ensures competitive exports, it will still require price changes to produce substantial increases in output.

Hence, over a period the desired objectives of exchange rate policy are short-term stability and long-term flexibility. The dangers to avoid are long-term fixity and short-term volatility. The only way of achieving these goals is a system that permits long-run change whilst avoiding violent short run fluctuations. Various policies are available to secure this end, but membership of the euro prevents them being implemented by establishing a permanent fixity which imposes deflation upon less competitive national economies. However, this does not reduce relative prices automatically; it does so by creating unemployment and stifling the future prospects for economic growth. That is what is meant by those who advocate EMU membership as a 'discipline' upon the British population.

The exchange rate between two currencies is a price like any other. Its movement enables the two economies to achieve trade and payments balance. If one country's exchange rate is over-valued its exports become more expensive in the foreign currency, while imports become cheaper in its own currency. Therefore export volumes tend to decline and import volumes to increase, so that eventually the trade balance moves into deficit and unemployment rises. Conversely, when a country lowers its exchange rate, exports became cheaper and expand, while imports are constricted. The trade balance usually improves[3] but at some contemporary sacrifice of real income due to higher internal prices.

The correct level for the exchange rate at any one time is that which enables an economy to combine full employment of productive resources simultaneously with approximate balance of payments equilibrium. A higher exchange rate generates overseas deficits and unemployment; a lower one leads to the build up of excessive foreign currency reserves and domestic inflation. However, it has been emphasised that this 'correct' exchange rate varies in value over time (Jay, 1990). The variety

---

3   The converse occasionally occurs, if import and export volumes do not change sufficiently to offset the price movements; the Marshall-Lerner condition states that the trade balance will improve when the sum of the elasticities of demand for exports and imports exceeds unity.

of influences affecting economic performance (trade balances, productivity, price movements, discoveries of natural resources etc.) combines to ensure that the 'correct' value of the exchange rate alters with the years. Therefore a country needs to retain its ability to adjust the external value of its currency. To fix it irrevocably forever is as difficult as attempting to maintain in perpetuity the rate of income tax or the price of oil. The endeavour to do so generates economic inefficiency, usually in the form of accelerating inflation or a rise in unemployment.

Consequently Britain's optimal strategy is to retain the national policy instruments required to increase its competitiveness in a socially acceptable manner. It is essential that the UK retains control over its interest rate, uses Bank of England intervention to smooth speculative fluctuations, encourages world-wide co-operation (through the G8) between central banks and aims for the maximum long term exchange rate flexibility combined with the maximum practical short term stability. Under such a regime, the exchange rate fulfils its role as facilitator of greater growth, higher living standards and full employment, without becoming an end in itself.

There is always a rate of exchange that enables each country to employ its productive resources fully. In an ever-changing environment, the rate frequently alters to secure simultaneous full employment and trade balance. Therefore, when formulating British economic policy outside the EU, any suggestion that the pound should 'shadow' the euro must be rebutted. Such targeting makes domestic objectives harder to achieve; in any case the pound moves more closely with the US dollar than with any European currency.

However, as the Chinese government has illustrated, it is possible for national to choose where they want the exchange rate to be and, over the long-term, to hold it there within narrow margins. Of course there will be short-term fluctuations, but these are not important. It is the medium-term trend that counts. The question then becomes one of which policies can governments pursue to change the exchange rate, and then maintain it near the preferred level? A range of options is available which can be co-ordinated to generate a viable, nation-wide strategy.

Firstly, is the monetary and interest rate stance that the government adopts. Strong evidence exists that tight monetary policies and the high interest rates, which accompany them, pull the exchange rate up, while more accommodating monetary policies and lower interest rates bring it down. Secondly, the actions of both the government and the central bank, when dealing with the foreign exchange market, exert a powerful influence in an area where expectations are crucial. If the government expresses a clear view that the exchange rate is too high or too low, the market will respond. Thirdly, the government possesses a defined strategy to eliminate the foreign trade imbalance. Such a strategy requires a commitment to achieving a long-term competitive exchange rate, which achieves balance of payments equilibrium at full employment. This rate will, of course, alter over time. Fourthly, tariff protection may be crucial in order to restrict the flows of imports to a level consistent with the targeted short-term exchange rate. Fifth, on the capital side of the balance of payments the government can control international financial flows to maintain a competitive exchange rate. Potential policies range from taxes to quantitative restrictions on speculative movements (Baimbridge and Burkitt, 1993).

However, if the value of the currency falls, there is a tendency for imports to stay initially at their previous volume, while the domestic revenue from exports falls because the exchange rate has gone down, the 'J curve' effect. A slow decline in the exchange rate generates a succession of 'J curve' effects flowing from each successive decrease, giving the impression that no improvement is in sight. Nonetheless the empirical evidence of exchange rate movements occurring in Britain and other countries, and of the availability of a battery of policy instruments to sustain a targeted external currency value, demonstrates that in the medium-term governments can determine exchange rates.

As illustrated in Chapter 5, Britain's exchange rate policy has lurched from the ultra fixed systems such as the Gold Standard, through Bretton Woods and the ERM, to the freely floating days when monetarism and the rule of markets swept through governments across the industrialised world. Rarely has the decision to enter, or exit, one particular system been for any proven economic reasons. Instead the main driving force is whatever the current vogue of politicians and their advisers happen to be.

This is clearly an inefficient method of managing an economy, and of determining peoples' employment potential and standard of living. Rather within the context of this discussion concerning the development of an active exchange rate policy to facilitate national economic renewal, we argue that its over-riding function is to convert domestic prices of all factors of production, including, labour, energy, raw materials, into international prices at such a level as to encourage economic growth through the full use of resources and simultaneously to achieve trade balance. If the exchange rate cannot fulfil these functions over a sufficient period of time (to counter fluctuations), this offers conclusive evidence that the exchange rate is misaligned, so that the existing system must come under scrutiny.

Whilst an exchange rate system to suit all economies for all seasons is an impossible reality, the brief analysis of the arguments concerning flexible and fixed exchange rates discussed in Chapter 5 illustrates the complexity of determining the exact exchange rate regime for a country. Two systems, however, offer the greatest potential for combining an exchange rate that secures balance of payments equilibrium with full employment.

Firstly, managed floating does not involve parities that the government is obliged to preserve. Instead the currency is free to float, but the authorities intervene to avoid what they regard to be undesirable consequences of excessive appreciation or depreciation. A weak currency may lead to excessive depreciation that the government may wish to avoid because of its repercussions on the domestic price of imports and the internal cost structure. Alternatively, countries with a strong currency may seek to avoid appreciation if they want to accumulate reserves and are indifferent to the effect on the money supply. Moreover, a country may even attempt to engineer the depreciation of its currency that would otherwise appreciate if the foreign exchange market were left to operate freely.

Secondly, multiple exchange rates offer a system whereby different exchange rates are enforced for different transactions either on the current or capital account. The IMF's official definition of a multiple exchange rate is 'an effective buying or selling rate which, as a result of official action, differs from parity by more than

1 per cent'. Multiple exchange rates can be viewed both as a form of exchange control (particularly over capital transactions) and as a rational response to the fact that different classes of goods have different price elasticities in world trade. Many countries, including Britain in the past with the 'dollar premium', charge a higher domestic price for foreign currency than the prevailing market rate for investment abroad in capital assets such as shares and property. Such a device acts in essence as a form of exchange control.

Misplaced Criticism

Supporters of continued EU membership argue that the degree of economic autonomy for the nation state outlined here is illusory, because globalisation and the integration of financial markets will not allow differences in economic policy to persist. Therefore the UK might as well join the single currency. Indeed, many left-of-centre supporters of economic and monetary integration profess the belief that only as part of a new euroland can governments become sufficiently powerful to operate a form of Euro-Keynesianism without financial markets causing terminal destabilisation via a currency crisis. However, both viewpoints are over-stated. For example, the experience of the UK economy between 1990 and 1992 demonstrated that being tied into a fixed exchange rate system at an uncompetitively high rate leads to a fall in output and a rise in unemployment.[4] However, departure from the ERM and the subsequent 20 per cent depreciation in sterling resulted in the resumption of economic growth, which facilitated a fall in unemployment to levels last experienced two-and-a-half decades earlier. Thus arguments that economic policy autonomy is impossible because of financial market integration are wrong, because both the UK's strategy and performance were significantly different from all other EU member states during this period; that is why it was so comparatively successful. Devaluation gave UK firms a much needed increase in competitiveness, which was not instantly lost due to inflation, as new classical theorists claim, but instead provided government with a freedom of manoeuvre that could have resulted in the adoption of either strategy outlined in this chapter or a multiplicity of alternatives.

A second argument for maintaining EU membership is the suggestion that the UK's European partners would engage in some form of trade protection, which would deny British firms access to the single internal market and therefore cause considerable damage to its economy should the UK remain outside the euro on a long-term basis. The argument is implausible. Firstly, the UK has suffered a substantial trade deficit with the rest of the EU since accession in 1973. Therefore, in the event of a trade war, our EU 'partners' would lose the most. Secondly, any such protectionist measures would fall foul of the Treaty of Rome, the Single European Act, the TEU and the World Trade Organisation's regulations. All are international treaties, binding their signatories to respect reciprocity of trade.

---

4   One estimate, made by Burkitt *et al.* (1996), concluded that the UK's two-year membership of the ERM cost an estimated £68.2 billion in 1992 prices (equivalent to 11.5 per cent of UK GDP), in terms of lost output and one-and-a-quarter million more unemployed.

Another argument favouring continued EU membership is that frequently associated with Tony Blair, namely that it will provide the UK with additional political influence over the future development of the EU. Independence, according to the argument, equals powerlessness.[5] However, the claim is spurious. Whilst the participants in the single currency may opt to discuss their common economic policy apart from other EU member states, there is no legal mechanism for any other decisions to be taken in this way. Thus the UK cannot be marginalised simply due to its non-participation in the single currency. Moreover, its position would be strengthened further by consultation and co-operation with other EU member states who have exercised their opt-out (Denmark and Sweden) or been deemed too divergent for immediate membership (Greece). Further enlargement of the EU will increase the number of member countries incapable or unwilling to sacrifice other policy objectives for conformity to EMU's 'one size fits all' policies. When such uniform monetary measures create areas of high structural unemployment, as they inevitably will, it is essential for opt-out nations to possess a collectively pre-agreed strategy of vetoing any plan to provide EU-wide aid to those areas. Problems created by the euro's operations should not be the responsibility of non-participants, but should be wholly financed by those embracing the single currency. Additionally, because *all* historical monetary unions not based upon political union have collapsed amidst substantial economic difficulties, these non-members would be wise to encourage the EU to formulate a contingency plan for the re-establishment of individual currencies if (or when) the demise of the euro occurs.

In reality, Britain enjoys an effective long-run choice concerning its future strategy; it can embrace an essentially European identity or, if it decides to opt-out of the euro, it can pursue a global strategy. Moreover, the advantages of free trade within the EU and the imposition of a common external tariff on outside imports have become progressively smaller since 1973, as restrictions on trade have been steadily diminished world-wide. Under the auspices of GATT and its successor, the WTO, the average tariff on industrial goods between developed countries has been reduced to just 3.8 per cent. Consequently, the industrialised nations are closer to the free trade ideal than they have ever been. In this gradually emerging new world economy, access to the EU single internal market for UK business is assured.

Britain need not fear that a long-term disengagement with movements towards further EU integration will lead to a powerless isolation. Britain is a member of the 'G8' industrial nations; its economy ranks as one of the largest in the world and the third largest in the EU. It is a member of the World Bank and the International Monetary Fund. It possesses a seat on the United Nations Security Council and remains the head of the Commonwealth, whose potential for expanded trade has recently been grossly neglected (West, 1995; Burkitt *et al.*, 1996). Moreover, Britain

---

5   A related, but separate, argument that the UK will lose its world influence if it remains outside EMU is the direct opposite of the truth. If subsumed into EMU, the UK will be seen as a duplicate mouthpiece for EU interests and there will be pressure for the EU to replace British, German and French individual participation on international bodies including the UN, IMF and G8. A distinct British influence over world events will, under such circumstances, be far smaller.

enjoys a substantial portfolio of overseas assets and investments, and attracts the highest level of inward investment in the EU. It is the world's second largest financial centre and global investor. It has more companies in the world's top 500 than any other EU country. The UK is well placed to be one of the most dynamic and innovative global economies (Taylor, 1995).

Among Britain's greatest assets, underpinning its global economic effectiveness is the English language. More than 1,400 million people live in officially English-speaking countries. One in five of the world's population speaks English. By next year, more than a billion will be learning it. It is the main language of books, newspapers, international business, academic conferences, science, technology, diplomacy and the Internet. Of all electronically stored information, 80 per cent is in English.

The widely held view that Britain has 'no alternative' but to participate in European integration is at odds with the facts. Instead a range of possible alternatives exists. Britain could remain a EU member and secure, under WTO rules, free trading arrangements with the EMU-zone through a series of mutually beneficial, bilateral agreements. It could explore the possibility of a closer relationship with the North American Free Trade Association, as recently suggested by Canadian opposition leaders. Now that formal negotiations have been launched to establish a free trade pact between Canada and the European Free Trade Association (Norway, Switzerland, Iceland and Liechtenstein), the UK could follow the same procedure. Above all, it should intensify its trading and investment links with the Commonwealth and the nations of the Pacific Rim. In these ways Britain would be able to pursue its true contemporary role of global trader and investor, while at the same time retaining its scope for a largely autonomous economic and social policy, such as the two possible strategies detailed above. Furthermore, outside the single currency, the choice between and among such strategies would be taken through the democratic process.

Conclusion

The design of a macroeconomic framework for a complex advanced economy depends upon a multiplicity of diverse factors, including recognition of its unique industrial structure, monetary and fiscal policy transmission mechanisms, the practice of wage formation, propensity for owner-occupation, national savings rates and technological progress. A combination of differences in consumer tastes, political choices, natural resources and centres of competitive excellence, together with the actions of institutions established to implement economic and social policy, necessitates differences in economic policy between nations. For example, the labour market operates very differently in the USA, where non-collective bargaining is the rule, than in Sweden where trade union representation is close to saturation at 90 per cent density, irrespective of whether their fiscal or monetary authorities followed a similar strategy. Moreover, exchange rate regimes tend to have a greater impact upon smaller, export-orientated nations than upon their larger neighbours, where only a relatively small proportion of GDP is traded. Consequently, it is extremely difficult for one international economic authority to replace national macroeconomic management by one common interest or exchange rate. It is simply that many economies of EU member states are too divergent cyclically and structurally from their neighbours for any claim of prior convergence to be convincing and, without such evidence, a common economic strategy is unlikely to be simultaneously in their individual interests.

In view of such fundamental weakness at the heart of the EU project, the decision to reject participation retains for national government the economic instruments vital to successful macroeconomic management. Exchange rates can fulfil their function of equalising the demand and supply for a currency by the variation of its price, thereby preventing a basic uncompetitive imbalance from causing mass unemployment and falling standards of living. Fiscal policy, freed from the twin restrictions of the TEU convergence criteria and the Stability and Growth Pact, can smooth cyclical fluctuations, avoiding periodic unemployment that wastes productive resources and generates associated human misery. The purpose of monetary policy is, then, to prevent unstable boom and slump conditions in housing and financial markets, whilst seeking to ensure a low interest rate for investors in productive capital. Supply-side policies, including selective labour market programmes and investment in the economy's physical and IT superstructure, do not require a rejection of the single currency to be applied, although the benefit of a macroeconomic structure tailored to the needs of the economy would provide a more fertile environment for their implementation. Thus, rather than being weakened by the refusal to be dominated by an EU agenda, which will often conflict with the interests of its economy, the UK would be both stronger and possess a superior ability to adapt to changing international market conditions. In the process, democratic choice would be enhanced and encourage the UK to end its undue preoccupation with events in a small corner of the European continent at the expense of a vigorous attempt to meet the growing demands of emergent markets across the globe.

In view of the overwhelming evidence supporting the maintenance of national self-determination of economic policy, two factors remain to provide the momentum towards further integrationalist economic participation. The first relates to the determination of a small political elite, together with the representatives of multinational corporations, to complete the European integration project; the former perhaps seek the increased influence a 'United States of Europe' would play in world events, whereas the latter desire to evade national regulatory regimes and thereby enhance profits. However, these small elites are neither representative of the wider British electorate, nor even of the majority of business. In a democracy, governments should act in the interests of all the people, which requires the rejection of abandoning national economic policy.

The second factor undermining the vigorous assertion of national independence is the fear of failure. The notion of the UK as a declining nation has long sapped its resolve to follow its own interests and has caused many to prefer safety in 'Fortress Europe', with economic policy dictated by outside 'experts'. Yet, as illustrated in this chapter, there is no reason for such defeatism. Fear is the enemy of innovation and as the one of the largest economies in the world; the UK possesses a significant number of advantages. The question remains whether these can be better realised within an EU model of deeper economic and political integration, a looser relationship with the EU, or through a more independent arrangement, possibly involving withdrawal as a first step towards this reorientation of priorities. This is a question for considered evaluation of all the evidence and not to be closed off due to political prejudice or an ill-thought-through agenda that conflicts with contemporary debate. This is an important question since it goes to the very heart of what Britain will make of itself and whether it places artificial limitations upon its ability to deliver the priorities espoused by its citizens.

Chapter 16

Conclusion

The question of Britain's relationship with the EU has resulted in a large literature over the years, although most of this has been political in nature, with few attempts made to produce an objective, economic analysis concerning Britain's optimal strategy towards its large neighbour. In some ways, this has been a difficult proposition, because rhetoric and a marked avoidance amongst many in the political elite to adequately debate all aspects of the issue has restricted the range of information. Nevertheless, a number of conclusions can be reached. Firstly, the combination of historical and contemporary consequences of EU membership almost certainly involves a net drain upon government resources and the dynamism of the economy. Budgetary contributions, CAP/CFP payments and inflationary consequences for consumer prices, together with the substantial losses concerned with the short-lived ERM membership are all unhesitatingly negative. Trade is more difficult to discern, although even here the estimate generated by this book is that the widening of the British-EU trade imbalance will have resulted in the loss of a significant number of British manufacturing jobs over the three decades of membership.

Britain's potential participation within EMU is likely to create further problems for the domestic economy, as a more efficient monetary transmission mechanism will exacerbate common interest rate changes, taken by the ECB on an average-need basis. This is likely to result in the UK suffering more than most continental neighbours from economic imbalances created by official economic policy measures that, whilst good for the EU as a whole, may create inflation and/or unemployment for the UK. A 'one-club-golfer' is hardly a good model to impose upon a complicated integration of individual economies that, because of the dynamic nature of capitalism, will each tend to converge and diverge in different ways due to internal and external changes in markets and the economic environment. Forcing a uniform economic approach upon each nation is therefore likely to compound economic difficulties.

The monetarist neo-liberal nature of the institutional framework established to sustain EMU is likely to dampen economic development in favour of financial orthodoxy. The ECB, for example, with its sole objective being the achievement of price stability, is likely to operate monetary policy asymmetrically to cement its reputation as anti-inflationary, but this will, in turn, constrain economic growth and cause unemployment to rise, or at least not fall as quickly as it would otherwise have done. The SGP, moreover, will continue to prevent nations from pursuing counter-cyclical fiscal policy, unless they have first secured budget surpluses in all but the worst years. Rather this is a measure that could only be justified if the government recycles this money into the provision of cheap risk capital to its indigenous productive industry, and otherwise is of dubious economic worth. In addition, potential issues of importance include fiscal federalism as a means of securing the stability of EMU, and the potential for developing a social policy dimension to the EU are considered, but practical problems involving cost and political polarisation imply that neither initiative is likely to be introduced in the manner that their advocates would prefer.

Having determined that the economic cost-benefit of past and continuing EU membership is likely to be *negative*, a number of alternative approaches are identified. These indicate that, far from continued economic integration being the only realistic alternative for a medium-sized European nation like the UK, there are a number of feasible options that may well produce superior economic performance. Indeed, this is perhaps the most important conclusion reached by this book – rather than the debate about Britain's future relationship with the EU being continually closed down by political elites who are frightened by the consequences of being forced into taking a decision in the issue, many of these alternatives actually look quite attractive.

Any government that seeks to serve its people and put their best interests before those of the governing political and business elites themselves, should always seek to determine policy after a careful consideration of all major and realistic alternatives, and having done so to periodically review this position in the light of future evidence. Three decades after Britain joined the EU, there is a wealth of evidence that should prompt a re-evaluation of the relationship, and there are a large number of alternatives that need to be carefully considered. It is our hope that the British government both has the openness and confidence to undertake such a re-evaluation, before it forms its opinion upon other measures, like EMU membership, the renegotiated constitution and, indeed, the future structural relationship between Britain and the EU.

Bibliography

Abbott, D. (2000), 'The Case Against the Maastricht Model of Central Bank Independence', in Baimbridge, M., Burkitt, B. and Whyman, P. (eds) *The Impact of the Euro: Debating Britain's Future*, London: Macmillan.

Abbott, K. (1997) 'The European Trade Union Confederation: Its Organisation and Objectives in Transition', *Journal of Common Market Studies*, **35**(3), 465–481.

Ackrill, R. (2005) 'The Common Agricultural Policy', in van der Hoek, M.P. (ed.) *Handbook of Public Administration and Policy in the European Union*, New York: CRC Press.

Addison, J.T. and Sieber, W.S. (1991) 'The Social Charter of the European Community: Evolution and Controversies', *Industrial and Labour Relations Review*, **44**(4), 597–625.

Agell, J. (1996) 'Why Sweden's Welfare State Needed Reform', *Economic Journal*, **106**(439), 1760–71.

Aglietta, M. and Uctum, M. (1996) *Europe and the Maastricht Challenge*, Research Paper 9616, Federal Reserve Bank of New York, New York.

Albert, M. (1993) *Capitalism Against Capitalism*, London: Whurr.

Alesina, A. (1988) *Macroeconomics and Politics*, NBER Macroeconomic Annual 1988, NBER, Cambridge Ma.

Alesina, A. (1989) 'Politics and Business Cycles in Industrial Democracies', *Economic Policy*, **8**, 58–98.

Alesina, A. and Grilli, V. (1991) *The European Central Bank: Reshaping Monetary Policies in Europe*, Discussion Paper 563, CEPR, London.

Alesina, A. and Perotti, R. (1998) 'Economic Risk and Political Risk in Fiscal Unions', *Economic Journal*, **108**(449), 989–1008.

Alesina, A. and Summers, L.H. (1993) 'Central Bank Independence and Macroeconomic Performance: Some Comparative Evidence', *Journal of Money, Credit and Banking*, **25**(2), 151–162.

Alesina, A., Blanchard, O., Galì, J., Giavazzi, F. and Ulhig, H. (2001) *Defining a Macroeconomic Framework for the Euro Area*, Monitoring the European Central Bank 3, CEPR, London.

Allsopp, C. and Artis, M.J. (2003) 'The Assessment: EMU Four Years on', *Oxford Review of Economic Policy*, **19**(1), 1–29.

Alogoskoufis, G. and Portes, R. (1991) 'The International Costs and Benefits from EMU', in the Economics of EMU, *European Economy*, Special Edition 1, Office for the Official Publications of the European Communities, Luxembourg.

Alogoskoufis, G. and Portes, R. (1992) 'European Monetary Union and International Currencies in A Tripolar World', in Canzoneri, M., Grilli, V. and Masson, P.R.

(eds) *Establishing A Central Bank: Issue in Europe and Lessons from the US*, Cambridge: Cambridge University Press.

Amoroso, B. and Jespersen, J. (1992) *Macroeconomic Theories and Policies for the 1990s: A Scandinavian Perspective*, New York: St Martins Press.

Anderson, K. and Tyers, R. (1993) 'Implications of EC Expansion for European Agricultural Policies, Trade and Welfare', *Centre for Economic Policy Research*, Discussion Paper 829.

Angeloni, I., Gaspar, V. and Tristani, O. (1999) 'The Monetary Policy Strategy of the ECB', in Cobham, D. and Zis, G. (eds) *From EMS to EMU*, London: Macmillan.

Arestis, P. and Sawyer, M. (1996) 'Making the Euro Palatable', *New Economy*, **3**(2), 89–92.

Arestis, P. and Sawyer, M. (2000) 'Deflationary Consequences of the Single Currency', in Baimbridge, M., Burkitt, B. and Whyman, P. (eds) *The Impact of the Euro: Debating Britain's Future*, London: Macmillan.

Arestis, P. and Sawyer, M. (2004) *Re-examining Monetary and Fiscal Policy for the 21st Century*, Cheltenham: Edward Elgar.

Artis, M.J. and Buti, M. (2001) 'Setting Medium-term Fiscal Targets in EMU', in Brunila, A., Buti, M. and Franco, D. (eds) *The Stability and Growth Pact: The Architecture of Fiscal Policy in EMU*, London: Palgrave Macmillan.

Aspinwall, M. (2003) Britain and Europe: Some Alternative Economic Tests, *Political Quarterly*, **74**(2), 146–157.

Atkinson, A.B. (1999) *The Economic Consequences of Rolling Back the Welfare State*, London: MIT Press.

Bade, R. and Parkin, M. (1988) Central Bank Laws and Monetary Policy, Working Paper, University of Western Ontario.

Baimbridge, M. (1997) 'Is EMU Ready for Take-off?', *The Review of Policy Issues*, **3**(4), 25–33.

Baimbridge, M. (2005) Euphoria to Apathy: EP Turnout in the New Member States; in Lodge, J. (ed.) *The 2004 Elections to the European Parliament*, London: Palgrave Macmillan.

Baimbridge, M. (2005) 'The Euro', in van der Hoek, M.P. (ed.) *Handbook of Public Administration and Policy in the European Union*, New York: CRC Press.

Baimbridge, M. (2006) 'The ECB in Theory and Practice', in Whyman, P., Baimbridge, M. and Burkitt, B. (eds) *Implications of the Euro: A Critical Perspective from the Left*, London: Routledge.

Baimbridge, M. and Burkitt, B. (1995a) 'Equitable Voting in the EU?: Options for Change', *Politics*, **15**(2), 79–87.

Baimbridge, M. and Burkitt, B. (1995b) 'Council of Ministers Voting Rights', *Politics Review*, **4**(3), 31–33.

Baimbridge, M. and Philippidis, G. (eds) (2008) *EU Enlargement: Challenges and Prospects*, Copenhagen Business School Press, Copenhagen.

Baimbridge, M. and Whyman, P. (1997) 'Institutional Macroeconomic Forecasting Performance of the UK Economy', *Applied Economics Letters*, **4**(6), 373–376.

Baimbridge, M. and Whyman, P. (2004a) 'Fiscal Federalism and EMU: An Appraisal', in Baimbridge, M. and Whyman, P. (eds) *Fiscal Federalism and European Economic Integration*, London: Routledge.

Baimbridge, M. and Whyman, P. (eds) (2004b) *Fiscal Federalism and European Economic Integration*, London: Routledge.

Baimbridge, M., Burkitt, B. and Whyman, P. (1997) 'A Critical British Perspective', *New Political Economy*, **2**(3), 488–492.

Baimbridge, M., Burkitt, B. and Whyman, P. (1998) *Evaluation of Convergence Criteria*, in 'Preparations for Stage Three of Economic and Monetary Union', Treasury Committee, House of Commons, HMSO, London.

Baimbridge, M., Burkitt, B. and Whyman, P. (1998) *Is Europe Ready for EMU? Theory, Evidence and Consequences*, Occasional Paper 31, London: The Bruges Group.

Baimbridge, M., Burkitt, B. and Whyman, P. (1999) Convergence Criteria and EMU Membership: Theory and Evidence, *Journal of European Integration*, **21**(4), 281–305.

Baimbridge, M., Burkitt, B. and Whyman, P. (1999a) *The Bank that Rules Europe? the ECB and Central Bank Independence*, London: The Bruges Group.

Baimbridge, M., Burkitt, B. and Whyman, P. (2000) 'An Overview of European Monetary Integration', in Baimbridge, M., Burkitt, B. and Whyman, P. (eds) *The Impact of the Euro: Debating Britain's Future*, London: Macmillan.

Baimbridge, M., Burkitt, B. and Whyman, P. (2002) 'The Bank that Rules Europe: the ECB and Central Bank Independence', in Holmes, M. (ed.) *The Eurosceptical Reader II*, London: Palgrave.

Baimbridge, M., Burkitt, B. and Whyman, P. (2005) *Britain and the European Union: Alternative Futures*, London: CIB.

Baimbridge, M., Espindola, R., Philippidis, G. and Whyman, P. (2008) *Current Issues in EU Enlargement*, London: Palgrave Macmillan.

Baimbridge, M., Harrop, J. and Philippidis, G. (2004) *Current Economic Issues in EU Integration*, London: Palgrave Macmillan.

Baker, D., Gamble, A., Ludlum, S. and Seawright, D. (1996) 'Labour and Europe: A Survey of MPS and MEPS', *Political Quarterly*, **67**(4), 353–371.

Bakhoven, A.F. (1989) *The Completion of the Single Market in 1992: Macroeconomic Consequences for the European Community*, Central Planning Bureau, No. 56, The Netherlands.

Balanyá, B., Doherty, A., Hoedeman, O., Maanit, A. and Wesselius, E. (2000) *Europe Inc: Regional and Global Restructuring and the Rise of Corporate Power*, London: Pluto Books.

Balassone, F. and Franco, D. (2001) 'Public Investment, the Stability Pact and the Golden Rule', in Brunila, A., Buti, M. and Franco, D. (eds) *The Stability and Growth Pact: The Architecture of Fiscal Policy in EMU*, London: Palgrave Macmillan.

Bank for International Settlements (1994) *Financial Structure and the Monetary Transmission Mechanism*, Switzerland: Basle.

Bank for International Settlements (1996) *Central Bank Survey of Foreign Exchange and Derivatives Market Activity*, Switzerland: Basle.

Bank of England (1992) 'The Foreign Exchange Market in London', *Bank of England Quarterly Bulletin*, **32**.

Bank of England (May 2002) *Practical Issues Arising from the Euro*, Bank of England, London.

Barclay, C. (1995) 'The Common Agricultural Policy and Eastern Europe', *House of Commons Library Research Paper*, No. 13, House of Commons, London.

Barnard, C. and Deakin, S. (1997) 'European Community Social Law and Policy: Evolution Or Regression?', *Industrial Relations Journal* (European Annual Review), 131–153.

Barr, D., Breedon, F. and Miles, D. (2003) 'Life on the Outside: Economic Conditions and Prospects Outside Euroland', *Economic Policy*, **37**, 573–613.

Barr, N. (1992) 'Economic Theory and the Welfare State: A Survey and Interpretation', *Journal of Economic Literature*, **30**, 741–803.

Barrel, R. and Te Velde, D.W. (2003) 'German Monetary Union and the Lessons for EMU', in Baimbridge, M. and Whyman, P. (eds) *Economic and Monetary Union in Europe: Theory, Evidence and Practice*, Cheltenham: Edward Elgar.

Barro, R. and Gordon, R. (1983) 'Rules, Discretion and Reputation in a Model of Monetary Policy', *Journal of Monetary Economics*, **12**(1), 101–121

Barro, R.J. (1997) 'Determinants of Economic Growth: A Cross-country Empirical Study', MIT Press, London.

Baumol, W.J. (1961) 'Pitfalls in Counter-cyclical Policies: Some Tools and Results', *Review of Economics and Statistics*, **43**(1).

Bayoumi, T. and Eichengreen, B. (1993) 'Shocking Aspects of European Monetary Integration', in Torres, F. and Giavazzi, F. (eds) *Adjustment and Growth in the European Monetary Union*, Cambridge: Cambridge University Press.

Bayoumi, T. and Masson, P.R. (1995) 'Fiscal Flows in the United States and Canada: Lessons for Monetary Union in Europe', *European Economic Review*, **39**, 253–274.

Bean, C.R. (1998) 'Discussion', *Economic Policy*, **26**, 104–07.

Begg, D., Canova, F., De Grauwe, P., Fatás, A. and Lane, P. (2002) *Surviving the Slowdown*, Monitoring Europe, 3rd Report of the CEPS Macroeconomic Policy Group, London.

Begg, I. (2000) 'Reshaping the EU Budget: Yet Another Missed Opportunity', *European Urban and Regional Studies*, **7**, 51–62.

Behnisch, A.J. (2002) 'For Britain, Joining Europe was Associated with National Decline and Loss of Great Power Status', *New Statesman*, 16 December.

Benn, T. (2006) 'The Establishment of a Commonwealth of Europe'; in Whyman, P., Baimbridge, M. and Burkitt, B. (eds) *Implications of the Euro: A Critical Perspective from the Left*, London: Routledge.

Berry, R., Kitson, M. and Michie, J. (1995) *Towards Full Employment: The First Million Jobs*, Full Employment Forum, London.

Berthold, N. and Fehn, R. (1998) 'Does EMU Promote Labour-market Reforms?', *Kyklos*, **51**(4), 509–536.

Bini-smaghi, L. and Vori, S. (1992) 'Rating the EC as an Optimum Currency Area: Is it Worse than the US?' in O'brien, R. (ed.) *Finance and the International Economy*, Oxford: Oxford University Press.

Black, C.M. (2000) *The European Union, Britain and the United States: Which Way to Go?*, Nixon Center Perspectives, **4**(2).

Blair, A. (2000) *Managing Change: A National and International Agenda of Reform?*, Speech Given At the World Economic Forum, Davos, Switzerland, 28 January.

Blanchard, O. and Katz, L. (1992) 'Regional Evolutions', *Brookings Papers on Economic Activity*, **1**, 1–61.

Blankart, C.B. and Kirchner, C. (2004) 'The Deadlock of the EU Budget: An Economic Analysis of Ways in and Ways Out', in Blankart, C.B. and Mueller, D.C. (eds) *A Constitution for the European Union*, MIT Press, Cambridge Ma.

Bodart, V. (1990) *Central Bank Independence and the Effectiveness of Monetary Policy: A Comparative Analysis*, International Monetary Fund, Central Banking Department, IMF, Washington DC.

Booker, C. and Jamieson, B. (1994) 'How Europe Cost Us £235bn', *Sunday Telegraph*, 9 October.

Breton, A. (1974) *The Economic Theory of Representative Government*, London: Macmillan.

Brown, A.J. (1985) *World Inflation Since 1950*, Cambridge: Cambridge University Press.

Brunila, A., Buti, M. and Franco, D. (eds) (2001) *The Stability and Growth Pact: The Architecture of Fiscal Policy in EMU*, London: Palgrave Macmillan.

Bruno, M. and Sachs, J.D. (1985) *Economics of Worldwide Stagflation*, Oxford: Blackwell.

Buechtemann, C.F. and Schupp, J. (1992) 'Repercussions of Reunification: Patterns and Trends in the Socio-economic Transformation of East Germany', *Industrial Relations Journal*, **23**(2), 90–106.

Buiter, W., Corsetti, G. and Roubini, N. (1993) 'Excessive Deficits: Sense and Nonsense in the Treaty of Maastricht', *Economic Policy*, **16**, 57–100.

Buiter, W.H. (1999) *Alice in Euroland*, CEPR Policy Paper No. 1, Centre for Economic Policy Research, London.

Buiter, W.H. (2003) 'Ten Commandments for a Fiscal Rule in the E(M)U', *Oxford Review of Economic Policy*, **19**(1), 84–99.

Bulmer, S. and Burch, M. (1998) 'Organising for Europe: Whitehall, the British State and the European Union', *Public Administration*, **76**, 601–28.

Burdekin, R.C.K, and Willett, T.D. (1990) *Central Bank Reform: The Federal Reserve in International Perspective*, Paper Prepared for the Special Issue of Public Budgeting and Financial Management.

Burkitt, B. (2006) 'The European Social Model', in Whyman, P., Baimbridge, M. and Burkitt, B. (eds) *Implications of the Euro: A Critical Perspective from the Left*, London: Routledge.

Burkitt, B. and Baimbridge, M. (1990) 'The Performance of British Agriculture and the Impact of the Common Agricultural Policy: A Historical Review', *Rural History*, **1**(2), 265–280.

Burkitt, B. and Baimbridge, M. (1990) 'Britain, the European Economic Community and the Single Market of 1992: A Reappraisal', *Journal of Public Money and Management*, **10**(4), 57–61.

Burkitt, B. and Baimbridge, M. (1991) 'The Cecchini Report and the Impact of 1992', *European Research*, **2**(5), 16–19.

Burkitt, B., Baimbridge, M. and Mills, J. (1993) *What Price the Pound? The Exchange Rate and Full Employment*, Full Employment Forum, Watford.

Burkitt, B., Baimbridge, M. and Reed, S. (1992) *From Rome to Maastricht: A Reappraisal of Britain's Membership of the European Community*, Sudbury: Anglia Press.

Burkitt, B., Baimbridge, M. and Whyman, P. (1996) *There is an Alternative: Britain and its Relationship with the EU*, Oxford: Nelson and Pollard.

Burkitt, B., Baimbridge, M. and Whyman, P. (1997) *A Price Not Worth Paying: The Economic Cost of EMU*, Oxford: Nelson and Pollard.

Busch, K. and Knelangen, W. (2004) 'German Euroscepticism', in Harmsen, R. and Spiering, M. (eds) *Euroscepticism: Party Politics, National Identity and European Integration*, Amsterdam: Rodopi.

Buti, M. and Giudice, G. (2002) 'Maastricht Fiscal Rules at Ten: An Assessment', *Journal of Common Market Studies*, **40**(5), 823–47.

Buti, M. and Martinot, B. (2000) 'Open Issues in the Implementation of the Stability and Growth Pact', *National Institute Economic Review*, **174**, 92–104.

Buti, M. and Nava, M. (2003) *Towards a European Budgetary System*, Group of Policy Advisors, European Commission, Brussels.

Buti, M. and van den Noord, P. (2003) *Discretionary Fiscal Policy and Elections: The Experience of the Early Years of EMU*, OECD Economics Department Working Paper No. 351.

Buti, M., Eijffinger, S. and Franco, D. (2003) 'Revisiting EMU's Stability Pact: A Pragmatic Way Forward', *Oxford Review of Economic Policy*, **19**(1), 100–111.

Buti, M., Franco, D. and Ongena, H. (1998) 'Fiscal Discipline and Flexibility in EMU: The Implementation of the Stability and Growth Pact', *Oxford Review of Economic Policy*, **14**, 81–97.

Butler, D. and Kitzinger, U. (1996) *The 1975 Referendum*, London: Macmillan.

Cabral, A.J. (2001) 'Main Aspects of the Working of the Stability and Growth Pact', in Brunila, A., Buti, M. and Franco, D. (eds) *The Stability and Growth Pact: The Architecture of Fiscal Policy in EMU*, London: Palgrave Macmillan.

Calmfors, L. and Driffill, J. (1988) 'Bargaining Structure, Corporatism and Macroeconomic Performance', *Economic Policy*, **6**, 13–62.

Calmfors, L. and Nyomen, R. (1990) 'Real Wage Adjustment and Employment Policies in the Nordic Countries', *Economic Policy*, **5**(2), 397–448.

Cambridge Econometrics (1990) *Regional Economic Prospects*, Cambridge: Cambridge Econometrics.

Cameron, D.R. (1984) 'Social Democracy, Corporatism, Labour Quiescence and the Representation of Economic Interest in Advanced Capitalist Society', in Goldthorpe, J.H. (ed.) *Order and Conflict in Contemporary Capitalism*, Oxford: Clarendon Press.

Canzoneri, M.B. and Diba, B.T. (2000) *The Stability and Growth Pact Revisited: A Delicate Balance or an Albatross?* Mimeo.

Carlin, W. and Soskice, D. (1990) *Macroeconomics and the Wage Bargain*, Oxford: Oxford University Press.

Casella, A. (2001) 'Achieving Fiscal Discipline through Tradable Deficit Permits', in Brunila, A., Buti, M. and Franco, D. (eds) *The Stability and Growth Pact: The Architecture of Fiscal Policy in EMU*, London: Palgrave Macmillan.

Cash, W. (2001) *The Associated European Area: A Constructive Alternative to a Single European State*, London: European Foundation.

Castelnuovo, E., Altimari, S.N. and Rodriguez-Palenzuela, D. (2003) *Definition of Price Stability, Range and Point Inflation Targets: The Anchoring of Long-term Inflation Expectations*. Background Study for ECB Governing Council, ECB, Frankfurt.

Cecchetti, S., Mcconnell, M.M. and Perez-Quiros, G. (1999) *Policy Makers Revealed Preferences and the Output-inflation Variability Trade-off. Implications for the European System of Central Banks*. Mimeo.

Cecchetti, S.G. and O'sullivan, R. (2003) 'The European Central Bank and the Federal Reserve', *Oxford Review of Economic Policy*, **19**(1), 30–43.

Cecchetti, S.G. and Wynne, M.A. (2003) 'Inflation Measurement and the ECBS Pursuit of Price Stability: A First Assessment', *Economic Policy*, **37**, 395–434.

Cecchini, P. (1988) *The European Challenge – The Benefits of a Single Market*, Aldershot: Wildwood House.

Cerny, P.G. (1990) *The Changing Architecture of Politics*, London: Sage.

Church, C. (1993) 'Switzerland and Europe: Problem or Pattern?', *European Policy Forum*.

Church, C. (2004) 'Swiss Euroscepticism: Local Variations on Wider Themes', in Harmsen, R. and Spiering, M. (eds) *Euroscepticism: Party Politics, National Identity and European Integration*, Amsterdam: Rodopi.

Coates, D. (1999) 'Models of Capitalism in the New World Order', *Political Studies*, **47**, 643–660.

Coenen G. (2003a) *Downward Nominal Wage Rigidity and the Long-run Phillips Curve: Simulation-based Evidence for the Euro Area*, Background Study for ECB Governing Council, ECB, Frankfurt.

Coenen G. (2003b) *Zero Lower Bound: Is it a Problem in the Euro Area?*, Background Study for ECB Governing Council, ECB, Frankfurt.

Committee for the Study of Economic and Monetary Union (1989) *Report on Economic and Monetary Union in the European Community* [Delors Report], Office for Official Publications of the European Communities, Luxembourg.

Corden, M. (2003) 'Monetary Integration: The Intellectual Pre-history', in Baimbridge, M. and Whyman, P. (eds) *Economic and Monetary Union in Europe: Theory, Evidence and Practice*, Cheltenham: Edward Elgar.

Costello, D. (1993) 'The Redistributive Effects of Inter-regional Transfers: A Comparison of the European Community and Germany', *European Economy*, Reports and Studies, **5**, 271–278.

Courchene, T.J. (1993) 'Reflections on Canadian Federalism: Are There Implications for European Economic and Monetary Union?', *European Economy*. Reports and Studies, **5**, 127–166.

Court of Auditors (1995) Annual Report Concerning the Financial Year 1994 Together With the Institutions' Replies, *Official Journal of the European Communities*, **38**(C303), 14 November, 1–328.

Crouch, C. (1985) 'Corporation in Industrial Relations: A Formal Model', in Grant, W. (ed.) *The Political Economy of Corporatism*, London: Macmillan.

CSO (1995) *Family Spending – A Report on the 1994–95 Family Expenditure Survey*, HMSO, London.

Cukierman, A. (1992) 'Central Bank Strategy, Credibility and Independence', Cambridge Ma: MIT Press.

Dalsgaard, T. and De Serres, A. (2001) 'Estimating Prudent Budgetary Margins for Eu Countries: A Simulated Svar Model Approach', in Brunila, A., Buti, M. and Franco, D. (eds) *The Stability and Growth Pact: The Architecture of Fiscal Policy in EMU*, London: Palgrave Macmillan.

Davidson, P. (1998) 'Post Keynesian Employment Analysis and the Macroeconomics of OECD Unemployment', *The Economic Journal*, **108**(448), 817–831.

De Grauwe, P. (1994) *The Economics of Monetary Integration*, Oxford: Oxford University Press.

De Grauwe, P. and Vanhaverbeke, W. (1993) 'Is Europe an Optimum Currency Area?', in Masson, P.R. and Taylor, M.P. (eds) *Policy Issues in the Operation of Currency Unions*, Cambridge: Cambridge University Press.

Dearlove, J. and Saunders, P. (2000) *Introduction to British Politics*, Polity, Cambridge.

Deva, N. (2002) *Who Really Governs Britain?*, Totnes: The June Press.

Dobson, W. (1991) 'Economic Policy Coordination: Requiem or Prologue?', *Policy Analysis in International Economics*, **30**, Washington: Institute for International Economics.

Dornbusch, R. (1988) 'The European Monetary System, the Dollar and the Yen', in Giovazzi, F., Micossi, S. and Miller, M. (eds) *The European Monetary System*, Cambridge: Cambridge University Press.

Dowd, K. (1989) 'The Case Against a European Central Bank', *The World Economy*, **12**(3), 361–372.

Dowd, K. (1994) 'The Political Economy of Central Banking', *Critical Review*, **8**(1), 49–60.

Dowrick, S. (1996) 'Sweden's Economic Performance and Swedish Economic Debate: A View from Outside', *Economic Journal*, **106**(439), 1772–79.

Doyle, M.F. (1989) 'Regional Policy and European Economic Integration, in Committee for the Study of Economic and Monetary Union', *Report on Economic and Monetary Union in the European Community* – Collection of Papers, Office for Official Publications of the European Communities, Luxembourg.

Dréze, J. and Bean, C.R. (1990) 'European Unemployment: Lessons from a Multicountry Econometric Study', *Scandinavian Journal of Economics*, **92**(2), 135–165.

EC Commission (1990) 'One Money, One Market', *European Economy*, **44**, Office for the Official Publications of the European Communities, Luxembourg.

EC Commission (1992) *Treaty on European Union*, Office for the Official Publications of the European Communities, Luxembourg.

ECB (2005) 'The Reform of the Stability and Growth Pact', *Monthly Bulletin*, August.

Edmonds, J. (2000) 'The Single Currency and the European Social Model', in Baimbridge, M., Burkitt, B. and Whyman, P. (eds) *The Impact of the Euro: Debating Britain's Future*, London: Macmillan.

Ehrmann, M., Gambacorta, L., Martinez-Pages, J., Sevestre, P. and Worms, A. (2003) 'The Effects of Monetary Policy in the Euro Area', *Oxford Review of Economic Policy*, **19**(1), 58–72.

Eichener, V. (1996) 'Die Ruckwirkungen Der Europaischen Integration Auf Nationale Politikmuster', in Jachtenfuchs, M. and Kohler-Koch, N. (eds), *Europasiche Integration*, Opladen, Leske and Budrich.

Eichengreen, B. (1990) 'One Money for Europe? Lessons from the U.S. Currency Union', *Economic Policy*, **10**, 118–187.

Eichengreen, B. (1992) 'Is Europe an Optimum Currency Area?', in Borner, S. and Grubel, H. (eds) *The European Community After 1992: Perspectives from the Outside*, London: Macmillan.

Eichengreen, B. (1992) 'Should the Maastricht Treaty be Saved?', *Princeton Studies in International Finance*, **74**, International Finance Section, Princeton University, Princeton.

Eichengreen, B. (1993a) 'European Monetary Unification', *Journal of Economic Literature*, **31**(3), 1321–1357.

Eichengreen, B. (1993b) 'Labour Markets and European Monetary Unification', in Masson, P.R. and Taylor, M.P. (eds) *Policy Issues in the Operation of Currency Unions*, Cambridge: Cambridge University Press.

Eichengreen, B. (1994) 'Fiscal Policy and EMU', in Eichengreen, B. and Frieden, J. (eds), *The Political Economy of European Monetary Integration*, Oxford: Westview Press.

Eichengreen, B. (2000) 'Saving Europe's Automatic Stabilisers', in Baimbridge, M., Burkitt, B. and Whyman, P. (eds) *The Impact of the Euro: Debating Britain's Future*, London: Macmillan.

Eltis, W. (1996) 'If EMU Happens Should Britain Join?', *International Currency Review*, **23**(3), 61–66.

Eltis, W. (2000) 'EMU Membership would Destabilise the British Economy', in Baimbridge, M., Burkitt, B. and Whyman, P. (eds) *The Impact of the Euro: Debating Britain's Future*, London: Macmillan.

Emerson, M. (1990) 'One Market, One Money', *European Economy*, **44**, Commission of the European Economies, Luxembourg.

Ermisch, J. (1991) 'European Integration and External Constraints on Social Policy: Is a Social Charter Necessary?', *National Institute Economic Review*, **136**, May, 93–108.

Ersboll, N. and Ludlow, P. (1995) *Preparing for 1996 and a Larger European Union*, Centre for European Policy Studies, Brussels.

Esping-Andersen, G. (1990) *The Three Worlds of Welfare Capitalism*, Cambridge: Polity Press.

EU (2000) *European Economy*, Economic Trends (Supplement A) No. 1/2, Office for the Official Publications of the European Communities, Luxembourg.

EU Commission (1996) *The Community Budget – 1996 Edition*, Office for the Official Publications of the European Communities, Luxembourg.

EU Commission (1997) 'The Stability and Growth Pact', *Infeuro*, Office for the Official Publications of the European Communities, Luxembourg.

EU Commission (1998) *Financing the European Union: Commission Report on the Operation of the Own Resources System*, Office for the Official Publications of the European Communities, Luxembourg.

EU Commission (2000) *Public Finances in EMU – 2000*, Report of the Directorate General for Economic and Financial Affairs, Brussels.

EU Commission (2002) *Public Finances in EMU – 2002*, Report of the Directorate General for Economic and Financial Affairs, Brussels.

EU Commission (2004a) *General Budget of the European Union for the Financial Year 2004*, Office for the Official Publications of the European Communities, Luxembourg.

EU Commission (2004b) *Allocation of 2003 EU Operating Expenditure by Member State*, Office for the Official Publications of the European Communities, Luxembourg.

European Central Bank (1998) *A Stability Oriented Monetary Policy Strategy for the ESCB*. Frankfurt: ECB.

European Central Bank (1999) *Monthly Bulletin*, Frankfurt: ECB.

European Central Bank (2001) *Monthly Bulletin*, Frankfurt: ECB.

European Central Bank (2002) *Evaluation of the 2002 Cash Changeover*, Frankfurt: ECB.

European Central Bank (2003) *Overview of the Background Studies for the Reflections on the ECBS Monetary Policy Strategy*, Frankfurt: ECB.

European Commission (1992) *Treaty on European Union*. Office for the Official Publications of the European Communities. Luxembourg.

European Commission (1996) *The Community Budget – 1996 Edition*. Office for the Official Publications of the European Communities. Luxembourg.

European Commission (1998) *A Review of Possible Own Resources for the European Union*, European Commission, Brussels.

European Commission (2003) *Second Progress Report on Economic and Social Cohesion*, European Union, Brussels.

European Communities (1991) *Amendments to the EEC Treaty – Economic and Monetary Union*, Conference of the Representatives of the Governments of the Member States – Economic and Monetary Union, CONF-UEM 1621/91.

European Monetary Institute (1997) *The Single Monetary Policy in Stage Three*, Frankfurt: EMI.

Eurostat Yearbook (1998–1999) *A Statistical Eye on Europe Data 1987–1997*

Feld, L.P. (2005) 'European Public Finances: Much Ado About Nothing', in van der Hoek, M.P. (ed.) Handbook of Public Administration and Policy in the European Union, New York: CRC Press.

Feld, L.P. and Kirchgassner, G. (2004) 'The Role of Direct Democracy in the European Union', in Blankart, C.B. and Mueller, D.C. (eds) *A Constitution for the European Union*, Cambridge Ma: MIT Press.

Feldstein, M.S. (1974) 'Social Security, Induced Retirement and Aggregate Capital Accumulation', *Journal of Political Economy*, **82**, 905–926.

Feldstein, M.S. (1976) 'Temporary Layoffs in the Theory of Unemployment', *Journal of Political Economy*, **84**, 937–957.

Fischer, J. and Giudice, G. (2001) 'Fiscal Surveillance Under the Pact: the Stability and Convergence Programmes', in Brunila, A., Buti, M. and Franco, D. (eds) *The Stability and Growth Pact: the Architecture of Fiscal Policy in EMU*, London: Palgrave Macmillan.

Fisher, S. and Cooper, J.P. (1973) 'Stabilisation Policy and Lags', *Journal of Political Economy*, **81**(4).

Fitoussi, J.-P. and Creel, J. (2002) *How to Reform the European Central Bank*, Centre for European Reform, London.

Fleming, J.M. (1971) 'On Exchange Rate Unification', *Economic Journal*, **81**, 467–488.

Flockton, C. (1998) 'Germany's Long-running Fiscal Strains: Unification Costs or Unsustainability of Welfare State Arrangements?', *Debatte*, **6**(1), 79–93.

Flood, C. (2002) 'The Challenge of Euroscepticism', in Gower, J. (ed.) *The European Union Handbook*, London: Fitzroy Dearborn.

Foreman-Peck, J. (1995) *A History of the World Economy: International Relations Since 1850*, London: Harvester Wheatsheaf.

Forster, A. (2002) *Euroscepticism in Contemporary British Politics: Opposition to Europe in the British Conservative and Labour Parties Since 1945*, London: Routledge.

Frankel, J.A. and Wei, S.J. (1993) *Trade Blocs and Currency Blocs*, CEPR Conference on the Monetary Future of Europe, Spain: La Coruna.

Frey, B.S. (1978) *Modern Political Economy*, Oxford: Martin Robertson.

Friedman, M. (1953) 'The Case for Floating Rates', in Friedman, M. (ed.) *Essays in Positive Economics*, Chicago: University of Chicago Press.

Friedman, M. (1953) 'The Lags of a Full Employment Policy on Economic Stability: a Formal Analysis', in Friedman, M. (ed.) *Essays in Positive Economics*, Chicago: University of Chicago Press.

Friedman, M. and Schwartz, A.J. (1991) 'Alternative Approaches to Analysing Economic Data', *American Economic Review*, **81**(1), 39–49.

Fukuda, H. (1995) Speech at Chatham House Conference, London, 29 March.

Funabashi, Y. (1989) *Managing the Dollar from the Plaza to the Louvre*, Institute for International Economics, Washington.

Gali, J. (2001) *Monetary Policy in the Early Years of EMU*. Paper Presented at the European Commission Workshop on the Functioning of EMU: Challenges of the Early Years.

Gali, J. and Perotti, R. (2003) 'Fiscal Policy and Monetary Integration in Europe', *Economic Policy*, **37**, 533–572.

Gaspar, V., Masuch, K. and Pill, H. (2001) *The ECB's Monetary Policy Strategy: Responding to the Challenges of the Early Years*. Mimeo.

Geddes, A. (2004) *The European Union and British Politics*, London: Palgrave.

George, S. (1998) *An Awkward Partner: Britain in the European Community*, Oxford University Press, Oxford.

George, S. (ed.) (1992) *Britain and the European Community: the Politics of Semi-detachment*, Oxford: Clarendon Press.

Ghosh, A.R., Gulde, A.-M. and Wolf, H.C. (2002) *Exchange Rate Regimes: Choices and Consequences*, Cambridge Ma: The MIT Press,

Glasman, M. (1997) 'The Siege of the German Social Market', *New Left Review*, **225**, 134–9.

Global Britain (1999) *UK Trade in 1998*, Global Britain, London.

Goodhart, C.A.E. (1992) 'National Fiscal Policy within EMU: the Fiscal Implications of Maastricht', in Goodhart, C.A.E. (ed.) *EMU and ESCB after Maastricht*, London School of Economics/financial Markets Group, London.

Goodhart, C.A.E. (1995) 'The Political Economy of Monetary Union', in Kenen, P.B. (ed.) *Understanding Independence: the Macroeconomics of the Open Economy*, Princeton University Press, Princeton.

Goodhart, C.A.E. and Hansen, E. (1990) 'Fiscal Policy and EMU', in Dornbusch, R., Goodhart, C.A.E. and Layard, R. (eds) *Britain and EMU*, Centre for Economic Performance, London School of Economics, December.

Goodhart, C.A.E. and Smith, S. (1993) 'Stabilisation', *European Economy*, Reports and Studies, **5**, 419–455.

Gould, B. (2006) 'Preface', in Whyman, P., Baimbridge, M. and Burkitt, B. (eds) *Implications of the Euro: A Critical Perspective from the Left*, London: Routledge.

Gramlich, E.M and Wood, P.R. (2004) 'Fiscal and Monetary Policies', in Baimbridge, M. and Whyman, P. (eds) *Fiscal Federalism and European Economic Integration*, London: Routledge.

Green, J. and Swagel, P.I. (1998) 'The Euro Area and the World Economy', *Finance and Development*, **35**(4), 8–11.

Grilli, V., Masciandoro, D. and Tabellini, G. (1991) 'Political and Monetary Institutions and Public Financial Policies in the Industrial Countries', *Economic Policy*, **13**, 341–392.

Gros, D., Jimeno, J., Monticelli, C., Tabellini, G. and Thygesen, N. (2001) *Testing the Speed Limit for the European Central Bank*, **4**, CEPR, London.

Gross, D. and Thygesen, N. (1992) *European Monetary Integration*, London: Longman.

Haberler, G. (1970) 'The International Monetary System: Some Recent Developments and Discussions', in Halm, G.N. (ed.) *Approaches to Greater Flexibility of Exchange Rates*, Princeton: Princeton University Press.

Hainsworth, P., O'Brien, C. and Mitchell, P. (2004) 'Defending the Nation: the Politics of Euroscepticism on the French Right', in Harmsen, R. and Spiering, M. (eds) *Euroscepticism: Party Politics, National Identity and European Integration*, Amsterdam: Rodopi.

Hallett, A.J.H. and Vines, D. (1993) 'On the Possible Costs of European Monetary Union', *The Manchester School*, **61**(1), 35–64.

Hansson, A. (1987) *Politics, Institutions and Cross-country Inflation Differentials*, Unpublished.

Harmsen, R. (2004) 'Euroscepticism in The Netherlands: Stirrings of Dissent', in Harmsen, R. and Spiering, M. (eds) *Euroscepticism: Party Politics, National Identity and European Integration*, Amsterdam: Rodopi.

Harrison, B. (1996) *The Transformation of British Politics 1860–1995*, Oxford: Oxford University Press.

Harrop, J. (2005) 'The Internal Market', in van der Hoek, M.P. (ed.) *Handbook of Public Administration and Policy in the European Union*, New York: CRC Press.

Hassel, A. (1999) 'The Erosion of the German System of Industrial Relations', *British Journal of Industrial Relations*, **37**(3), 483–505.

Healey, N. (2000) 'The Case for European Monetary Union', in Baimbridge, M., Burkitt, B. and Whyman, P. (eds) *The Impact of the Euro: Debating Britain's Future*, London: Macmillan.

Henderick, M. (1998) *The Euro and Co-operative Enterprises*, Manchester: Co-operative Press.

Henley, A. and Tsakalotos, E. (1995) 'Unemployment Experience and the Institutional Preconditions', in Arestis, P. and Marshall, M. (eds) *The Political Economy of Full Employment*, Cheltenham: Edward Elgar.

Henrekson, M. (1996) 'Sweden's Relative Economic Performance: Lagging Behind or Staying on Top?', *Economic Journal*, **106**(439), 1747–59.

Hindley, B. and Howe, M. (1996) *Better-off Out? The Benefits or Costs of EU Membership*, IEA Occasional Paper 99, London: Institute of Economic Affairs.

Hirst, P. and Thompson, G. (1996) *Globalisation in Question: The International Economy and the Possibilities of Governance*, Cambridge: Polity Press.

HM Treasury (1997) *UK Membership of the Single Currency: An Assessment of Five Economic Tests*, HMSO, London.

Hofstede, G. (1980) *Culture's Consequences*, London: Sage.

Holland, S. (1995) 'Squaring the Circle: the Maastricht Convergence Criteria, Cohesion and Employment', in Coates, K. and Holland, S. (eds) *Full Employment for Europe*, Nottingham: Spokesman.

Honohan, P. and Lane, P.R. (2003) 'Divergent Inflation Rates in EMU', *Economic Policy*, **37**, 357–394.

Hopkins, S. (1995) 'The Council of Ministers', *Politics Review*, **4**(3), 32.

Horn, G.a. and Zwiener, R. (1992) 'Wage Regimes in a United Europe', in Barrell, R. and Whitley, J. (eds) *Macroeconomic Policy Co-ordination in Europe*, London: Sage.

Hutton, W. (1994) *The State We're In*, London: Cape.

Incomes Data Services (1990) *European Report*, **340**, April.

Ingram, J. (1962) *Regional Payments Mechanisms: The Case of Puerto Rico*, North Carolina: University of North Carolina Press.

Ingram, J. (1969) 'Comment: the Currency Area Problem', in Mundell, R.A. and Swoboda, A.K. (eds) *Monetary Problems of the International Economy*, Chicago: University of Chicago Press.

International Monetary Fund (2001) *World Economic Outlook Database*, IMF, Washington DC.

International Monetary Fund (2002) *Concluding Statement of the IMF Mission on the Economic Policies of the Euro Area – in the Context of the 2002 Article IV Consultation Discussions with the Euro Area Countries*, IMF, Washington DC.

Issing, O., Gaspar, V., Angeloni, I. and Tristani, O. (2001) *Monetary Policy in the Euro Area: Strategy and Decision Making at the European Central Bank*, Cambridge: Cambridge University Press.

Italianer, A. and Vanheukelen, M. (1993) 'Proposals for Community Stabilisation Mechanisms: Some Historical Applications', *European Economy*, Reports and Studies, **5**, 495–510.

Jackman, R., Pissarides, C. and Savouri, S. (1990) 'Labour Market Policies and Unemployment in the OECD', *Economic Policy*, **5**(2), 449–490.

Jamieson, B. (1995) *Worlds Apart?*, Occasional Paper No.19, London: The Bruges Group.

Jamieson, B. (1998) *Britain: Free to Choose*, London: Global Britain.

Jarvis, V. and Prais, S.J. (1989) 'Two Nations of Shopkeepers', *National Institute Economic Review*, **128**, May, 58–74.

Jay, D. (1990) *The European Monetary System: The ERM Illusion*, Labour Common Market Safeguards Committee, London.

Johnson, G. (1991) *World Agriculture in Disarray*, London: Macmillan.

Johnson, K.H. (1994) 'International Dimension of European Monetary Union: Implications for the Dollar', *International Finance Discussion Paper*, **496**, Washington: Board of Governors of the Federal Reserve System.

Kaergard, N. and Henriksen, I. (2003) 'Historical Experience with Monetary Unions: The Case of Scandinavia 1875–1914', in Baimbridge, M. and Whyman, P. (eds) *Economic and Monetary Union in Europe: Theory, Evidence and Practice*, Cheltenham: Edward Elgar.

Kalecki, M. (1943) 'Political Aspects of Full Employment', *Political Quarterly*, October-December, 322–331.

Karanassou, M. and Snower, D. (1998) 'How Labour Market Flexibility Affects Unemployment: Long-term Implications of the Chain Reaction Theory', *The Economic Journal*, **108**(448), 832–849.

Kavanagh, D. (2000) *British Politics: Continuities and Change*, Oxford: Oxford University Press.

Keller, B. and Sorries, B. (1997) 'The New Social Dialogue: Procedural Structuring, First Results and Perspectives', *Industrial Relations Journal* (European Annual Review), 77–98.

Kenen, P.B. (1969) 'The Theory of Optimum Currency Areas: An Eclectic View', in Mundell, R.A. and Swoboda, A.K. (eds) *Monetary Problems of the International Economy*, Chicago: University of Chicago Press.

Kenen, P.B. (1989) *Exchange Rates and Policy Coordination*, Ann Arbor: University of Michigan Press.

Kenen, P.B. (1995) *Economic and Monetary Union in Europe: Moving Beyond Maastricht*, Cambridge: Cambridge University Press.

Kenen, P.B. (1995) 'What Have we Learned from the EMS Crises?', *Journal of Policy Modelling*, **17**(5), 449–461.

Klaeffling M. and Lopez-Perez, V. (2003) *Inflation Targets and the Liquidity Trap*, Background Study for ECB Governing Council, Frankfurt: ECB.

Knutsen, P. (1997) 'Corporatist Tendencies in the Euro-polity: The EU Directive of 22 September 1994 on European Works Councils', *Economic and Industrial Democracy*, **18**(2), 289–323.

Konstanty, R. and Zwingmann, B. (1996) 'Arbeitsschutzeform – Bleibt Deutschland Schlu-lict in Europa?', WSI-*meittelungen*, **49**(2), 56–70.

Kopecky, P. (2004) 'An Awkward Newcomer? EU Enlargement and Euroscepticism in the Czech Republic', in Harmsen, R. and Spiering, M. (eds) *Euroscepticism: Party Politics, National Identity and European Integration*, Amsterdam: Rodopi.

Korkman, S. (2001) 'Should Fiscal Policy Co-ordination Go Beyond the SGP?', in Brunila, A., Buti, M. and Franco, D. (eds) *The Stability and Growth Pact: The Architecture of Fiscal Policy in EMU*, London: Palgrave Macmillan.

Korpi, W. (1985) 'Economic Growth and the Welfare System: Leaky Bucket or Irrigation System?', *European Sociological Review*, **1**, 97–118.

Korpi, W. (1996) 'Eurosclerosis and the Sclerosis of Objectivity: On the Role of Values Among Economic Policy Experts', *Economic Journal*, **106**(439), 1727–46.

Kpmg. (2000) *Europe's Response to EMU*, KPMG Consultants, London.

Krugman, P. (1980) Vehicle Currencies and the Structure of International Exchange, *Journal of Money, Credit and Banking*, **12**.

Krugman, P. (1984) The International Role of the Dollar: Theory and Prospect; in Bilson, J.F.O. and Marston, R.C. (eds) *Exchange Rate Theory and Practice*, Chicago: University of Chicago Press.

Kydland, F.E. and Prescott, E.C. (1977) Rules Rather than Discretion: The Time Inconsistency of Optimal Plans, *Journal of Political Economy*, **85**, 473–99.

Lamfalussy, A. (1989) 'Macro-coordination of Fiscal Policies in an Economic and Monetary Union in Europe', in Committee for the Study of Economic and Monetary Union [Delors Report] (ed.) *Report of Economic and Monetary Union in the European Community*, Office for the Official Publications of the European Communities, Luxembourg.

Lash, S. and Urry, J. (1987) *The End of Organised Capitalism*, Oxford: Polity Press.

Lawrence, R. and Schultz, C. (1987) (eds) *Barriers to European Growth: A Transatlantic View*, Washington DC: Brokings Institution.

Layard, R., Nickell, S. and Jackman, R. (1991) *Unemployment: Macroeconomic Performance and the Labour Market*, Oxford: Oxford University Press.

Leach, R. (2000) EU Membership: What's the Bottom Line? IOD Policy Paper, London: Institute of Directors.

Leibfried, S. (1994) 'The Social Dimension of the European Union: En Route to Positively Joint Sovereignty?', *Journal of European Social Policy*, **4**(4), 239–262.

Leibfried, S. and Pierson, P. (1995) 'The Dynamics of Social Policy Integration', in S. Leibfried and P. Pierson (eds) *Fragmented Social Policy: The European Community's Social Dimension in Comparative Perspective*, Washington DC: Brookings Institution.

Lindbeck, A., Molander, P., Persson, T., Petersson, O., Sandmo, A., Swedenborg, B. and Thygesen, N. (1994) *Turning Sweden Around*, London: MIT Press.

Lockwood, C. (1994) 'Play the EU Game: You Can Waste Millions', *Daily Telegraph*, 16 November.

Lumley, R. (1996) 'Labour Markets and Employment Relations in Transition: The Case of German Unification', *Employee Relations*, **17**(1), 24–37.

Macdougall, D. (1977) *The Role of Public Finance in the European Communities*, Office for the Official Publications of the European Communities, Brussels.

Macdougall, D. (1992) 'Economic and Monetary Union and the European Community Budget', *National Institute Economic Review*, May, 64–68.

Macdougall, D. (2003) 'Economic and Monetary Union and the European Community Budget', in Baimbridge, M. and Whyman, P. (eds) *Economic and Monetary Union in Europe: Theory, Evidence and Practice*, Cheltenham: Edward Elgar.

Macrae, C.D. (1977) 'A Political Model of the Business Cycle', *Journal of Political Economy*, **85**, 239–263.

Madsen, J.B. (1998) 'General Equilibrium Macroeconomic Models of Unemployment: Can They Explain the Unemployment Path in the OECD?', *The Economic Journal*, **108**(448), 850–867.

Magnifico, G. (1973) *European Monetary Unification*, New York: Wiley.

Majocchi, A. and Rey, M. (1993) 'A Special Financial Support Scheme in Economic and Monetary Union: Need and Nature in the Economics of Community Public Finance', *European Economy*, Reports and Studies, **5**, 459–480.

Mangano, G. (1998) 'Measuring Central Bank Independence: A Tale of Subjectivity and of its Consequences', *Oxford Economic Papers*, **50**(3), 468–492.

Marginson, P. and Sisson, K. (1996) 'Multinational Companies and the Future of Collective Bargaining: A Review of the Research Issues', *European Journal of Industrial Relations*, **2**(2), 173–97.

Marsden, D. (1992) 'Incomes Policy for Europe? Or Will Pay Bargaining Destroy the Single European Market?', *British Journal of Industrial Relations*, **30**(4), 587–604.

Marsh, D. (1992) *The Bundesbank – the Bank that Rules Europe*, London: Heinemann.

Marshall, M.G. (1995) 'Lessons from the Experience of the Swedish Model', in Arestis, P. and Marshall, M. (eds) *The Political Economy of Full Employment*, Cheltenham: Edward Elgar.

Masson, P.R. (1996) 'Fiscal Dimensions of EMU', *Economic Journal*, **106**(437), 996–1004.

Masson, P.R. and Melitz, J. (1990) 'Fiscal Policy Independence in a European Monetary Union', *Open Economies Review*, **2**.

Masson, P.R. and Taylor, M.P. (1993) 'Common Currency Areas and Currency Unions: An Analysis of the Issues, Parts I and II', *Journal of International and Comparative Economics*, **1**(3–4), 231–294.

Masson, P.R. and Taylor, M.P. (1993), 'Currency Unions: A Survey of the Issues', in Masson, P.R. and Taylor, M.P. (eds) *Policy Issues in the Operation of Currency Unions*, Cambridge: Cambridge University Press.

Masson, P.R. (1996) 'Fiscal Dimensions of EMU', *Economic Journal*, **106**(437), 996–1004.

Mayes, D.G. (2003) 'The Euro and the Stabilisation of the Eastern European Economy', in Baimbridge, M. and Whyman, P. (eds) *Economic and Monetary Union in Europe: Theory, Evidence and Practice*, Cheltenham: Edward Elgar.

McCallum, J. (1983) 'Inflation and Social Consensus in the Seventies', *Economic Journal*, **93**(372), 784–805.

McGiffen, S.P. (2001) *The European Union: A Critical Guide*, London: Pluto.

McKay, D. (1999) *Federalism and the European Union: A Political Economy Perspective*, Oxford: Oxford University Press.

McKay, D. (2001) *Designing Europe: Comparative Lessons from the Federal Experience*, Oxford: Oxford University Press.

McKinnon, R. (1963) 'Optimum Currency Areas', *American Economic Review*, **53**, 717–725.

McKinnon, R. (2003) 'Monetary Regimes, Collective Fiscal Retrenchment and the Political Economy of EMU', in Baimbridge, M. and Whyman, P. (eds) *Economic and Monetary Union in Europe: Theory, Evidence and Practice*, Cheltenham: Edward Elgar.

Melitz, J. (1997) 'The Evidence about the Costs and Benefits of EMU', *Swedish Economic Policy Review*, **4**, 359–410.

Micco, A., Stein, E. and Ordonez, G. (2003) 'The Currency Union Effect on Trade: Early Evidence from EMU', *Economic Policy*, **37**, 315–356.

Michie, J. (2000) 'The Economic Consequences of EMU for Britain', in Baimbridge, M., Burkitt, B. and Whyman, P. (eds), *The Impact of the Euro: Debating Britain's Future*, London: Macmillan.

Michie, J. (2006), 'Economic Consequences of EMU for Britain', in Whyman, P., Baimbridge, M. and Burkitt, B. (eds) *Implications of the Euro: A Critical Perspective from the Left*, London: Routledge.

Midelfart-Knarvik, K.H. and Overman, H.G. (2002) 'Delocation and European Integration. Is Structural Spending Justified?', *Economic Policy*, 323–359.

Miller, V. and Dyson, J. (1994) The European Communities (Finance Bill), *House of Commons Library Research Paper*, 94/117, London.

Milne, I. (1998) *The Facts about Direct Investment*, London: The June Press.

Milne, I. (2004) *A Cost Too Far? An Analysis of the Net Economic Costs and Benefits for the UK of EU Membership*, London: The Institute for the Study of Civil Society.

Milner, S. (2004) 'For an Alternative Europe: Euroscepticism and the French Left Since the Maastricht Treaty', in Harmsen, R. and Spiering, M. (eds) *Euroscepticism: Party Politics, National Identity and European Integration*, Amsterdam: Rodopi.

Minford, P. (1996) *Britain and Europe: the Balance Sheet*, Liverpool Macroeconomic Research.

Minford, P. (1996) 'Corporatism, the Natural Rate and Productivity', in *Trade Unions and the Economy: Into the 1990s*, Employment Institute, London.

Minford, P. (2000) 'The Single Currency – Will it Work and Should We Join?', in Baimbridge, M., Burkitt, B. and Whyman, P. (eds) *The Impact of the Euro: Debating Britain's Future*, London: Macmillan.

Minford, P., Mahambare, V. and Novell, E. (2005) *Should Britain Leave the EU? An Economic Analysis of a Troubled Relationship*, Cheltenham: Edward Elgar.

Missale, A. (2001) 'How Should the Debt be Managed? Supporting the Stability Pact', in Brunila, A., Buti, M. and Franco, D. (eds) *The Stability and Growth Pact: The Architecture of Fiscal Policy in EMU*, London: Palgrave Macmillan.

Mitchell, A. (1993) *Democracy and Monetary Policy*, Memorandum submitted to the Treasury and Civil Service Committee.

Mitchell, A. (2006) 'Euro Versus the People', in Whyman, P., Baimbridge, M. and Burkitt, B. (eds) *Implications of the Euro: A Critical Perspective from the Left*, London: Routledge.

Molle, W. (2003) 'Are EU Policies Good or Bad for Convergence?' Paper Presented at the Experts Workshop, *Cohesion in the European Union*, College of Europe, Bruges.

Monks, J. (2000) 'A Single Currency for Europe – Considerations for Workers', in Baimbridge, M., Burkitt, B. and Whyman, P. (eds) *The Impact of the Euro: Debating Britain's Future*, London: Macmillan.

Mundell, R.A. (1961) 'A Theory of Optimum Currency Areas', *American Economic Review*, **51**, 657–665.

Muscatelli, V.A. (1998) 'Political Consensus, Uncertain Preferences, and Central Bank Independence', *Oxford Economic Papers*, **50**(3), 412–430.

Musgrave, R.A. and Musgrave, P.B. (1973) *Public Finance in Theory and Practice*, London: Mcgraw-Hill.

Myrdal, G. (1957) *Economic Theory and Underdeveloped Regions*, London: Duckworth.

Nairn, T. (1972) *The Left Against Europe?*, London: Penguin.

National Consumer Council (1995) *Agricultural Policy in the European Union*, National Consumer Council, London.

Nevin, E. (1990) *The Economics of Europe*, London: Macmillan.

Nickell, S. (1998) 'Unemployment: Questions and Some Answers', *The Economic Journal*, **108**(448), 802–816.

Nordhaus, W.D. (1975) 'The Political Business Cycle', *Review of Economic Studies*, **42**, 169–190.

Notermans, T. (2000) 'Europeanisation and the Crisis of Scandinavian Social Democracy', in Geyer, R., Ingebritsen, C. and Moses, J.W. (eds) *Globalisation, Europeanisation and the End of Social Democracy?*, London: Macmillan.

Oates, W.E. (1972) *Fiscal Federalism*, New York: Harcourt-Brace and Jovanovich.

Oates, W.E. (2004) 'An Essay on Fiscal Federalism', in Baimbridge, M. and Whyman, P. (eds) *Fiscal Federalism and European Economic Integration*, London: Routledge.

OECD (1986) *Flexibility in the Labour Market*, OECD, Paris.

Organisation for Economic Cooperation and Development (1986) *Flexibility in the Labour Market*, OECD, Paris.

Organisation for Economic Cooperation and Development (2001) *Economic Outlook*, OECD, Paris.

Ormerod, P. (1999a) 'The Euro-attack on Jobs', in Bush, J. (ed.), *Everything You Always Wanted to Know about the Euro*, London: New Europe.

Ormerod, P. (1999b) 'A Currency for Jobs?', *European Journal*, July, 7–8.

Ormerod, P. (2006) 'The Euro: An Outsider's Perspective', in Whyman, P., Baimbridge, M. and Burkitt, B. (eds) *Implications of the Euro: A Critical Perspective from the Left*, London: Routledge.

Owen, D. (2006) 'Foreword', in Whyman, P., Baimbridge, M. and Burkitt, B. (eds) *Implications of the Euro: A Critical Perspective from the Left*, London: Routledge.

Pain, N. and Young, G. (2004) 'The Macroeconomic Impact of UK Withdrawal from the EU', *Economic Modelling*, **21**(3), 387–408.

Panic, M. (1992) *European Monetary Union: Lessons from the Classical Gold Standard*, London: Macmillan.

Peele, G. (2004) *Governing the UK: British Politics in the 21st Century*, Oxford: Blackwell.

Pennant-Rea, R., Bean, C.R., Begg, D., Hardie, J., Lankester, T., Miles, D.K., Portes, R., Robinson, A. Seabright, P. and Wolf, M. (1997), *The Ostrich and the EMU – Policy Choices Facing the UK*, Centre for Economic Policy Research, London.

Petchey, J. and Wells, G. (2004) 'Australia's Federal Experience', in Baimbridge, M. and Whyman, P. (eds) *Fiscal Federalism and European Economic Integration*, London: Routledge.

Peters, T. (1995) 'European Monetary Union and Labour Markets: What to Expect', *International Labour Review*, **134**(3), 315–332.

Phelps, E.S. and Zoega, G. (1998) 'Natural-rate Theory and OECD Unemployment', *The Economic Journal*, **108**(448), 782–801.

Pisani-Ferry, J., Italianer, A. and Lescure, R. (1993) 'Stabilisation Properties of Budgetary Systems: A Simulation Analysis', *European Economy*, Reports and Studies, **5**, 513–538.

Pissarides, C. (1997) 'The Need for Labour Market Flexibility in European Economic and Monetary Union', *Swedish Economic Policy Review*, **4**(2), 513–546.

Podmore, W. and Katz, P. (1998) 'Sovereignty for What? Why European Monetary Union is Just the Start', London: Tribune.

Porter, M.E. (1990) *The Competitive Advantage of Nations*, London: Macmillan.

Posen, A. (1993) 'Why Central Bank Independence Does Not Cause Low Inflation: There is no Institutional Fix for Politics', in O'Brien, R. (ed.) *Finance and the International Economy*, **7**, Oxford: Oxford University Press.

Posen, A. (1998) 'Central Bank Independence and Disinflationary Credibility: A Missing Link', *Oxford Economic Papers*, **50**(3), 335–359.

Prais, S.J. and Wagner, K. (1988) 'Productivity and Management: The Training in Foremen in Britain and Germany', *National Institute Economic Review*, **123**, February, 34–47.

Redwood, J. (2000) 'Sterling Democracy or European Bureaucracy?', in Baimbridge, M., Burkitt, B. and Whyman, P. (eds) *The Impact of the Euro: Debating Britain's Future*, London: Macmillan.

Rhodes, M. (1992) 'The Future of the Social Dimension: Labour Market Regulation in Post-1992 Europe', *Journal of Common Market Studies*, **30**(1), 23–51.

Richards, D. and Smith, M.J. (2002) *Governance and Public Policy in the United Kingdom*, Oxford: Oxford University Press.

Rogoff, K. (1985a) 'The Optimal Degree of Commitment to an Intermediate Monetary Target', *Quarterly Journal of Economics*, **100**, 1169–1190.

Rogoff, K. (1985b) 'Can International Monetary Policy Coordination be Counter-productive?', *Journal of International Economics*, **18**, 199–217.

Romer, P.M. (1994) 'The Origins of Endogenous Growth', *Journal of Economic Perspectives*, **8**(1), 3–22.

Rompuy, P.V., Abraham, F. and Heremans, D. (1993) 'Economic Federalism and the EMU', in the Economics of EMU – Background Studies, *European Economy*, **44**, 109–135.

Rostagno, M., Hiebert, P. and Pérez-Garcìa, J. (2001) 'Optimal Debt Under a Deficit Constraint', in Brunila, A., Buti, M. and Franco, D. (eds) *The Stability and Growth Pact: The Architecture of Fiscal Policy in EMU*, London: Palgrave Macmillan.

Rowthorn, B. and Glyn, A. (1990) 'The Diversity of Unemployment Experience Since 1973', in Marglin, S.A. and Schor, J.B. (eds) *The Golden Age of Capitalism: Reinterpreting the Post-war Experience*, Cambridge: Clarendon Press.

Royal Society of Edinburgh (2004) *Inquiry Into the Future of the Scottish Fishing Industry*, RSE, Edinburgh.

Sala-i-Martin, X. and Sachs, J. (1992) 'Fiscal Federalism and Optimum Currency Areas: Evidence for Europe from the United States', in Canzoneri, M.B. *et al.* (eds) *Establishing A Central Bank: Issues in Europe and Lessons from the US*, Cambridge: Cambridge University Press.

Sapir, A. and Sekkat, K. (1999) 'Optimum Electoral Areas: Should Europe Adopt a Single Election Day?', *European Economic Review*, **43**, 1595–1619.

Sapir, A., Sekkhat, K. and Weber, A. (1994) *The Impact of Exchange Rate Fluctuations on European Union Trade*, CEPR Discussion Paper, 104.

Sarno, L. and Taylor, M.P. (2002) *The Economics of Exchange Rates*, Cambridge: Cambridge University Press.

Sawyer, M. (1995) 'Obstacles to Full Employment in Capitalist Economies', in Arestis, P. and Marshall, M. (eds) *The Political Economy of Full Employment*, Cheltenham: Edward Elgar.

Sawyer, M. and Arestis, P. (2006) 'What Type of European Monetary Union?', in Whyman, P., Baimbridge, M. and Burkitt, B. (eds) *Implications of the Euro: A Critical Perspective from the Left*, London: Routledge.

Schaltegger, C.A. and Frey, R.L. (2004) 'Fiscal Federalism in Switzerland: A Public Choice Approach', in Baimbridge, M. and Whyman, P. (eds) *Fiscal Federalism and European Economic Integration*, London: Routledge.

Schoors, K. and Gobbin, N. (2005) 'Enlargement', in van der Hoek, M.P. (ed.) *Handbook of Public Administration and Policy in the European Union*, New York: CRC Press.

Shore, P. (2006) 'Fighting Against Federalism', in Whyman, P., Baimbridge, M. and Burkitt, B. (eds) *Implications of the Euro: A Critical Perspective from the Left*, London: Routledge.

Simon, D. (2000) 'EMU and the Opportunities for British Business', in Baimbridge, M., Burkitt, B. and Whyman, P. (eds) *The Impact of the Euro: Debating Britain's Future*, London: Macmillan.

Sisson, K. and Marginson, P. (1995) 'Management: Systems, Structures and Strategy', in Edwards, P. (ed.) *Industrial Relations: Theory and Practice in Britain*, Oxford: Blackwell.

Sleath, P. (1995) 'Fish Facts', *European Journal*, 20 March.

Snoddon, T.R. (2004) 'Fiscal Institutions, Regional Adjustment and Convergence in Canadas Currency Union: Lessons for EMU', in Baimbridge, M. and Whyman, P. (eds) *Fiscal Federalism and European Economic Integration*, London: Routledge.

Spahn, B. (1993) 'The Consequences of Economic and Monetary Union for Fiscal Relations in the Community and the Financing of the Community Budget, in the Economics of Community Public Finance', *European Economy*, Reports and Studies, **5**, 543–584.

Spiering, M. (2004) 'British Euroscepticism', in Harmsen, R. and Spiering, M. (eds) *Euroscepticism: Party Politics, National Identity and European Integration*, Amsterdam: Rodopi.

Stanners, W. (1993) 'Is Low Inflation an Important Condition for High Growth?', *Cambridge Journal of Economics*, **17**(1), 79–107.

Stark, J. (2001) 'Genesis of a Pact', in Brunila, A., Buti, M. and Franco, D. (eds) *The Stability and Growth Pact: The Architecture of Fiscal Policy in EMU*, London: Palgrave Macmillan.

Steedman, H. (1988) 'Vocational Training in France and Britain', *National Institute Economic Review*, **126**, 57–70, November,

Stewart-Brown, R. (1999a) 'In Search of the Benefits of the Single Market', *Eurofacts*, 3–4, 23 April.

Stewart-Brown, R. (1999b) 'The Economic Consequences for the UK of the Single Market', *Eurofacts*, 6–7, 6 August.

Strange, G. (1997) 'The British Labour Movement and Economic and Monetary Union in Europe', *Capital and Class*, **63**, 13–24.

Streeck, W. (1992) *Social Institutions and Economic Performance: Studies of Industrial Relations in Advanced Capitalist Economies*, London: Sage.

Streeck, W. and Schmitter, P.C. (1991) 'From National Corporatism to Transnational Pluralism: Organised Interests in the Single European Market', *Politics and Society*, **19**(2), 133–164.

Sunnus, M. (2004) 'Swedish Euroscepticism: Democracy, Sovereignty and Welfare', in Harmsen, R. and Spiering, M. (eds) *Euroscepticism: Party Politics, National Identity and European Integration*, Amsterdam: Rodopi.

Surico, P. (2003) 'Asymmetric Reaction Functions for the Euro Area', *Oxford Review of Economic Policy*, **19**(1), 44–57.

Svensson, L.E.O. (2002) *A Reform of the Eurosystems Monetary Policy Strategy Is Increasingly Urgent*, Briefing Paper, Committee on Economic and Monetary Affairs, European Parliament.

Svensson, L.E.O. (2003) *How Should the Eurosystem Reform Its Monetary Strategy?*, Briefing Paper, Committee on Economic and Monetary Affairs, European Parliament.

Swinburne, M. and Castello-Branco, M. (1991) *Central Bank Independence: Issues and Experience*, International Monetary Fund Working Paper No. 91/58, IMF, Washington DC.

Szczerbiak, A. (2004) 'Polish Euroscepticism in the Run-up to EU Accession', in Harmsen, R. and Spiering, M. (eds) *Euroscepticism: Party Politics, National Identity and European Integration*, Amsterdam: Rodopi.

Taylor, M. (1995) *A Single Currency – Implications for the UK Economy*, Institute of Directors, London.

Teague, P. (1991) 'Introduction to the Cross-national Research', Seminar on *Workers Rights in Europe*, London School of Economics and Political Science, London, 13 April.

Teague, P. (1997) 'Lean Production and the German Model', *German Politics*, **6**(2), 76–94.

Teague, P. (1998) 'Monetary Union and Social Europe', *Journal of European Social Policy*, **8**(2), 117–139.

The Economist (1991) 'Japanese Spoken Here', *The Economist*, 14 September.

The Economist (2005) 'A Working Model', *The Economist*, 13 August.

Thirlwall, A.P. and Barton, C.A. (1971) 'Inflation and Growth: The International Evidence', *Banca Nazionale Del Lavoro – Quarterly Review*, **98**, 682–695.

Tinbergen, J. (1952) *On the Theory of Economic Policy*, North-Holland, Amsterdam.

Tobin, J. (1994) 'Speculators Tax', *New Economy*, **1**, 104–109.

Tondl, G. (2002) 'Will the New EU Regional Policy Meet the Challenges of Enlargement?', in Cuadrado-Roura, J. and Parellada, M. (eds) *Regional Convergence in the European Union: Advances in Spatial Science*, Springer, Heidelberg.

Tondl, G. (2005) 'European Union Regional Policy', in van der Hoek, M.P. (ed.) *Handbook of Public Administration and Policy in the European Union*, New York: CRC Press.

Toniolo, G. (1988) *Central Banks Independence in Historical Perspective*, Berlin: Walter de Gruyter.

Tower, E and Willett, T.D. (1970) 'The Concept of Optimum Currency Areas and the Choice Between Fixed and Flexible Exchange Rates', in Halm, G.N. (ed.) *Approaches to Greater Flexibility of Exchange Rates*, Princeton: Princeton University Press.

Trades Union Congress (1993) *European Common Currency*, London: TUC.

Treaty of Nice (2000) Intergovernmental Conference on Institutional Reform, 12 December 2000, Conference of the Representatives of the Governments of Member States, Nice.

Turner, L. (1996) 'The Europeanisation of Labour: Structure Before Action', *European Journal of Industrial Relations*, **2**(3), 325–344.

Unctad (1996) *Trade and Development Annual Report*, New York: UNCTAD.

United States International Trade Commission (2000), *The Impact on the US Economy of Including the United Kingdom in a Free Trade Arrangement with the United States, Canada and Mexico*, Investigation No. 332–409, Publication 3339, August.

van der Hoek, M.P. (ed.) (2005) *Handbook of Public Administration and Policy in the European Union*, New York: CRC Press.

van der Ploeg, F. (1993) 'Macroeconomic Policy Co-ordination: Issues During the Various Phases of Economic and Monetary Integration in Europe', in The Economics of EMU, *European Economy*, Special Edition, **1**, 136–164.

Vaubel, R. (1976) 'Real Exchange Rate Changes in the European Community: The Empirical Evidence and its Implications for European Currency Unification', *Weltwirtschaftliches Archiv*, **112**, 429–470.

Vaubel, R. (1978) *Strategies for Currency Unification*, J.B.C. Mohr, Tubingen.

Verdun, A. (2005) 'A History of Economic and Monetary Union', in van der Hoek, M.P. (ed.) *Handbook of Public Administration and Policy in the European Union*, New York: CRC Press.

Viren, M. (2001) 'Fiscal Policy, Automatic Stabilisers and Policy Co-ordination in EMU', in Brunila, A., Buti, M. and Franco, D. (eds) *The Stability and Growth Pact: the Architecture of Fiscal Policy in EMU*, London: Palgrave Macmillan.

von Hagen, J. (1992) 'Fiscal Arrangements in a Monetary Union: Evidence from the US', in Fair, D.E. and De Boissieu, C. (eds) *Fiscal Policy, Taxes and the Financial System in An Increasingly Integrated Europe*, Kluwer, Deventer.

von Hagen, J. (1993) 'Monetary Union and Fiscal Union: A Perspective from Fiscal Federalism', in Masson, P.R. and Taylor, M.P. (eds) *Policy Issues in the Operation of Currency Unions*, Cambridge: Cambridge University Press.

von Hagen, J. (2003) 'EMU: Monetary Policy Issues and Challenges', in Baimbridge, M. and Whyman, P. (eds) *Economic and Monetary Union in Europe: Theory, Evidence and Practice*, Cheltenham: Edward Elgar.

von Hagen, J. and Brückner, M. (2002) 'Monetary Policy in Unknown Territory: The European Central Bank in the Early Years', *Zei Working Paper*, B18.

Wagner, R.E. (1977) 'Economic Manipulation for Political Profit: Macroeconomic Consequences and Constitutional Implications', *Kyklos*, **30**, 395–410.

Walsh, J., Zappala, G. and Brown, W. (1995) 'European Integration and the Pay Policies of British Multinational', *Industrial Relations Journal*, **26**(2), 84–96.

Warr, P. (1987) *Work, Unemployment and Mental Health*, Oxford: Oxford University Press.

Watson, M. (2006) 'The European Social Model: Between a Rock and a Hard Place?', in Whyman, P., Baimbridge, M. and Burkitt, B. (eds) *Implications of the Euro: A Critical Perspective from the Left*, London: Routledge.

Weber, A.A. (1991a) 'Reputation and Credibility in the European Monetary System', *The European Economy*, **12**, 57–102.

Weber, A.A. (1991b) 'EMU and Asymmetries and Adjustment Problems in the EMS, in the Economics of EMU', *European Economy*, Special Edition, **1**.

West, K. (1995) *Economic Opportunities for Britain and the Commonwealth*, London: Royal Institute for International Affairs.

Wheare, K.C. (1963) *Federal Government*, Oxford: Oxford University Press.

Whyman, P. (1997a) 'Fiscal Policy Consequences of Economic and Monetary Union in Europe', Working Paper No. 97/1, Department of Social and Economic Studies, University of Bradford, Bradford.

Whyman, P. (1997b) *Fiscal Federalism and EMU: A Proposal for a European Federal Transfer Scheme*, Working Paper No. 97.10.5, Department of Social and Economic Studies, University of Bradford.

Whyman, P. (2001) 'Can Opposites Attract? Monetary Union and the Social Market', *Contemporary Politics*, **7**(2), 113–128.

Whyman, P. (2001) 'The Impact of Economic and Monetary Union Upon British Business', *European Business Journal*, **13**(1), 28–36.

Whyman, P. (2002) 'British Trade Unions and EMU: Natural Supporters or Conflicting Interests?', *Industrial Relations*, **41**(3), 467–476.

Whyman, P. (2006) 'Trade Unions and EMU', in Whyman, P., Baimbridge, M. and Burkitt, B. (eds) *Implications of the Euro: A Critical Perspective from the Left*, London: Routledge.

Whyman, P., Burkitt, B. and Baimbridge, M. (2000) 'Economic Policy Outside EMU: Strategies for A Global Britain', *Political Quarterly*, **71**(4), 451–462.

Whyman, P., Burkitt, B. and Baimbridge, M. (2006) 'A Post-Keynesian Strategy for the UK Economy', in Whyman, P., Baimbridge, M. and Burkitt, B. (eds) *Implications of the Euro: A Critical Perspective from the Left*, London: Routledge.

Windolf, P. (1989) 'Productivity Coalitions and the Future of European Corporatism', *Industrial Relations*, **28**(1), 1–20.

Winters, L.A. (2003) 'EMU and the Rest of the World: Thinking About the Effects on the Real Economy', in Baimbridge, M. and Whyman, P. (eds) *Economic and Monetary Union in Europe: Theory, Evidence and Practice*, Cheltenham: Edward Elgar.

World Bank (1993) *The East Asian Miracle: Economic Growth and Public Policy*, Oxford: Oxford University Press.

Wynne, M. and Rodriguez-Palenzuela, D. (2002) 'Measurement Bias in the HICP: What Do We Know and What Do We Need to Know?', ECB Working Paper, 131, Frankfurt: ECB.

Wyplosz, C. (1993) 'Monetary Union and Fiscal Policy Discipline, in the Economics of EMU – Background Studies', *European Economy*, **44**, 165–184.

Wyplosz, C. (2003) 'Policy Challenges Under EMU', in Baimbridge, M. and Whyman, P. (eds) *Economic and Monetary Union in Europe: Theory, Evidence and Practice*, Cheltenham: Edward Elgar.

Yates T. (1998) 'Downward Nominal Rigidity and Monetary Policy', Bank of England Working Paper, **82**, Bank of England, London.

Yates, T. (2002) 'Monetary Policy and the Zero Bound to Interest Rates: A Review', ECB Working Paper, **190**, ECB, Frankfurt.

Index